CAREER GUIDANCE

CAREER GUIDANCE

Who Needs It,
Who Provides It,
Who Can Improve It

BY

Eli Ginzberg

McGRAW-HILL BOOK COMPANY

New York   St. Louis   San Francisco   Düsseldorf
London   Mexico   Sydney   Toronto

Library of Congress Catalog Card Number: 72-150776

FIRST EDITION

07-023284-9

TO

The Rockefeller Foundation
The Ford Foundation
The Field Foundation
The Carnegie Corporation
The Rockefeller Brothers Fund
The Russell Sage Foundation

FOR THEIR ASSISTANCE TO THE

Conservation of Human Resources Project
Columbia University
1941–1971

Conservation of Human Resources
Guidance Study Staff

Eli Ginzberg, Ph.D. (Economics), *Director*
A. Barton Hepburn Professor of Economics, Graduate School of Business, Columbia University

Ivar E. Berg, Ph.D. (Sociology), *Senior Research Associate*
Professor of Sociology, Graduate School of Business, and Associate Dean of Faculties, Columbia University

Marcia Freedman, Ph.D. (Education), *Senior Research Associate*
Adjunct Associate Professor of Education (Guidance), Teachers College, Columbia University

Jesse S. Goodman, Ph.D. (College Counseling), *Research Associate*
Assistant Professor, College Counseling and Student Development, Hunter College

Stanley J. Segal, Ph.D. (Counseling Psychology),
Senior Research Associate Professor, College Counseling and Student Development, and Associate Dean of Students, Hunter College

Alice M. Yohalem, M.A. (Economics), *Research Associate*

Ruth Beinart, M.A., Research Assistant (1968–69)

Roberta Handwerger, B.A., Research Assistant (1967–68)

Mary Hagigeorgiou, Secretary to the Director

Sylvia Leef, Administrative Assistant

CONTENTS

PART III: GUIDEPOSTS

PART IV: POLICY

PREFACE

The origin and working methods that inform this study are set forth in Chapter 1. The many persons who contributed to the final product are mentioned below, both for the record and so that I can thank them.

My greatest debt is to the members of my staff. Although my name appears on the title page, those listed on the staff page are in every sense of the term co-authors. Professor Berg drafted Chapter 5 and served as the staff's rhetorician; Professors Goodman and Segal provided the principal inputs for Chapters 8 through 11 and for Chapter 13; Dr. Marcia Freedman played a critical role in helping to outline the entire book, in sharpening our approaches, and, in association with Mrs. Alice Yohalem, in revising the manuscript. To the extent that the book is clear and balanced, the major credit goes to Mrs. Yohalem, who worked over every sentence, every page, every chapter to insure that it reflects what we want to say; in addition, she drafted Chapter 12.

Mrs. Sylvia Leef, my Administrative Assistant for many years, typed and retyped the thousands of yellow sheets on which I wrote the successive drafts, an undertaking she alone was capable of executing. And she did so with unfailing good humor.

My unflappable secretary, Mrs. Mary Hagigeorgiou, saw to it that the successive drafts made their way to and from the bevy of secretaries who helped us and within the stipulated time period.

The readability of the finished product reflects the willingness of my wife, Ruth S. Ginzberg, to devote her free hours to editing the manuscript. This was an undertaking that went beyond her marriage vows and for which I am grateful.

Dr. Ralph Tyler permitted me to impose on our long-term friendship and agreed to serve as our principal consultant. He not only participated actively in the three conferences which are noted below but also read through the entire manuscript with care and gave us the benefit of his wide knowledge and acute judgment.

I thank the Director of Pupil Personnel Services and Research of "Suburbantown," who must remain anonymous so as not to reveal the identity of the community.

When the study was first launched (December 1, 1966), Professor C. Gilbert Wrenn, the Chairman of the Panel on Counseling and Selection of the National Manpower Advisory Committee, invited me to present our preliminary plans to the members of his committee who are listed below. We greatly profited from this exchange:

Panel on Counseling and Selection

C. Gilbert Wrenn
Arizona State University

Marvin Adelson
System Development Corporation

Harold F. Cottingham
Florida State University

William C. Cottle
Boston College

Willis E. Dugan
American Personnel and Guidance
Association, Inc.

Margaret J. Gilkey
Dade County Public Schools
Miami, Florida

Edward Gross
University of Minnesota

Stewart C. Hulslander
University of Michigan

Karl R. Kunze
Lockheed-California Company

Blanche Paulson
Bureau of Pupil Personnel Services
Board of Education
Chicago, Illinois

Otto Pragan
AFL-CIO

Edward C. Roeber
Indiana State University

Herbert E. Striner
The W. E. Upjohn Institute
for Employment Research

Albert S. Thompson
Teachers College
Columbia University

David V. Tiedeman
Harvard University

Toward the end of our study, in the winter of 1969, the Conservation Project held three conferences on information, theory, and policy, respectively, with the following leaders in the field of guidance and cognate disciplines. Again, we learned much of value.

Conference on Educational and Occupational Information

Max Baer
B'nai B'rith Vocational Service

Helen Birtwell
Vocational Advisory Service

Joseph Bernier
General Learning Corporation

Edward Chase
New American Library

Daniel Creamer
National Industrial Conference Board

John Myers
National Industrial Conference Board

Robert Hoppock
New York University

Martin Katz
Educational Testing Service

Philip Perrone
University of Wisconsin

Howard Rosen
U.S. Department of Labor

Paul M. Smith, Jr.
North Carolina College

Sol Swerdloff
U.S. Department of Labor

David V. Tiedeman
Harvard University

Albert S. Thompson
Columbia University

Ralph Tyler
Science Research Associates

Seymour Wolfbein
Temple University

Conference on Theory and Practice

Benjamin Barbarosh
Paramus, N.J., School District

Edward Bordin
University of Michigan

Robert Dentler
Center for Urban Education

Edmund Gordon
Columbia University

Martin Katz
Educational Testing Service

S. M. Miller
New York University

John Rothney
University of Wisconsin

Buford Stefflre
Michigan State University

Donald Super
Columbia University

Ralph Tyler
Science Research Associates

Charles Wilson
I.S. 201, New York City

Conference on Guidance Policy

Arthur Brayfield
Claremont Colleges

Harold Dunne
United Automobile Workers

Charles Dailey
Dartmouth College

Willis E. Dugan
American Personnel and
Guidance Association, Inc.

John Fischer
Columbia University

Fred Hechinger
The New York Times

Walter Johnson
Michigan State University

Jacob Kaufman
Pennsylvania State University

Karl Kunze
Lockheed-California Company

Jacob Landers
Asst. Superintendent Schools, N.Y.C.

Charles Odell
U.S. Employment Service

Richard Pearson
College Entrance Examination
Board

David Pritchard
U.S. Office of Education

Felix Robb
Southern Association of
Colleges and Schools

Bruce Shear
N.Y. State Education Dept.

Milton Schwebel
Rutgers University

Ralph Tyler
Science Research Associates

Bennetta Washington
Office of Economic Opportunity

Paul Woodring
Fairhaven College

Harold Wool
U.S. Department of Defense

Thomas J. Skelly
U.S. Rehabilitation Services
Administration

The Rockefeller Brothers Fund underwrote the cost of this study. Moreover, having agreed that I would have sole responsibility for carrying it out, the foundation's staff never interfered. Every research director can appreciate the value of such a relationship. But as the dedication indicates, I have always been fortunate in my relationships with my sponsors.

Conservation of Human Resources   ELI GINZBERG
Columbia University
June 1970

PART I

FRAMEWORK

1

FOCUS

IN 1951, my colleagues and I published *Occupational Choice: An Approach to a General Theory,* which was one of the first efforts to conceptualize the process of career decision-making.[1] Since then, our research has been concerned primarily with the development and utilization of human resources, ranging from the uneducated to the talented. As a consequence we have been repeatedly concerned with problems of career development and career guidance.

These concerns had a central place in the following of our works:
The Optimistic Tradition and American Youth, 1962
Talent and Performance, 1966
Life Styles of Educated Women, 1967
The Middle-Class Negro in the White Man's World, 1967.[2]

In 1967, the Rockefeller Brothers Fund, which had supported our research on educated women, indicated its interest in an appraisal of the potentialities of educational and vocational guidance to assist women and members of minority groups, in particular, in making more effective use of the new career options that were becoming available to them.

Our research group, the Conservation of Human Resources Project, Columbia University, accepted the offer of the Rockefeller

3

Brothers Fund to underwrite a broad-scale inquiry into career guidance, and added to its interdisciplinary staff, based in economics, sociology, education, and manpower, two psychologists whose professional careers had been in the field of guidance and counseling. With this reinforcement we were able to establish a broad framework in which to carry out the inquiry. Our plan provided for a study of the socio-economic factors which largely determine the opportunities and constraints that people encounter in establishing and implementing their career plans, as well as of the psychological processes in growth and development which determine how individuals act in the present and plan for the future.

We define career guidance as *a process of structured intervention aimed at helping individuals to take advantage of the educational, training, and occupational opportunities that are available*. We are therefore concerned with the philosophy of guidance counselors, the actions they take in the performance of their tasks, and the goals they seek to accomplish. As in other personal services, one cannot study guidance without becoming involved with the guidance profession. The fact that many people maintain good health without recourse to physicians, and others manage to educate themselves with only incidental help from teachers, is not to say that physicians and teachers do not usually play a strategic role in health and education but only that favorable results do not necessarily depend on them. The same is true of career guidance. Many young people resolve their career decisions satisfactorily with little or no help from guidance personnel. We therefore distinguished at the outset and throughout our investigation between structured guidance interventions which are part of an institutionalized system and informal processes whereby individuals acquire understanding and perspective about the educational and occupational world. The two are related but they are certainly not identical.

A preliminary word about our concentration on educational and vocational guidance. Every person in our society is constrained to attend school for many years, to consider the type of work and life he would like to pursue, and to make choices and decisions informed by these preferences. Moreover, he must relate his development to the opportunities and options available to him. Educational and vocational guidance therefore represents a pivotal intervention.

Work, and education and training for work, represent a critical arena of human activity. Hence guidance directed toward assisting individuals to choose among different types of work and to prepare for work is a critical intervention to help them clarify their developmental experiences and the world of reality.[3]

Education seeks to help the individual develop his capacities and interests and its effectiveness depends in considerable measure on how well he makes use of his present and potential options. Since the educational-training system is both complex and dynamic, many individuals are unable to negotiate it effectively on their own. They need help, but many of them cannot obtain it from family or friends who have had limited exposure to the educational system and that often several decades earlier.

While we do not believe that education should be solely or even primarily preparation for work, we do believe that since all males and increasing numbers of females spend most of their adult lives at work, the relations between education and work cannot be ignored. If they are, young people will be unable to understand the important linkages between the two. A young person who does not avail himself of his educational opportunities often will have difficulty in earning a livelihood. While education and work must be distinguished, they are sequentially linked at the beginning of an individual's life and are increasingly intertwined in adulthood as our technological society puts a premium on continued learning. Since most young people spend about thirteen years in school, and many others spend sixteen years or more, there clearly is need for educational guidance.

Our second concern is with guidance related to the world of work —that is, help in locating a job, moving to a better job, acquiring skills that can facilitate career progression, finding a new career if forced to retire early, adjusting to an urban labor market after having grown up on a farm, re-entering employment after a period spent at home raising children. All of these dimensions appear to be critical since they help to determine whether a person works, the wages he earns, his opportunities for advancement, and the satisfactions he derives from working.

Although our study is concerned not only with young people in school but with all persons—young, mature, and elderly—who have educational, training, or occupational problems, it has some important limits that should be indicated. First, we are concerned with people who fall within the normal range; thus we do not explore the special problems presented to guidance by persons who are severely impaired by a serious mental, emotional, or physical disability. Moreover, we do not consider marked intrapsychic and interpersonal problems which interfere with the successful adjustment of individuals to school and work. Finally, we have only touched upon the potentially important arena of choices and decisions about non-work activities.

Since words can be confusing as well as clarifying, we will seek to remove a few semantic stumbling blocks. Theoreticians and practitioners frequently use the terms *guidance* and *counseling* interchangeably, but at other times they make a sharp distinction between the two. Often the two terms are used together, as when "guidance counselor" defines the person in the school hierarchy responsible for helping young people to make educational and occupational decisions.

While we do not want to be more puristic than the profession itself, we will distinguish between guidance and counseling, although we may not always observe our own differentiation. *Guidance* includes a wide range of functions which are directed toward helping individuals make optimum use of their alternatives in acquiring an education and in pursuing a career, such as providing information and assisting in its interpretation, testing and appraising individuals, counseling, placement, and follow-up. Many people provide guidance: parents, teachers, peers, coaches, sergeants, foremen, employment officials, and counselors whose specific task is to provide guidance services.

Counseling, on the other hand, is a specialized function. It is usually but not always part of a guidance program. At times, counseling is the only type of assistance offered in a guidance program. According to one leader in the field, "Counseling denotes a professional relationship between a trained counselor and a client which is designed to help the client understand and clarify his view of his life space so that he may make meaningful and informed choices consonant with his essential nature and his particular circumstances in those areas where choices are available to him."[4]

Another term that is often ambiguous is *career*. Commonly, the term connotes a meaningful progression in a person's working life: a physician who starts as an intern and ends up as professor of surgery has a career; so does a politician who starts out as a state legislator and later is elected to the U.S. Senate; likewise an engineer who, after some years in technical and sales work, enters the executive ranks and becomes a vice-president of a major corporation. Since most blue- and white-collar workers seldom move more than a few rungs up the skill and income ladder during the course of their working lives, their work experience, in the conventional sense, with its limited progression can not be called a career.

At different points in our analysis, we use related terms such as job, position, occupation, employment, work, and career; however, we have found that the last term best encompasses the long-run objectives and consequences of a man's experiences in the world of work, although many do not achieve substantial progression. Our use of the term does not imply that we believe all men seek a career or that most succeed in achieving one.

Having briefly described the inception and focus of our study, we will now present our approach and discuss its implementation. We set ourselves the task of looking at career guidance broadly—that is, at the needs of the entire population and the array of institutions within which guidance services are provided. Our first challenge was to construct a framework broad enough to encompass the diversity of educational and vocational problems encountered by males and females, whites and blacks, the rich and poor, those from urban and rural backgrounds, at different stages in their development—in school, out of school, in the Armed Forces, in job training, at work, at home.

Since guidance is provided in tens of thousands of schools, in several thousand offices and suboffices of the Employment Service, and in hundreds of other settings, it is impossible to describe the typical or the average range and quality of services or to assess the variation between extremes. Thus any finding, favorable or unfavorable, about any facet of the present guidance system can always be challenged. Guidance is carried on under vastly differing conditions in terms of the resources available, implicit and explicit goals, the quality of leadership and supervision, client's needs and desires.

We therefore adopted the following devices. First, we assiduously avoided looking for or making use of what appeared to be extreme situations. Second, we avoided postulating that all difficulties we uncovered reflect professional inadequacies of the counselor involved. We assumed that improved selection, training, supervision, retention within the profession would be beneficial to guidance. But we felt that we must realistically assess the prospects of transforming the field and not limit ourselves solely to improvements in personnel.

An attempt to assess a profession when reliable information about current practices is inadequate and when such key factors as counselor competence and client needs cannot be specified would be self-defeating. We therefore concentrated on the needs of different individuals and groups for guidance services and on the ways in which existing institutions are responding. We were thus alerted to the non-congruence, even conflict, that often exists between persons needing help and those who provide it. We have sought to study guidance as a social process and to understand how it operates, not according to the prescriptions found in textbooks but as it actually is. In pursuing this approach, the Conservation staff determined at the outset not to undertake a large sample survey of the operation of career guidance in the United States from either the viewpoint of the purveyors or of the users of guidance services. We made this decision even though preliminary exploration had indicated that the amount of solid information available about the actual provision of guidance services was much less than we wanted and needed to know. Matters of cost aside, we concluded that the information which could be obtained from a new national survey would still leave a great many critical questions unanswered.

As an alternative we decided to study the major investigations that had recently been completed as well as those nearing completion which might provide data we might tap. One of our senior staff, a counseling psychologist with a research orientation, made a trip around the country to explore potential data banks. We would be happy if we could report that he uncovered great riches and that our evaluation is more solid because of what he found. But the truth is that he uncovered only a few nuggets. We may have missed some valuable studies, but we made an effort to learn about the principal investigations

Our most important investment was a continuing interdisciplinary seminar in which we sought by research, analysis, and discussion to develop a meaningful synthesis between the sociological and psychological factors that together determine career decision-making and to which career guidance, if it is to be effective, must be responsive.

The notes and selective bibliography at the end of this book will provide the interested reader with an overview of our coverage of the literature and identify the sources from which we drew the most help, although it does not include more than a minority of the items we reviewed. We made no effort to cover the literature exhaustively, but sought for help in conceptualizing and evaluating how the present guidance system sees its tasks and discharges them.

We made a special effort to establish contact with various research centers which were engaged in studies that seemed to be closely related to our own:

Harvard Graduate School of Education and Teachers College, Columbia University, where work has been under way to assess the potentialities of the computer for career exploration and decision-making.

Pennsylvania State University, which has carried out studies in depth of vocational education and which has probed the quantity and quality of guidance services.

Ohio State University, which has engaged in a nation-wide survey of the organization of guidance services in different types of secondary schools and which has collected data on these services from principals, teachers, pupils, and parents.

The University of Maryland, the regional center selected under a grant by the federal government to explore the roles of pupil personnel specialists, including guidance counselors.

American Institutes of Research, formerly at Pittsburgh and currently at Palo Alto, which collected and has been analyzing data generated by *Project Talent*, including information about the guidance services provided to high school students.

The University of Missouri, which is the headquarters for an ambitious long-term study to evaluate school guidance services.

We also visited and consulted at length with the staffs of the key institutions engaged in providing guidance and counseling services to different groups, including the Employment Service, vocational rehabilitation, and community agencies.

We do not want to skip lightly over the help that we received. But we cannot report that the research findings to which we became privy, often prior to publication, had a *major* influence in shaping our investigation. As frequently happens in research, the findings of one investigation are not directly apposite to the concerns of another.

We were pleased to take advantage of an offer that came early in our investigation to use a suburban school district in the New York metropolitan region as a case study to help us formulate and sharpen our approaches. Members of our staff spent considerable time in "Suburbantown" seeking to capture the many dimensions of its school guidance services, which are recognized as well above average.

In addition we consulted with representative leaders of the guidance profession and with other leaders from allied fields, particularly at the beginning and at the end of our study. The National Manpower Advisory Committee, a statutory body established under the Manpower Development and Training Act of 1962, had a Panel on Counseling and Selection which included many leaders of American guidance.[5] The Panel, chaired by Professor C. Gilbert Wrenn, evinced a particular interest in our study when it was first announced. Through the courtesy of its chairman, we were invited to make a presentation of our objectives and design and to benefit from an incisive interchange with its members. We learned much from this early encounter both about the traps to avoid and areas where we were likely to find opportunities to move ahead.

During the course of our investigation, members of our staff talked with literally hundreds of counselors in different guidance settings. The most constructive interchanges, however, were those with the carefully selected experts at the three working conferences the Conservation Project organized to review its emerging findings and recommendations. The first conference was on information, the second on theory and practice, and the third on policy. Each conference met for three sessions. The names of the participants are listed in the Preface.

We also established and maintained contact with key policy-making bodies at federal, state, and local levels as well as with the headquarters of the American Personnel and Guidance Association.

Thereby we were better able to keep abreast of current developments, especially those involving new strategies, new programs, new staffing patterns. The recent proliferation of federally financed manpower training and related programs created a welcome background for innovation, some of which has been of direct importance for career guidance. While we did not attempt to monitor all of these new activities, we sought to learn about the major innovations in order to appraise their significance.

Throughout, we sought to avoid oversimplifying a complex problem through easy answers. Others would have handled our charge differently. We sought to be responsive and responsible in seeking to shed new light on an important social function.

What follows is an overview of the structure of this book. The first six chapters comprise the *Framework* within which we set forth the social dimensions of career guidance. We begin by calling attention to the surfacing of guidance into a position of prominence in the 1960s, when our legislators looked to it to facilitate the functioning of major new public programs. This is followed by a historical essay which reviews the major transformations of guidance during its first half-century of development, as it responded to such diverse forces as the advancement of knowledge about human development and problems of social and economic adjustment. We then scrutinize the major claims that the leadership has advanced for guidance and assess these claims within the reality conditions that put limits on all services provided to the American people.

The next chapter delineates the ways in which key institutions channel people and thus shape their career opportunities and outcomes. The last chapter in *Part One* is addressed to the socioeconomic system, which both creates opportunities and places constraints on the career development of individuals and groups.

In *Part Two* we shift to the *institutions* through which career guidance operates. After a review of the different strategies which have informed the guidance movement, all of which still operate in varying degrees, we discuss the ways in which guidance personnel are recruited and trained and the types of careers open to them. Next we consider the major settings in which guidance counselors carry on their work and the tensions that arise and the resolutions that are effected between them and the people who hire and direct them. In "Suburbantown" we probe more deeply into one setting, that of school guidance and counseling. The last two chapters in *Part Two* are devoted respectively to client assessment and career information since people who make educational and career decisions should know more about themselves and about the world in which they study and work.

Part Three, Guideposts, is a transition from the analysis of environmental and institutional determinants to the concluding section, which is concerned with the future of the field. For the reasons adumbrated in Chapter 13, it is not possible at present to undertake and carry through a scientifically based evaluation of guidance. Hence all judgments and appraisals must be indirect and we must settle for first approximations. Chapter 14 presents a typology of the principal ways in which people in the United States pursue work and careers. The last chapter in *Part Three* summarizes the stance of the guidance profession toward itself and its immediate future.

This brings us to *Part Four,* which encompasses the three chapters on policy. We present first our detailed recommendations to the guidance profession, then to the public, and we conclude with a sketch of likely developments in the society at large during the 1970s that will set the parameters within which guidance can be strengthened and improved.

It is our hope that this book will enable Americans to judge whether their enthusiasm during the 1960s about guidance and its potential assistance in realizing important educational and occupational objectives was firmly grounded and what actions are required by both the profession and the public to assure that guidance will be able to fulfill new and important responsibilities.

2

CHALLENGE AND

RESPONSE

THE GUIDANCE MOVEMENT, which got under way in the second decade of this century, expanded slowly and although it underwent several significant transformations in the ensuing fifty years it attracted little attention and even less support from government policy-makers. While guidance had been given a role to play in several federal programs, notably the Employment Service and vocational rehabilitation, it was not until the end of the 1950s that the lawmakers, faced with new challenges, took an intensified interest in its potentiality to contribute to the realization of important national goals.

In the late 1950s and in the 1960s the nation was shaken by a series of educational, employment, and social crises that dramatized the failure of existing institutions to be responsive to new challenges. Shortcomings were revealed in the ability of the family, the school, the labor market to prepare people adequately for work and citizenship. In the belief that these failures endangered our domestic and foreign relations, the policy-makers looked for remedies. Since fundamental reforms in the educational, social, and economic spheres were not then on the nation's agenda, the lawmakers looked for programs that might prove helpful without dis-

13

turbing the basic institutions. They wanted programs that would promise much and cost little. Out of this background came new interest in expanding guidance services in the hope and expectation that this might lead to improved individual and group performance.

The surfacing of guidance into national consciousness began with the trauma suffered by the American people after the launching of Sputnik in 1957, when the widely held belief in the supremacy of our technology was suddenly undermined. It was incomprehensible to most Americans, those in leadership positions as well as the man in the street, that presumably technologically backward Russians, living under a rigid Communist dictatorship should be the first to enter the Space Age. While it was not immediately clear why the Russians were able to get a head start in the race to conquer space, it was not long before the investigation centered on the shortcomings of our educational system on the assumption that education, as the principal engine of progress, had faltered.

In the following year, the Eisenhower administration, despite its distaste for expanding the involvement of the federal government in areas customarily reserved to the states and to the private sector, came forward with a program to remedy the defects in the spheres of American science, technology, and manpower that Sputnik had thrown into relief. It recommended broad new federal financing for graduate instruction in defense-related fields, and included support for the training of high school counselors.

During the Congressional hearings on the administration proposal, the U.S. Commissioner of Education, Dr. Lawrence G. Derthick, called attention to the following deficiencies in existing school systems: a shortage of counselors, lack of testing and counseling in rural schools, and poor pupil records. These deficiencies, he stated, were resulting in the loss of much potential talent. This point was further developed by Marion Folsom, Secretary of Health, Education and Welfare, when he called the attention of the Congressmen to the fact that "skilled counselling services can help students develop their capacities more fully ... and encourage [them] to remain in school, to work harder in basic academic courses, and to prepare for college."

Several Congressmen were skeptical and some were hostile to this suggestion. Representative Landrum suggested that appropriations for athletics might prove a better investment. Others proposed that schools turn their backs on foolish experimentation and advised them to concentrate on the 3 R's. The following exchange took place between the Chairman of the House Committee and the Undersecretary of HEW:

> *Barden:* If you have the right kind of teacher you can keep the counsel [sic] out.
>
> *Perkins:* Of course the teacher and the counselor are virtually the same thing. If a teacher is not counseling I feel he is not a good teacher.
>
> *Barden:* However, if you pass this law, you will have more folks running around as a counselor, knowing everything, telling everybody how to live and what to do. I have had some experience with them. I don't mean that they are bad folks. They are not. They are well-intentioned and fine folks but they haven't bumped against the practical side of the thing like the teacher.... If you have the right kind of teacher you can cut that paragraph about the counseling and save some money....

Dr. Derthick intervened and pointed out that "the counselor will know a lot about occupational guidance and vocational opportunities, will know a lot about financial aid and will know a lot about test interpretation that you could not expect the classroom teacher to carry in her mind." The Chairman was unpersuaded, but the counseling section remained in the bill.[1]

The bill as passed in 1958 was titled the National Defense Education Act (NDEA). It followed the recommendations of the administration by making funds available for graduate study in several disciplines, primarily the physical sciences, which were judged to be critically important to establish and maintain leadership in areas deemed essential to national security. In order to identify and facilitate the progress of talented youth, Congress also made funds available for strengthening existing school guidance services and for the training of school counselors. Guidance services were singled out as a major facilitating mechanism to accomplish an important national objective.

When the Act was first passed, only secondary school guidance programs were eligible for NDEA funds. By 1964, through successive amendments, NDEA funding could be used throughout an entire gamut of the educational system from elementary schools to junior colleges and technical institutions, and training support was provided for elementary as well as for secondary school counselors.

The next resort to guidance as a response to a social challenge was triggered by the rising rate of juvenile delinquency. In the early 1960s President Kennedy's Committee on Juvenile Delinquency decided to experiment with new and ambitious programs to re-direct delinquents and potential delinquents from antisocial into constructive activities, particularly into skill training and paid employment. These programs, such as Mobilization for Youth in New York City, placed heavy reliance on guidance services. Coun-selors were used to help attract young people into these programs; to assess the types of remedial educational and occupational train-ing they required; to provide support and encouragement to those who found the sledding hard; to attempt to remove frictions be-tween enrollees and their families; to seek out employment oppor-tunities for them; and otherwise to help them to get onto and stay on a track where the end was a steady job at an adequate wage, not a renewed encounter with the police and prison.

This was among the first large-scale efforts to utilize guidance services for a socially disadvantaged population. It was hoped that improved guidance services would attract clients and effect changes in their attitudes and behavior or, at the least, demonstrate the necessary adaptations in conventional guidance approaches that would be required if these groups were to be helped.

A third challenge to policy-makers in the 1960s was increasing unemployment. In his Economic Message to the Congress in 1961, President Kennedy stated that he was asking the Secretary of Labor to take steps to improve the Employment Service. He said: "This will require expanded counseling and placement services for work-ers or jobseekers (a) in depressed areas; (b) in rural areas of chronic underemployment; (c) displaced by automation and tech-nological change in factories and on farms; (d) in upper age brackets; and (e) recently graduated from college and high school."

The Employment Service began to reorient its operations in 1962 along the lines directed by the President and, in the same year, Congress passed the Manpower Development and Training Act

(MDTA) which, in the perspective of history, must be recognized as a major breakthrough in federal manpower policy. The original thrust of the Act was to retrain skilled adults displaced by economic and technological change; however, by 1963 amendments were passed that shifted its emphasis to the disadvantaged. Henceforth remedial education, pre-skill training, and other services could be provided for the hard-to employ. The Employment Service is the principal operating arm of this manpower program and its local offices were charged with the responsibility for counseling, testing, and referral to training of workers entitled to the benefits under the Act.

The Manpower Development and Training Act was enacted primarily to help adults. In fact, a limitation was placed on the funds that could be used for young people. But as leaders in and out of government studied and learned more about the malfunctioning of our economy and society, they became increasingly concerned about the plight of poorly educated young people, among whom members of minority groups were conspicuously overrepresented. Dr. James B. Conant had warned of the "social dynamite" represented by large numbers of undereducated, underskilled, alienated youth, school dropouts and school pushouts, who were standing on street corners because they had no alternative.[2] Here was a further challenge to policy-makers.

After failing to win the approval of Congress for a Youth Employment Act, the Secretary of Labor in the fall of 1964 announced the establishment of a national network of Youth Opportunity Centers (YOC's) as part of the Employment Service, which were to build on experimental programs that had been under way for some time in St. Louis, New Haven, and other cities. The objective of this program was to encourage young men and women, out of school and out of work, to come to these Centers for counseling and appraisal as a result of which it was hoped that some would be helped to find jobs, others would be encouraged to return to school, and still others would be referred to a training program.

The provision of guidance and counseling services was fundamental to the operation of these centers. Within three years of the program's establishment, 170 centers had opened with a total annual budget of $40 million, and the Employment Service, realizing that it could not possibly staff this new undertaking with its existing manpower resources, financed an emergency training program for youth counselors in the summers of 1964 and 1965.

In the early 1960s, an increasingly active and militant Negro minority indicated that it would no longer wait to be accepted as full citizens and it determined to take matters in its own hands to secure the rights to which it was entitled.

The most meaningful response to this challenge would have been the eradication of the pervasive racial discrimination that characterized most sectors of American society. But even if the elimination of discrimination could have been elicited, it would not have compensated for centuries of deprivation. For the blacks to make significant gains would require that they gain access to educational and training opportunities in order to qualify for preferred employment from which they had formerly been barred. The MDTA was further amended and additional legislation was passed to expand opportunities for minorities. By 1967 there were at least twenty-eight distinct job training programs directed at "disadvantaged workers," a disproportionate number of whom were Negroes, Spanish-speaking Americans, and Indians.

These programs provided a wide range of services, but almost all of them explicitly included guidance support. The assumption was that skill training, by itself, would not assure job readiness in a population that had had little prior contact with the world of industrial work.

Since this population group was so unlike that to which guidance had traditionally addressed its efforts, many improvisations were required. Among the most successful has been the recruitment and short-term training of persons from among the disadvantaged groups themselves who have demonstrated some capacity for leadership and who can, therefore, guide by personal example. The Community Action Programs, funded primarily by the Office of Economic Opportunity, have been in the forefront of this type of counselor recruitment.

From the foregoing examples we find that in the 1960s the federal government looked to career guidance to play a leading role in five important areas of national policy:

The conservation of talent

The reduction of juvenile delinquency

The employment of the hard-to-employ

The removal of racial discrimination

The establishment of youth at work

An important backdrop to this enthusiastic reliance in the 1960s on expanded guidance services to help the nation meet and resolve urgent social problems was provided by the discussions and conclusions reached by the Golden Anniversary White House Conference on Children and Youth (1960) attended by 7,700 delegates. They called for the strengthening of guidance services to assist various groups of youngsters (rural, school dropouts, the talented) to improve their preparation for and adjustment to work; to help minority groups to overcome the educational and occupational barriers that blocked their career development; to add to the productivity and effectiveness of the American educational system; to prevent or at least reduce juvenile delinquency. The delegates recommended a vast increase in the number of school counselors.[3]

The 1960s also saw substantially enlarged Congressional appropriations for vocational rehabilitation and a broadened charter which included many more potential eligibles for its services. Since rehabilitation counselors play a crucial role in restoring the handicapped, here was a further vote of confidence in guidance. During the second half of the sixties expanded and improved efforts were also made by the Departments of Defense and Labor to provide educational and vocational counseling and guidance for servicemen, before and after their return to civilian life.

The new emphasis on guidance was not limited to the government. At the conclusion of his review of secondary education carried out under a grant from the Carnegie Corporation, Dr. Conant placed stress on strengthening guidance services. In *The American High School Today* he specifically recommended that:

—Counseling start in elementary school.

—There be better articulation between counseling in the junior and senior high schools.

—There be one full-time counselor for every 250 or 300 pupils in high school.

—Counselors have experience as teachers but that they devote virtually all their time to counseling.

—More use be made of tests and measurements of aptitudes and achievements.

—The aim of the counselor be to supplement parental advice.

—The counselors be sympathetic to the elective programs in the schools which develop marketable skills.[4]

In his companion volume, *Slums and Suburbs,* Dr. Conant reached the following conclusions with respect to suburban schools:

—The main problem for guidance in wealthy suburban schools is to guide the parent whose college ambitions for his child outrun his child's abilities.

—In order to educate both parent and child about the realities of college admission, expert guidance must begin early.

With respect to schools in large-city slums, he recommended that the schools be given responsibility for the educational and vocational guidance of youth after they leave school until they reach the age of twenty-one.[5]

Starting with Conant's suggestion that the ghetto high school retain a supporting relationship with its former students until they reach twenty-one, John W. Gardner, then President of the Carnegie Corporation, suggested in his Annual Report for 1960 that more guidance specialists would be needed in the years ahead to aid people of all ages negotiate the complex educational-training institutions that are increasingly characteristic of our advanced technological society. The fact that some years later HUD decided to underwrite the construction and staffing of a limited number of community service centers where residents of the neighborhood could obtain a wide array of services, including information about services available elsewhere, reinforced Gardner's recommendation that more reliance be placed on guidance as a facilitating mechanism.

In the 1960s new or expanded efforts at educational and vocational guidance were also introduced by such diverse private and voluntary organizations as corporate enterprise, community action groups, and an array of social welfare organizations in efforts to encourage young people to stay in school, to help many who had dropped out to return, to direct others, adults as well as youths, into new training or employment opportunities, and to help them utilize these opportunities.

How can we explain this sudden widespread enthusiasm for guidance from so many different sectors of American society? The post-World War II period had witnessed an elongation and increased specialization of the educational and training systems at a time when dynamic change continued to characterize the occupational structure and the world of work. The expectations of many youths and adults about the opportunities to which they were entitled and about the results that they could anticipate from gaining access to them introduced one more complicating factor. A large number of persons found that they were unable to cope effectively with the fast-changing scene and thus were unable to capitalize effectively on the opportunities that were developing.

Since guidance claimed to be uniquely qualified to help individuals become more aware of themselves in the context of external realities, it seemed to offer a mechanism for improving the educational and occupational development of many who were encountering difficulties or who were floundering. It was anticipated that improved guidance would enable many to adapt more successfully to training and employment so that they could better realize their potential and increase their career satisfactions.

This concern with helping the individual learn about and make use of the options that American society offers was congruent with the temper and orientation of the times. President Eisenhower did not contemplate a major restructuring of American institutions: neither did Presidents Kennedy or Johnson. Johnson was the most ambitious with regard to social reform, but he tempered his advocacy of racial reforms after 1965, when he realized that black activists were operating on assumptions quite different from his own. They wanted changes, big changes, immediately. President Johnson was committed to maximum *possible* speed.

Similar tensions between the minority who wanted major institutional changes and the overriding majority who were willing to go along with carefully designed and controlled reforms surfaced with regard to education, employment, youth, delinquency, poverty —in fact, all the critical issues that await solution. The majority in an affluent America were willing to support measures to reduce the numbers living in poverty, to increase everyone's opportunity to go to college regardless of financial status, and to insure that men who are able and willing to work be helped to get and hold jobs. The new faith in guidance was in the American tradition, which is committed to the belief that if opportunities are expanded, people will respond and thereby improve their circumstances. Guidance was believed to be a key to bring the people who needed access to opportunity into contact with the opportunities that were continually opening up. Whether the numbers who needed opportunities were in accord with the numbers of opportunities available was a question not on the agenda.

In the perspective of American development, we can readily appreciate the recognition that guidance acquired in the public arena of the 1960s. We suddenly had to acknowledge shortcomings in our society: in education, employment, race relations. But there was no inclination on the part of either the public or its leaders to entertain radical proposals aimed at transforming our basic institutions. They preferred to admit that our institutions have defects, but to argue that they also have strengths. The challenge was to shore them up; to make improvements; to add appendages where necessary. Above all, they believed it is important to give people access to those institutions that could help them in their career development. And it was this that an expanded guidance system might be expected to do.

3

TRANSFORMATIONS

GUIDANCE WAS NOT a new service when it was thrust into the limelight. It had been in existence for many years, and to understand its present status and to acquire perspective on its future directions requires knowledge of its origins and development. This chapter will present a broad outline of the history of guidance. We will, however, present a thematic rather than a sequential historical reconstruction. We will delineate the environment which gave birth to vocational guidance and the dominant institutional and ideological forces that helped to shape it. We will juxtapose its present to these beginnings to highlight the major transformations which occurred in the intervening three score years. In discussing these transformations we will pay particular attention to the developments in psychology, the mother discipline on which guidance is so directly dependent.

It is generally agreed that 1908 marks the institutionalization of vocational guidance; in that year Frank Parsons established the Vocation Bureau in Civic Service House in Boston. As with most institutions, the roots went farther back. One student has traced them to the beginnings of systematic inquiry into genetics and psychology in the last quarter of the nineteenth century and the perception of a few educators that a new discipline, which comprised the study of man, could make education more responsive to students' needs at the same time that it could assist students in making the transition from school to work.[1]

Parsons saw the task of vocational guidance as embracing the following:

An analysis undertaken by student and counselor together of the student's capabilities, interests, and temperament.

The student's study of occupational opportunities, requirements, and employment statistics.

A comparison undertaken by student and counselor together of these two sets of information.[2]

Parsons concentrated his efforts on helping underprivileged children when they were completing their formal education—at about fourteen—and about to look for a job. Since these youngsters were from low-income or immigrant families, their relatives had limited knowledge of the increasingly differentiated job market and its opportunities and requirements and thus were unlikely to be able to advise and help them. Moreover, these young people were ill prepared to assess themselves, to know their strengths and their weaknesses; they knew even less about how to relate self-assessment to the shaping of an occupational plan.

Parsons came out of the social work–social reform tradition whose spiritual leader was Jane Addams of Hull House. In fact he himself had established a settlement house in Boston which attempted to raise the educational sights of young men and women who were already in the labor force. Although most reformers were dissatisfied with the ways in which industrialism and money-making were undermining human social values, they were not revolutionaries. Instead, they attempted to help young people adjust to the social order. As Lasch says about Jane Addams, "She proceeded to look for ways of reconciling people to their work . . . her own efforts served often to have as their aim only to make [society's] parts run more smoothly."[3]

The major instrument for helping young people adjust to society was the school. The reformers at the turn of the century, under the leadership of John Dewey, sought to make the school more responsive to the needs of the individual and more effective in realizing the goals of a democratic society.

Lawrence Cremin, the historian of progressive education, has singled out the following four principal objectives of these early educational reformers:

—To broaden the program and function of the school to include direct concern for health, vocation, and the quality of family and community life.

—To apply in the classroom the pedagogical principles derived from new scientific research in psychology and the social sciences.

—To tailor instruction more and more to different kinds and classes of children who were brought within the purview of the school.

—To support the radical assumption that culture could be democratized without being vulgarized.[4]

As Lasch points out, "The settlement movement and the movement for progressive education run parallel at every point."[5] Science, rationality, planning programs were all part of the new faith and Parsons belonged to the reform church. In his first and only report to the Executive Committee of the Vocation Bureau, he looked forward to the training of experts in the art of vocational guidance who would be supplied with every facility and device that science could devise for testing the senses and capacities and the physical, intellectual, and emotional makeup of the child. Moreover, he looked forward to the day when vocational guidance would "become a part of the public school system in every community."[6] Within the next few years both objectives were on the way to being realized. Harvard University offered a course for the training of guidance counselors, and several cities, including Cincinnati, Minneapolis, Boston, and Philadelphia, expanded their school services to include vocational guidance. During these first years, the National Vocational Guidance Association was founded and a specialized journal was published; it was an auspicious start.

At the end of six decades these are the characteristics of the guidance movement:

—The client population no longer consists of only underprivileged children, but includes all children. Emphasis is put on services to youngsters in junior and senior high school, but there are also limited guidance services for pupils in elementary school as well as for those pursuing higher education.

—While young people continue to be the major clients of the guidance movement, significant groups of adults, particularly disabled persons and those who have difficulty in finding or keeping jobs, also receive attention.

—The earlier exclusive focus on vocational planning has broadened to include educational planning and even decision-making in general.

—There has been a pronounced shift away from supplying the client with occupational information in favor of helping him understand his abilities and his goals.

—While formal structures have been developed for the training of individuals who will provide guidance services, and a significant proportion of today's counselors have had this training, many employed in the field have had only a limited amount of specialized instruction in guidance.

—The present armamentarium of guidance contains a great variety of approaches and instruments but currently its principal reliance is on counseling.

Let us consider briefly the forces that transformed a narrow service for a limited number of young people provided under philanthropic auspices by non-specialists to a broadly defined service available to students in most secondary schools and to selected adult groups in other settings, primarily supported by tax revenues and provided increasingly by specialists.

When Parsons' *Choosing a Vocation* was published posthumously in 1909, only one out of more than eleven seventeen-year-olds graduated from high school. The first objective of vocational guidance, then, as one of its contemporary leaders put it, was "to serve the great armies of child laborers who were leaving the public schools to become wage earners under unfavorable conditions."[7] Shortly, however, child labor laws, accelerated industrialization, higher incomes, trade union growth, Americanization of the immigrant population, enlarged expenditures for public education all conspired to keep young people longer in school. By 1920 the proportion of seventeen-year-olds who were high school graduates had almost doubled, by 1930 it had almost doubled once again, and even during the blistering depression of the 1930s the upward trend continued so that the proportion of students who graduated from high school in that decade increased from slightly under 30 per cent to slightly over 50 per cent! Projections for 1970 show that the rate has risen to a point above 80 per cent.[8]

When vocational guidance was institutionalized at the end of the first decade of this century, the completion of elementary school was the norm. Six decades later the norm is the completion of high school. In the intervening years the secondary educational system has had to embrace a greatly enlarged and more heterogeneous student body.

During the same period there was a parallel increase in the proportion of eighteen- to twenty-one-year-old youths enrolled in college. In 1910, approximately 5 per cent of this age group were in college. By 1924 this proportion had doubled. By the end of the depressed 1930s, it had reached 16 per cent. After World War II, there were further increases and today the proportion is nearing 40 per cent.[9]

The educational revolution characterized by the vast expansion in the proportion of young people who remain in school not for eight years but for twelve to sixteen years lies at the heart of the transformation of vocational guidance. The educational establishment had to adjust its structure and operations to be responsive to the needs and interests of its much larger and more heterogeneous student body and the introduction of guidance services appeared to be one answer.

The second major transformation of guidance was a result of the depression of the 1930s and its concomitant shortage of jobs for both adults and youth. At no time during the decade did the unemployment rate drop below 10 per cent and at the nadir, 1933, it was hovering around 25 per cent. When account is taken of underemployment, the situation was even bleaker.

In *Matching Youth and Jobs,* prepared for the American Youth Commission and published in 1940, Howard R. Bell stated that in the late thirties there was a "backlog of nearly 4,000,000 between the ages of fifteen and twenty-four who were then out of school and totally unemployed." And, the author reported, "Each year about 1,750,000 boys and girls in the United States offer their services as beginning workers."[10]

Bell's study, based on extensive research, stated that only about one in four high school students received any kind of vocational guidance; that only 6 per cent of the almost 23,500 white junior and senior high schools employed one or more counselors who spent at least half of their time in guidance; and that since about 2,300 counselors provided services to about 7,200,000 pupils, the resulting ratio was one counselor for every 3,200 pupils.[11]

As the title of the book indicates, Bell wanted a better adjustment between the young people and the world of work, which he thought would result if the counseling were more relevant, guidance services were strengthened, and assessment and placement services in the community were improved. The inquiries into the problems of youth undertaken by the American Youth Commission followed efforts initiated earlier in the decade at the Employment Stabilization Research Institute at the University of Minnesota that were predicated on the belief that vocational diagnosis could reduce unemployment and labor turnover by bringing about a better match between workers and work.

The passage of the Wagner-Peyser Act in 1933, which established the U.S. Employment Service, provided *inter alia* for "employment counseling and placement services for handicapped persons." During the next few years almost all of the states created employment services in 341 local offices. Here testing and counseling were available to two special groups: youth and handicapped adults. By the end of the decade, experts had learned that job maladjustment is a misfortune not confined to the young; adults often encounter serious job problems. The experts therefore recommended that counseling and testing be made available to all persons with work adjustment problems, regardless of age. But the war intervened and the pressure that had been building up to expand the counseling and testing services of the Employment Service was deflected to meet mobilization requirements.

During the 1930s there was also considerable expansion in the efforts of philanthropic and community service organizations to provide various types of vocational services to youth and adults. Because of the deficit of jobs, most of these efforts were directed to the strengthening of informational services and to improvement of assessment and counseling techniques.

Those who were involved in efforts to strengthen vocational guidance understood that it was not a cure-all for unemployment, but they believed that a better guidance system could facilitate the re-employment of some of the unemployed, even while the depression was under way, and that it could contribute to better utilization of workers and to workers' satisfaction when the depression was over.

During the immediate post-World War II years, guidance expanded its services to aid the large number of veterans with GI benefits in deciding whether to attend college or to enter job training. In addition, as we have noted, during these years guidance was under pressure to help large numbers of disabled and disadvantaged persons as the federal government established new programs to assist in their training and employment.

We see, then, that the vastly increased commitment of the American people to secondary and higher education affected the role of guidance services as did expanding efforts to provide special assistance to disadvantaged groups to become employed and self-supporting.

Pervasive changes have characterized the American scene since the first decade of this century. These changes, brought about by wars, the growth of urbanization and megalopolis, revolutions in science and technology, the radically altered role of women, new patterns of race relations, the growth of disposable income, improvements in health and increases in longevity, decreases in working time and increases in leisure time, individually and collectively, have altered the framework within which guidance operates. But we must look to its internal life—to its intellectual foundations, its value orientations, its techniques—to understand the dynamics of the transformations that have carried guidance a long distance from what one writer has called the "bare-bones of vocational guidance of the classical sort."[12] To do this, we must trace the changes that occurred in its mother discipline, psychology. When psychology changed, guidance was not far behind.

The Binet-Simon scale of intelligence made its American debut at about the time that Parsons was launching the Vocation Bureau. Otis adapted the individual IQ test for group administration and the second decade of the twentieth century saw a veritable explosion of measurement, testing, quantification in educational psychology. Most researchers did not attempt to refine the instruments of measuring intelligence, but quickly moved on to measure achievement. Cremin reports that in 1918, when the National Society for the Study of Education published its yearbook *The Measurement of Education Products,* one of the authors described over one hundred standardized tests of achievement then in use in elementary and secondary schools.[13] Edward L. Thorndike, a leader among the experimentalists, enunciated his credo that same year. If the purpose and end of education are to bring about changes in human beings, he said, then research must be directed to measuring these changes. "Whatever exists at all exists in some amount."[14]

The quantifiers were helped by World War I. Dr. Robert Yerkes of Yale University, in his capacity as president of the American Psychological Association, offered his services and those of his colleagues to help develop a screening instrument that would facilitate the Army's utilization of the large numbers of men who were being called into service. The Army Alpha, the test they developed, was easy to administer and score and it helped the Army to weed out the grossly incompetent, to identify potential officer material, and otherwise to classify and assign men. Psychology thus won its spurs. It demonstrated that it had a major contribution to make to the efficiency of large organizations. Small wonder that, during the 1920s, both education and industry attempted to capitalize on it.

In addition to tests of intelligence and achievement, the psychometricians developed a wide range of aptitude tests. Once it was postulated that an individual's performance potential could be assessed, and once jobs could be analyzed with regard to the skills required to perform them, the stage was set for turning vocational guidance into a "science." In 1928, when he was at the University of Wisconsin, Clark L. Hull published his pioneering work, *Aptitude Testing,*[15] in which he looked forward to the construction of a machine that would permit the matching of men and jobs based on aptitude scores and occupational skill requirements.

It is not surprising that vocational guidance became first attracted to and then addicted to testing. The school counselors had daily evidence of the extent to which the educational establishment was using tests to help sort and assign pupils. And they knew from their reading about and contacts with industry that employers were resorting increasingly to tests to help screen, assign, and even promote workers. As one enthusiast put it, "Few sources surpass standardized tests in efficiency, economy, reliability, validity and comparability from student to student."[16] He then commented that tests have the further advantage of being relatively immune to accusations of teacher bias and favoritism. It was many years before theoreticians and practitioners understood the limitations of testing. It was not until the mid-1950s that Ghiselli demonstrated that most aptitude tests had not been properly validated.[17] Even the most hallowed instrument, the IQ test, was found to be less pure and less stable than had been originally believed. Experts began to realize that test scores of young children are affected by their prior developmental experiences and exposures, in particular their knowledge of language, but that children with low test scores who have access to superior learning environments can increase their performance significantly.

A further limitation that was slowly recognized was the substantial spread in intelligence, aptitude, and achievement scores among successful workers in the same field. Moreover, there is substantial overlap in the qualifications of workers in lower- and higher-ranking jobs. Under these circumstances, there was little meaning to "scientific" attempts to "match men and jobs."

But efforts directed toward objective data collection and quantification were reinforced in the 1930s as investigators began to explore new dimensions of vocational choice and adjustment. E. K. Strong, Jr., and G. F. Kuder, following different empirical approaches, the first based on the preferred avocational activities of men in different occupations and the latter on clusters of preferences among students for different activities, provided two approaches to measuring "interests," which were, it was presumed, an important determinant of vocational choice. In the early 1930s, the Minnesota Multiphasic Personality Inventory was developed, aimed at uncovering critical aspects of an individual's thought and behavior patterns which went beyond his capacities and interests but which were relevant to his eventual success at work.

The "trait and factor" approach dominated the academic landscape of vocational guidance almost from its beginnings until the end of World War II. Many influences operated in its favor: the leadership of gifted experimental psychologists, such as Thorndike and Hull; reinforcement from military and industrial use; technological adaptation which cut the per capita costs of administering and scoring test results to a figure that school systems could afford; congruence with the dominant intellectual trend that glorified quantification; and, not least, the aggressive selling techniques of the publishers of the various test instruments.

Although World War II represented the single largest demonstration of the use of objective tests for personnel management—approximately 18 million men of military age were screened, selected, classified, assigned, promoted on the basis of test scores—the war's end saw a major shift in the emphasis of vocational guidance from testing to counseling.

There are different ways of describing and interpreting the facts. We can say, for example, that the academic community in the United States finally caught up with Freud and Piaget. In 1964, Cecil H. Patterson summarized the contrast between the earlier and the later approaches as follows: "The process, following Parsons, was conceived essentially as a logical, rational one, in which the feelings, attitudes, and aspirations of individuals tended to be neglected. During the last decade this concept has changed, with increasing emphasis upon feelings and emotions fostered by the development of psychotherapy and therapeutic counseling."[18]

The proto-leader of the new approach was Carl Rogers, a professor at the University of Chicago, who had been working for some years with emotionally disturbed individuals. Rogers stipulated six conditions as necessary for constructive personality change:

1. Two persons are in psychological contact.
2. The first, whom we shall term the client, is in a state of incongruence, being vulnerable or anxious.
3. The second person, whom we shall term the therapist, is congruent or integrated in the relationship.
4. The therapist experiences unconditional positive regard for the client.
5. The therapist experiences an empathic understanding of the client's internal frame of reference and endeavors to communicate this experience to the client.
6. The communication to the client of the therapist's empathic understanding and unconditional positive regard is to a minimal degree achieved.[19]

By adapting Freud's theory and methods for use by non-medically and non-psychiatrically trained personnel, Rogers opened new vistas for guidance by stressing the contribution of a non-directive strategy through counseling rather than through specific advice-giving.

The Freudian revolution had been making inroads onto the American scene during the 1930s, when many refugee psychoanalysts settled in this country, and the "mental health movement" received a tremendous impetus from the war itself when it was revealed that large numbers of soldiers and sailors were ineffective because of emotional disabilities.[20] The educated public was ready for the psychological revolution which followed the return of peace and many in the guidance establishment were also ready and eagerly joined it.

The old trait-and-factor approach had left the individual out of the career decision-making process, while the new approach placed him in the center. The reformers moved quickly to capture the old strongholds. By 1951 vocational guidance had been pushed aside in favor of a new field—counseling psychology. In Super's words in offering a description of this new field, "While it includes vocational guidance, it goes beyond it to deal with the person as a person, attempting to help him with all types of life adjustments. Its underlying principle is that it is the adjusting individual who needs help, rather than merely an occupational, marital, or personal problem which needs solution."[21]

Edward S. Bordin describes the emergence of counseling psychology as the time when "counselors began to shift their attention and emphasis from the issue of what information they could give their clients to that of understanding their aspirations and impulses, their fears and their needs. . . . Their efforts are turned toward achieving a comprehensive understanding of their clients as striving people. . . . Psychological counseling has as its aim influencing the individual's maturation and integration at the profoundest level possible."[22]

Although he had played a leading part in the early 1950s in the attempt to capture the guidance field for counseling psychology, C. Gilbert Wrenn found it necessary in the early 1960s to warn against extremism. "Let there be no more placing of help with problems of feelings and self-concept above psychologically meaningful voca-

tional counseling."[23] In the same essay, Wrenn called attention to
the fact that recent data revealed that "vocational counseling was
definitely at the bottom of the totem pole."[24]

By the early 1960s David Tiedeman was also ready to reaffirm
that the external reality had to be reintroduced as a critical dimension of vocational development. He talked of "the congruence of
person and society" and emphasized the role of decision-making
for vocational development.[25]

Just as theory and technique had reinforced each other earlier
to enshrine the trait-and-factor approach, in the post-World War II
period the technique of psychological counseling received reinforcement not only from Freudian theory but also from the large number
of contemporary scholars who, in exploring occupational choice,
work, career development, talent, placed heavy weight on the developmental aspects of career decision-making, on emotional factors, even on the unconscious.[26]

The victory of counseling psychology was made even more certain
by trends within the educational establishment as well as in society
at large. Once the high school became the aging vat for all adolescents and more and more eighteen-year-olds went on to college, it
was inevitable that counselors would encounter many young people
with developmental difficulties. If a young person were in conflict
with his parents, if he were depressed because he could not enter
into a satisfactory heterosexual relationship, if he were associating
with youths who were in trouble with the law-enforcement authorities, he needed help. He might not be able to cope with his school-
work or make career plans unless he could resolve, or at least reduce, the emotional pressures to which he was exposed. School
counselors felt, therefore, that unless they attempted to assist with
these behavioral and personality problems, they could not be helpful
with respect to vocational decision-making.

The environment surrounding many school counselors supported
this new approach since this was the period when progressive
education was advancing its "life adjustment" doctrine. Following
World War II, the educational leadership attempted to make the
secondary school experience more responsive to the needs of the
individual student. The leadership stressed emotional health, preparation for future learning, personal satisfactions and achievements,

wise decision-making, and realizable goals. Most of these desiderata
were a distance from the classic aim of education, the acquisition
of basic knowledge, but the leadership felt that these new goals
were essential if many young people were to lead satisfactory lives
and contribute to the democracy of which they are a part.[27]

The linkage between progressive education and guidance was
made explicit in the middle 1950s by Robert K. Mathewson in his
Strategy for American Education. The following excerpts indicate
what these links would finally be, as formulated by an enthusiast of
the new approach:

> The entire education process would become a guidance program.
> All educational activities would be focused on individual develop-
> ment.
> Led by trained guidance personnel, personal development func-
> tions would permeate the educational program.
> Guidance psychologists in charge of personal development would
> carry out their individual counseling functions in close connection
> with their group work.
> Since group work would deal with personal-social orientation and
> adjustment needs and problems of students . . . the guidance process
> should be much more intensive and extensive than that found in any
> school today.[28]

The author maintained that while teachers "frequently are expected to have a so-called guidance viewpoint and a knowledge of
some guidance practices . . . in the individual-social educational program all teachers would have to possess this extra knowledge and
competence to a marked degree."[29] A critical reviewer, Paul Woodring, was amazed by the author's strategy "to extend guidance programs until they become the entire program of the school,"[30] but in
point of fact Mathewson was even more ambitious. He recommended the establishment of Community Guidance Centers "to
produce a continuing guidance service in all its aspects for out-of-
school youth and adults . . . with respect to choices and adjustments
or problems not primarily met during the in-school years."[31]

In an insightful article, Lee J. Cronbach explains why in the past
educators were left largely on their own to deal with trait psychology, mental health, and personality theory. In Cronbach's view,

the experimental and theoretical psychologists broke away as early as the 1920s from studying problems of critical concern to education. They have only recently returned to the exploration of structure and styles of thought and learning which are basic to the educational process.[32] The same sentiment that encouraged the schools to move toward life-adjustment education pushed guidance in the direction of counseling for life rather than for careers.

One more spoke must be put in place. The tasks that educators and guidance specialists set themselves as well as those which are set for them by others are rooted in the dominant ideological and political milieu. Dean Schwebel of Rutgers University recently stated (in introducing a discussion on guidance by Margaret Mead and the author) that the receptive attitude of school counselors toward non-directive counseling in the 1950s and their continuing endorsement of it can be understood only against the backdrop of the dominant political environment. The 1950s were Eisenhower years, when both the leadership and the public retreated from dealing with the many unsolved problems of American society. Implicit in this posture was a preoccupation with the problems of the individual. We had recently survived a major war and a minor war. And war had led not to peace, but to an armed truce. Many were disillusioned about attempting to resolve large problems. Instead they opted for modest goals, such as helping the individual deal more effectively with himself and his immediate environment —family, job, neighborhood. Halmos, in *The Faith of the Counsellors,* makes much the same point when he talks about "post-political man," and sees counselors as "responsible for a revival of interest in the rehabilitation of the individual and a loss of interest in the rehabilitation of society."[33]

It is hard to challenge Schwebel and Halmos. They surely have a point. But they may have stretched it. If our thematic reconstruction is correct, the major varieties of guidance—Parsons' realism, trait-and-factor analysis, and counseling psychology—were all committed to helping individuals make a more satisfactory adjustment to the world in which they must live and work. Time has seen shifts in the emphases that engage guidance specialists—from helping underprivileged children obtain suitable jobs to assisting young people from affluent families improve their decision-making about their life problems. But career guidance has always been concerned with the individual.

However, it is only recently that challenges presented by the unmet career needs of the poor, of blacks, and of women, have indicated the extent to which the individual is constrained by his environment. Moreover, guidance itself has been constrained by its social role. These are among the key issues with which guidance must contend in the decade ahead.

4

ASSUMPTIONS

WE HAVE SEEN that career guidance broadened its area of concern over the years and changed its *modus operandi*. But one must look further to discover what guidance proposes to do for the American people who look increasingly to it for assistance in solving many problems. This chapter will review the key hypotheses and goals that shape contemporary guidance and will consider them in light of the social realities within which guidance functions. Thus it can be viewed as the introduction to a systematic attempt to assess the interplay between guidance and society.

It is difficult to determine the essence of a social process such as guidance that is characterized by great diversity in objectives, approaches, and results. Nevertheless, the effort must be ventured if judgments are to be reached about current operations and recommendations made about future actions. As a convenience, we will delineate a number of propositions that command the allegiance of many theoreticians and practitioners of guidance and juxtapose these premises with a discussion of the conditions which determine the environment within which guidance operates.

Guidance services can add significantly to the prospect of a satisfying life. This faith is predicated on the following presumptions.

Ours is an increasingly complex and specialized world in which a young person finds it difficult to learn about himself and the external realities sufficiently to form even a tentative strategy for the future. While he gets some help with his decision-making from his parents, teachers, peers, and other informal advisors as he grows up, it is unlikely that these resources can provide him with the background and support he needs to optimize his choices.

Many proponents of guidance contend that well-trained practitioners with specialized skills in counseling and assessment and with knowledge of occupational trends are more likely than uninformed advisors to be able to help the young person make informed decisions about his future, thereby contributing to his life satisfactions.

However, brief inputs which are typical of the guidance intervention process are unlikely to have long-range impact. In view of the changes that occur during the process of development, it is difficult to predict from observing the boy of today what will satisfy the man of tomorrow. The concept of work or life satisfaction has never been adequately defined, much less measured. Guidance proponents would be on safer ground if they staked their claim on being able to improve short-range career decisions rather than to affect the quality of human life. One might ask whether, in our present ignorance about human aspirations and behavior, it is likely that access to any professional service, even access over a long period of time, is likely to enhance significantly the satisfaction or happiness a person will achieve.

Practitioners help their clients improve their career decision-making by enhancing their perceptions about themselves and reality. The major thrust of guidance is centered around interchanges between counselor and counselee. The objective of counseling is to help the counselee make better decisions about his future by increasing his knowledge of his own interests and of what he hopes to achieve.

The belief of many counselors in the critical role of psychological factors in career decision-making leads them to explore the deeper levels of personality when they find that their client is blocked from dealing effectively with his career problems. Because of their preoccupation with intrapsychic processes and the shortage of time for consultation, many practitioners devote considerable effort to testing their clients' interests, aptitudes, or personality and to interpreting these tests. They assume that the additional knowledge thus gained will assist the counselees in developing a mature self-concept.[1] As long as a student who does mediocre work in mathematics and indifferent work in science continues to want to become a scientist, he is likely to make the wrong plans and decisions about his future. Test results, if accepted, could help him develop a more realistic strategy.

Since the performance and potential of young people who go through our present school system are constantly being assessed, and since workers are judged by their performance on the job, the emphasis on special testing in guidance has lately been questioned. We know, for example, that the contribution that tests can make to improved career decision-making depends in considerable measure on how they are interpreted and used by the client. The role of the guidance specialist is critical. He often carries the whole responsibility for administering, scoring, and interpreting test results though he may have had relatively little training in psychological testing.[2]

A related question concerns the adequacy of the training of those who engage in probing types of counseling. While psychology is the core discipline in the training of counselors, most instruction is didactic, not clinical. Many guidance students have never been exposed to a practicum to enable them to test their skills under experienced supervision.

In addition, practitioners, in stressing individual assessment, have downgraded the exploration and evaluation of external realities. Thus the individual client engaged in decision-making may learn more than he needs to know about himself and less than he should know about the world.

Guidance assumes that Americans have options with respect to their educational and vocational goals. Most families are able to raise their children without help from government or philanthropy. Moreover, all communities provide free elementary and secondary schooling. And every state provides some opportunities for those who qualify to obtain a higher education; although financial ability remains a factor, it is a diminishing one with the expansion in the 1960s of scholarship and loan funds and the growth of community

colleges. Furthermore, many Americans who are not college graduates have achieved careers in business, the arts, sports, communications, and other fields of endeavor.

Guidance specialists share, with most Americans, the belief that
a man is largely in control of his own fate. However, guidance has
paid relatively little attention to the ways in which the economic
and social status of some families restricts the opportunities for
education and work available to their children. Although some people from low-income families are able to acquire a college education
and enter a preferred occupation, the vast majority of those who
grow up in disadvantaged families are handicapped. The middle-
class model which guidance counselors use does not take account of
the impact on personal development of low family income, racial
and ethnic minority status, and residence in communities and states
with low taxing power leading to poor public services.

Guidance counselors do not appear to appreciate the extent to
which the psyche of the individual, on which their work has focused,
is shaped and reshaped by the environment within which young
people grow up. Emotional development is not the result solely of
the interactions of the child with his parents and siblings, important
as these relations are. The relations of spouses to each other and to
their children are affected by the reality pressures which govern
their lives. A family's income, the neighborhood in which they live,
the housing they can afford, and the schools to which their children
have access are environmental forces that also leave their mark on
the development of the young.

Interpersonal relations within the family are not determined by
income alone, but they are surely influenced by income. The son of
a wealthy man may well be disturbed if neither parent has more
than casual interest in him and if they leave his rearing to servants.
On the other hand, some children, despite limited family resources,
receive love and support from their parents and grow up with
secure emotional backgrounds. But the probability of sound development is greater when families do not have to rear their offspring
under conditions of deprivation.

The period since the end of World War II has seen the rapid expansion of suburbia as a haven for middle-class white American
families. This trend has coincided with the rapid increase in the

numbers and proportion of young people attending college. In most sections of the country, suburban taxpayers and school boards have sought to improve the quality of education available in their communities and have added special services, such as guidance, largely for students bound for college.

Since affluent communities are in the best position to expand and improve their school services, it is not surprising that guidance counselors in such localities have come to place heavy weight on assisting young people to be admitted to college. When counselors are hired, it is made clear to them that college advising is one of their primary responsibilities. In other communities, where the trend to college is less pronounced, many guidance counselors tend to select from among the total student body those who are college-bound, since they know how to help these young people. School counseling has become more and more counseling for college.[3]

Guidance assumes the existence of alternative choices for most people but has concentrated attention upon those with the largest number of alternatives. In recent years guidance services have been expanded to help disadvantaged persons, but many practitioners fail to appreciate that these persons require far more than self-insight. In the absence of options, guidance can seldom make a significant contribution.

All young people should have access to guidance throughout all, or most, of their schooling and more guidance services should be made available to adults. This proposition is derived from the first one, which sees guidance as having the capability of improving the quality of life. Without challenging the faith on which the theorem rests, we raise some questions to test its implications. Survey data indicate that typically a young person in high school sees a guidance counselor two to four times annually for less than twenty minutes per conference.[4] If guidance services are to be expanded in college and, as many advocate, established in elementary schools, and if more services are to be made available to adults who are no longer in school, the clear implication is that guidance will confront a major manpower crisis which, for reasons outlined below, will not be readily resolved.

But before looking more closely at the current needs and the expected manpower shortages, we should note that survey and sample data repeatedly indicate that many young people, especially from higher socio-economic families, consistently report that their career decision-making is more influenced by advice sought from and given by parents, friends, and teachers than by guidance counselors. It is likely that the young people are reporting correctly the sources of their help, but it does not necessarily follow that they have acted to their own advantage. All we know is the nature of their action.[5]

Disregarding for the moment this important caveat about where young people go for assistance in career decision-making, we find authoritative support from the leadership of guidance and its friendly allies for the proposition that the number of guidance counselors should be rapidly increased to three times its present level.[6]

There are many difficulties in the path of achieving such a spectacular expansion in the supply of guidance counselors in a short period of time—in addition to the unwillingness of Congress to appropriate the required funds. The U.S. Office of Education has approved under the NDEA only a limited number of graduate centers for training—about 35 out of 261 which purport to train secondary school counselors![7] Recruitment into the field is complicated by state legislation requiring that only persons with teaching licenses and experience can be certified as school counselors, the group accounting for approximately 70 per cent of all guidance counselors. There is a steady outflow from guidance calculated at around 10 per cent per annum. In light of the qualifications guidance personnel are expected to have—graduate education, empathy, counseling skills, knowledge of the labor market—the prevailing salary level, an average of less than $10,000 annually, and the limited opportunities for promotion underscore the difficulties which will attend any attempt at an early resolution of the manpower dilemma.[8]

The leadership is distressed that the suggested ratio of 1 counselor to about 300 students in secondary education, a standard that was accepted by various authorities in the 1960s, is still more breached than observed. The effective national ratio at the beginning of the 1970s is probably around 1 to 550.[9] While some leaders are not convinced, the weight of opinion among those directly involved in guidance appears to be in favor of introducing guidance services into the elementary school. Currently the nation-wide guidance staff in elementary schools totals about 3,000. If the new objective were to be implemented it would require more than a tenfold expansion.[10]

There are also deficiencies in guidance staffing in junior and senior colleges, and in graduate and professional schools. In light of the heavy dropout rate that characterizes all levels of higher education, there is a strong *a priori* case for a strengthened system of guidance services.

The rapid expansion of manpower training and related programs during the past decade, especially those focused on helping the hard-to-employ, has spotlighted a substantial requirement for guidance specialists capable of relating effectively to deprived populations.

In addition, other groups, such as adults searching for new jobs or careers, the disabled, ex-prisoners, women returning to work, workers approaching retirement age, would make much heavier use of guidance services if they were available.

We now recall that behind the various calculations of "need" is the faith that the activities of counselors are clearly beneficial and that more counselors would add to the general welfare. But when we begin to look for hard evidence to support this belief, it is not easy to find. The clients who report satisfaction with guidance services are more numerous than those who are disappointed. And there is evidence that because of manpower stringencies, many persons fail to receive as much service as they want or counselors consider desirable.[11] However, consumer satisfaction with or professional claims about a service must not be equated with tests of adequacy.

A further constraint on accepting the position that argues that unmet needs for guidance require a vast expansion in the supply of guidance counselors would be to assess the solution against alternative use of resources. Many an elementary school principal would opt for a reading specialist, and many an employment office manager for a job development specialist, rather than for an additional guidance counselor.[12]

Guidance is a profession. Guidance has met certain criteria of a profession through the establishment of a limited number of major teaching and research centers; the expansion of organizations whose memberships are limited to qualified persons dedicated to a professional code of behavior; the publication of technical journals and the sponsorship of scholarly meetings; and broad agreement that a counselor should have completed at least two years of graduate study in an approved program and have had at least six months of supervised field work.

But the leadership realizes that the foregoing criteria have been only partially met. And the more critical recognize additional difficulties. Establishing and gaining adherence to a set of educational requirements is only a part, and the easier part, of specifying the characteristics of a profession.

The distinctive aspect of guidance is that it primarily functions in close association with other services, with education, vocational rehabilitation programs, and the Employment Service. These relationships can be a source of strength since they help to focus the work of guidance counselors. Their services help young people to make better use of their educational opportunities; they assist the disabled to obtain occupational training which will enable them to become self-supporting; and they facilitate the job placement of others.

Another source of strength from this alignment is the willingness of the taxpayer to validate guidance at least to the present level of support. If past practice is a guide to the future, we know that once the American people have made a commitment to provide a service, it usually makes additional resources available if there is strong pressure for the service. As we noted earlier, during the 1960s Congress repeatedly attested its belief that more guidance services were necessary to assure the success of a wide array of new programs in education, and in combating delinquency, unemployment, poverty, and racial discrimination, although to date its appropriations have not matched its words.

In addition to these advantages, there are also dangers when a field becomes so dependent on others. Since more and more bond issues for schools have gone down to defeat at the hands of irate taxpayers, local school boards have been forced to retrench and guidance services have been among those cut back.

Additional vulnerabilities attach to a field whose status derives in large measure from providing a supporting service. In the absence of competition from the nonprofit and private sector, government services tend to be of indifferent quality. Although some guidance specialists work for community agencies and a few are self-employed or on the staffs of profit-making enterprises, the non-governmental sector is small. Consequently, the individual who contemplates guidance as a career field must be willing to see his future as a member of a government bureaucracy. Of course, guidance personnel are not alone in this regard; the same obtains for military officers, diplomats, space scientists, teachers, conservationists, and other specialists whose primary source of employment is the government. Nevertheless, the fact remains that guidance does not have an independent life.

While every professional must work within constraints—the physician must be responsive to the demands of the hospital, the engineer to management, the diplomat to the State Department, the virtuoso to the conductor—we cannot quiet the impression that most guidance counselors have limited scope to determine their objectives, working methods, and accountability.

Guidance counselors are capable of performing their functions competently. The nub of a counseling relationship is the establishment of a bond of faith and trust between the counselee and the counselor. Such a relationship depends in the first instance on emotional rapport and empathy. Unless the counselee feels that the counselor has liking and respect for him, a willingness to accept him, and a desire to help him, rapport will not be established—and without it no significant change in the client's behavior is likely to occur.

Considerable research has been undertaken which points to the fact that many who enter the helping professions are themselves suffering from emotional difficulties. Often they succeed in overcoming these difficulties and are later able to help others. But many carry their unresolved problems with them into their work to the disadvantage of all who come in contact with them. While efforts have been made to devise screening mechanisms to identify psychologically disturbed persons before they enter training, the simple truth is that, in the absence of overt pathology, these efforts have not generally succeeded.[13]

The making of a guidance specialist requires more than education and empathy; skill in counseling and knowledge about the complex social and economic reality are also required. A young person who acquires a degree in guidance but who has not had an opportunity to counsel, to be supervised, or to improve his skills through trial, error, and criticism may need many years to learn how to listen, interpret, and respond to what he hears in a counseling session. Moreover, he must have broad knowledge of the complex educational, training, and occupational systems; he must know how to find the facts and figures that his counselee may need to make a sound decision.

We have also called attention to the critical importance of empathy in the effective performance of the counselor and the difficulties of selecting personnel with this quality. But we have not noted so far the dominant mode of training of counselors, which is largely part-time instruction after the trainee has completed his day's work. Moreover, the fact that most training programs are located in schools of education gives a special character to most guidance training.

Psychology is the core discipline for both education and guidance. Its strengths derive from its ability to provide a framework for understanding the processes of both cognition and emotional development; however, the dominance of psychology has been secured because it has developed an elaborate array of techniques useful in assessing individuals. Since the schools must handle large numbers of students characterized by great diversity in ability, interests, and values, they have eagerly sought help in this staggering managerial task. In this, psychology has been by far the most helpful discipline.

The ability of guidance to borrow liberally from both education and psychology also has drawbacks. In the halls of academe, where competition among established disciplines is intense and where competitors close ranks against interlopers, guidance has found it difficult to establish its own domain. Indicative of these difficulties is the fact that at one of the principal training and research centers, Teachers College, Columbia University, several of the most distinguished members of the guidance fraternity are members of the Psychology, not the Guidance, Department!

Guidance is an applied field. The closest analogies are social work and clinical psychology. There is always the danger that an applied field may remain too closely tied to its mother discipline, which cannot provide it sufficient nourishment. Moreover, guidance needs much closer ties with the social sciences because counselors need to know a great deal about the world of work and the paths into it.

Most guidance counselors are trained in part-time programs for a total of thirty graduate points heavily centered around didactic courses in psychology; they receive limited instruction in the dynamics of the labor market; they are not helped to integrate and synthesize knowledge from various disciplines; the evangelism of their instructors is permitted to blur the establishment of reasonable criteria of performance; practitioners are taught and come to believe that theirs is an all-purpose armamentarium as relevant for helping the black dropout as the white college-bound youth; many can enter the field only if they have been teachers; they do not control their practice and must work in settings where their objectives are set by others. In light of these circumstances, the question of counselor competence can hardly be ignored.

In conclusion, we will recapitulate the major positions that have been delineated and queried to illustrate the gap between the affirmations of the guidance leadership and the realities within which the profession functions.

—Guidance claims that it can enhance the life and work of its clientele, but this proposition has yet to be proved.

—Guidance counselors, in helping the individual concentrate on adding to his self-awareness, pay little attention to helping him probe and assess reality.

—Guidance assumes that all people have options to plan for their future; in fact many do not.

—Guidance assumes that all young people and adults could benefit from access to its services but has failed to demonstrate how the logistical barriers to accomplish this could be removed.

—Guidance sees itself as a profession although it lacks many of the hallmarks.

—Guidance assumes that the practitioner is competent; in fact many have been inadequately selected, trained, and supervised.

5

PATHWAYS INTO

WORK

THE PRECEDING CHAPTER raised questions about many assumptions underlying contemporary guidance, and directed attention to the impact of reality on the potential of the guidance counselor to help people plan for their future. In this chapter we will take a closer look at how the institutional framework opens up and closes out opportunities as young people pass through our elongated preparatory process. In the next chapter we will consider the totality of forces affecting the career and life chances of various groups in the population and consider what this means for guidance.

The heart of the long preparatory process in contemporary society is centered in the educational system, the several parts of which stand in a ladder-like arrangement. One must pass through the lower levels before he can reach the higher ones. Moreover, in order to be admitted into one of the preferred occupations, he must have achieved a stipulated level of education. The day is almost over when a man like the late Supreme Court Justice Benjamin Nathan Cardozo could *read* law, or when a future surgeon could go directly from high school to medical school. And in many states, many mundane occupations, such as hairdressing or undertaking, are open only to those who have pursued formal training and have been licensed.

Currently on any one day in this country there are about 60 million persons enrolled in school: approximately 7 million are in college; more than double that number are in high school; and over double that number again are in elementary school.[1] Such a large number, which accounts for nearly one out of every three persons in the total population, makes it essential that the educational system cope with large groups in an orderly fashion. It must use procedures attuned to mass selection, assignment, testing, promotion, graduation. Otherwise, the system would collapse from the sheer weight of numbers.

But the policies and procedures that the schools follow to handle their tremendously demanding logistical problem inevitably determine in considerable measure what happens to pupils as they pass through the system. We shall describe the channeling and the sorting that goes on during the long preparatory process, first within the educational system and later within training and initial employment settings, and shall then identify the points of tangency where guidance can affect the career options, plans, and outcomes of young people.

The home is the first important learning environment for the child, and the early years of life are critically important for human development. In his authoritative book *Stability and Change in Human Characteristics*,[2] Benjamin Bloom makes some telling points. He states that about half of the total growth of the average child's general intelligence has occurred by the time he is four. He finds important linkages between models of language to which the child is exposed at home and his developing verbal capacities which he believes are closely related to intelligence. In Bloom's view the child's early environment is of "enormous influence" on his later development. But Bloom has also stressed that if instead of relying on a single IQ score, reliance is placed on tests like Thurstone's seven primary mental abilities, we find that 50 per cent of the population is gifted by being in the highest decile in one or more of those abilities. And "If we should increase the number of abilities by a factor of three or more, we are likely to find that most of the population is gifted on one or more of these abilities." He has also emphasized that "The improvement of education and other environments is really the only means available to a civilized society for the improvement of the lot and fate of man."[3]

Many social and educational reformers have recently been committed to the belief that the best way to handle the learning difficulties of the poor child is to establish compensatory programs prior to his entrance into school—hence the popularity of Head Start. But there is no hard evidence that several hours daily of nursery-kindergarten experiences during the third to the sixth year, even under conditions that include counseling mothers to alter their rearing practices to improve school readiness, will assure that these children will be at the same starting point as those from middle-class homes and will thereafter be able to progress normally. Both home and school must be restructured if Head Start is to provide a meaningful link. And the best ways to bring about constructive changes remain elusive. A report on the impact of Head Start, carried out for the Office of Economic Opportunity in 1968–1969, concluded: "In sum the Head Start children could not be said to be *appreciably* different from their peers in the elementary grades who did not attend Head Start in most aspects of cognitive and effective development...."[4] While the supporters of the program pointed to shortcomings in the design and interpretation of the evaluation they were not able to present clear-cut findings that pointed to success. Those who look for simple answers would do well to remember the conclusion reached by Robert Coles in his recent study *Teachers and the Children of Poverty:* "No school, no teacher, no pupil exists in a social and political vacuum."[5]

Nearly 20 per cent of all three- and four-year-old children and about 90 per cent of five- and six-year-olds are enrolled in school. Most children receive their formal introduction to the educational system at the age of five but almost a million of them have previously attended nursery school, including Head Start programs.[6]

Children arrive at school, at kindergarten or the first grade, with quite different backgrounds which affect the ease with which they will adjust to the demands of the classroom, their interest in what transpires, and their ability to cope with the several tasks they are expected to master, particularly learning to read.

As we noted earlier, American psychologists have been concerned for a long time with the study of individual differences. Here we must note that school principals have sought to make use of the findings and techniques of psychology to help them cope more effectively with their large enrollments. The large urban systems took the lead in grouping children in elementary school according to their "tested" ability to learn. Until the middle 1960s, when in several large cities such as New York the parents of minority group children protested, IQ tests were employed to help in class assignment. Recently, reliance has been placed on a "reading readiness" test or allied instrument. Thus children are often labeled bright, average, or slow within their first year in school.

The pervasiveness of such a practice was reported by the Research Division of the National Education Association, which found in a 1965–1966 survey that 28 per cent of all elementary school systems with enrollments of 300 or more grouped all children carefully and another 43 per cent grouped a minority. In systems with enrollments of 100,000 or more, about half of all children were carefully grouped.[7]

This helps to explain why a concerned principal of an integrated elementary school in New York City spends considerable time becoming acquainted with her first and second graders to insure that black and Puerto Rican children are not automatically assigned to a slow class. She has found that the system tends to designate most children from minority groups as slow learners and to assign them accordingly.

The basic rationale for grouping and tracking is to enable children to learn at their own pace. The experts have warned about the psychological damage that can accrue to a child who is unable to keep up with his classmates. But informed observers have also become concerned because at the end of six years of school those who have been assigned to classes for slow learners have fallen far below the norm for their age group and often have not learned to read or handle numbers. As one school principal has said, "Homogeneous grouping tends to freeze children into an almost pre-ordained pattern—early stratification creates failure."[8]

By the end of the sixth grade, grouping patterns in many school systems have kept the slow learners—i.e., the poor readers—together for sufficient years so they are a group apart. In an article in *Transaction* Estelle Franks states that many teachers believe that there are two groups of children—those from middle-class homes, most of whom are interested and willing to learn, and those from lower-income homes, most of whom have neither capacity nor interest to learn and therefore cannot be effectively taught.[9]

Where does the pressure for grouping come from? Teachers are one source: most of them believe that it is easier to teach a homogeneous class. As just noted, psychologists are another. But the most vociferous proponents of grouping have been middle-class parents who are afraid that, otherwise, the level of teaching will be adjusted to the slower learners and that their children will suffer. We recently explored with the school authorities in "Suburbantown" the possibility of a controlled experiment in which a group of children would not be given any group tests during the first six grades. The major hurdle they saw was parental opposition.

We have only recently acknowledged the extent to which the elementary school fails young people who most need help. A disturbingly large proportion of children from low-income and minority-group homes, as well as a small minority of white children from middle-income homes, do not learn to read effectively. The key word is *effectively*, for most students eventually learn the alphabet, learn to spell simple words, and are able to read simple sentences. But their mastery is marginal and they expand their vocabulary so slowly that for most of them reading becomes a painful rather than a pleasurable experience, a prelude to later school failure. By the time they are fourteen they are often behind their age group by two or three years in reading and arithmetic. According to Jeanne Chall, who has undertaken the definitive review of the research in this area, failing to learn to read is usually not a function of limited intelligence but reflects the difficulty that some children have in mastering the component elements.[10]

Children see themselves as others see them. If during their first years in school they associate primarily with others who are labeled as slow they are likely to consider themselves slow and to *be* slow. Once the school has labeled a child, his new teacher tends to see the label, not the person. In 1965 Rosenthal and Jacobson carried out an experiment in California which provided evidence on this point. Teachers were informed that some randomly chosen pupils in their classes were "growth sprinters." Over the course of the year these pupils showed a significant gain in their achievement scores. While the techniques and analysis of the investigators have been questioned, and it would be wrong to suggest that if all teachers have high expectations for their class all pupils in turn will excel, the obverse seems reasonable: teachers who assume that certain children can learn only with difficulty can prove their case.[11]

Much has recently been written about the damage unsympathetic teachers and a rigid educational system inflict on young children, particularly in ghetto schools, and how a poor educational system inhibits their ability to learn. The charges that have been levied against teachers and administrators run the gamut from racial bigotry to laziness; from a preoccupation with discipline to a simple lack of pedagogical competence. The schoolmen, who have been put on the defensive, have argued that the difficulties these children experience stem not from shortcomings in curriculum, teaching staff, or administration, but from personal attributes or environmental conditions beyond the control of the school—children come to school sleepy, hungry, and uninterested in learning.

Both positions have oversimplified a complex situation. The simple explanation that racial antagonism between the white teacher and black child is the primary cause of serious learning difficulties is hard to accept, since for many years Negro children in the South were taught exclusively by Negro teachers and these children also show retardation. The failure of Southern black children might be explained by reference to the value conflicts between the middle-class teacher and the poverty-stricken child, as well as by the poor preparation of many of their teachers. Coles reports a Southern Negro principals' remark: "It's the whole attitude of the system to us—and I guess we feel it ourselves. I mean, I *know* we feel it. I sit in those meetings with my staff and I hear my teachers, *Negro teachers,* talking like someone in the Klan."[12]

It has often been emphasized that poor children in the Northern ghetto are frequently instructed by the least competent members of the teaching staff, those who have just entered the system, those who are serving as substitutes, those with temporary licenses. In some of the more deprived neighborhoods of New York City these categories sometimes account for the majority of the teaching staff. This interpretation is more difficult to ignore.

With regard to children from Mexican-American, Puerto Rican, and other Spanish-speaking homes, the school authorities have recognized that their problems are compounded by the fact that for most of these youngsters English is a foreign language which they must learn in school almost from scratch. But educators have tended to overlook the extent to which many blacks are brought up hearing and speaking a dialect that hampers them in learning standard English when they enter school.

We have slowly realized that learning is a sequential process that occurs within the social framework of both home and school and that is dependent on the individual's unique personality. Children come to school with different modes of looking at themselves and the outside reality. If the school is oblivious of this fact, or ignores it, it may structure a learning situation to which many children cannot respond. If the school labels them dull, they may never learn much, at least from books, because the effort has not been made to bridge the gap between what they know and what they are supposed to learn.

Learning involves interpersonal and group relations. If parents do not show appreciation for and teachers do not demonstrate interest in the accomplishments of the child, he will probably not learn much. Since schools must control conduct as well as instruct, conflicts can easily arise in which pupils look upon their teachers and the administrative staff as unfriendly and hostile persons and they are likely not to learn—in fact they may use non-learning as a counterattack on a system that is oppressing them. And many will never acquire the self-confidence they need in order to learn. It is easy for schools to fail and many do. To paraphrase Coles, without heart there can be no hope; without hope there will be no learning. To quote one of his young interviewees: "The way I see it, if whitey really wanted us to make the scene, he'd clue us in ... and brother would we get the message."[13]

Thus many children, particularly from low-income families, fail to acquire basic skills in the early years of school. As a result they are cut off from most of the educational and occupational options that are open later on to the majority.

A precondition which must be met before guidance can be helpful in the career development of young people is that their early schooling provide them with the fundamental skills that will enable them to take advantage of a variety of options that exists in and out of school. Guidance cannot compensate for a major failure of the educational system. And guidance is not in a strategic position to

improve the effectiveness of the elementary school whose performance rests largely on the concern and competence of the principal
and the teaching staff.

During the first six years a child spends in school he is routed
along one track or another in accordance with the assessments made
by his teachers and the administrative hierarchy. In rare cases, an
enterprising parent may intervene and convince the bureaucracy
to shift his youngster to a different group. But at the end of the
sixth grade pupils have, for the first time, options about subjects of
study. The principal choices the student has for the following year
usually are in the areas of foreign language and mathematics. Often
school authorities seek to prevent students from taking courses they
believe pupils will find difficult; the advisory system therefore tends
to shunt those who have been on the slow track into less demanding
curricula. And, occasionally, even when students have been pro-
gressing normally, they may be advised to avoid more difficult
subjects if they are not expected to enter the college-preparatory
curriculum in high school. Thus, choices made at the age of eleven
or twelve may later block entrance into preferred courses of study.
One of the district superintendents in the New York City school
system who had previously been a principal of a junior high school
told us of her difficulties in eliminating grouping and tracking. She
discovered, upon inquiry, that "some of the schools were grouping
as early as kindergarten," and when she pushed the administration
of these schools to explain how they could assess ability at such an
early point in the child's life, they admitted that the principal criterion was the socio-economic status of the family. She had to fight
the "reluctance of teachers to think in terms other than ability
groupings, rank ordering of classes, and other systems of separating
pupils by quality" and to remind the feeder schools that "homogeneous groupings were not ordained by God, only by 110 Livingston
Street [headquarters of the New York City Board of Education]."

To overcome some of the invidious results of administration-
teacher-counselor determinations of the programs young people were
encouraged to pursue, she insisted that her junior high school offer
every child initially a full program, including algebra and a foreign
language, with only minor gradations as to enrichment. Her philosophy was to have the school offer the courses and to let "the children

flunk themselves out if they can't handle it. They are not flunked out in advance by being denied the opportunity."

The next decision point comes as students enter the ninth year, when they have choices of many more curriculum alternatives. Specialized high schools are found primarily in large cities. The comprehensive high school, which serves a section or the whole of a community, usually has several distinctive programs: the college preparatory, the quasi-college preparatory, and the non-college, to follow the language used by Cicourel and Kitsuse. A more conventional description is academic (pre-college), vocational, commercial, and general.

Several points should be noted about the sorting that is accomplished at the transition to high school. In the absence of strongly expressed preferences by their parents or themselves, those who have taken college-preparatory courses, such as foreign languages and algebra, and who have been able to keep up with the work will be encouraged to stay on the academic track. Similarly, those who have been tagged as poor students and whose earlier course selections and class marks have tended to confirm this judgment will often be kept out of the academic program. Either they fail the screening criteria established for admission to the academic program or, if there are no criteria, they are persuaded (if persuasion is necessary) to avoid a program for which they are not prepared and for which they have not demonstrated aptitude. The group whose tracking is less predetermined consists of young people who have taken academic courses but who have not done particularly well and who come from families whose children usually do not go to college. These young people often opt for the general, vocational, or commercial program in preference to the academic—depending on how they, their parents, and their advisors assess their interest and ability to cope with the different curricula. A critical question to raise in connection with this group is whether they appreciate the implications of not remaining on the academic track and whether their guidance counselors alert them to the dangers of prematurely closing out options. In contrast, students with similar records of performance who are from families who expect their children to attend college are usually permitted to enter an academic curriculum. As Cicourel and Kitsuse point out, in the school which they studied, ability alone did not determine assignment to college-preparatory courses. Judgments about the socio-economic status of the pupils also played a role. If the counselor decided that a student's family was unlikely to pay for college, he was shunted off into the easier courses.[14]

Once the track decision has been made, there is relatively little opportunity for change except in one direction—away from the academic and the vocational into the general curriculum, where the requirements are less demanding. But by the time a mediocre or weak student comes to the end of his tenth year, he may be bored with his educational experience. He will be increasingly aware of the limited amount of useful knowledge he is acquiring. And he will be increasingly inclined to raise questions about the relevance of schooling for his future.

This is how Schafer and Polk interpret the feelings of such adolescents:

> Because school tasks, demands, rewards are seen (by students with reading and other difficulties) as having no payoff in the future the school course becomes meaningless and empty.... If they are not achieving it is only reasonable to expect that their perceptions of future occupational payoff will be highly pessimistic....[15]

Arthur Pearl adds that "growing failure may be also in part due to a growing recognition that there is no payoff in the system for them."[16] This helps to explain why about one out of four young persons drops out of school before earning a high school diploma or certificate. While a small percentage are forced to leave because family misfortune puts pressure on them to earn money, because of pregnancy, or because of trouble with the law, the vast majority who fail to finish have been "turned off." They find that the school environment is oppressive and offers nothing to compensate for its restrictions.[17] Some students do not drop out but are pushed out: the authorities seize on any excuse to reduce their rolls, especially if their school is operating at or above capacity. It has been suggested that, in some schools, counselors are advised by the administration to ease students out. Some believe that they are helping the young man when they suggest that he get his working papers and find a job; others are simply responding to pressure from their principals.[18]

An extra year or two in high school adds little to the knowledge and competence of many young people. But dropping out at the tenth or eleventh year is risky for the young person because a diploma, even one earned by completing the general curriculum, keeps more educational and employment options open to him.

It is easy to understand why young people who are performing poorly in their studies lose interest in school and drop out before they earn a high school diploma. But what of the others? Recent research suggests that in addition to family background, which plays a significant role in determining who goes to college and who does not, the climate of the school, the relative importance that is attached to academic, athletic, or social affairs, affects the outcome. Edward McDill and his collaborators concluded from their study of twenty co-educational high schools that the "individual student's academic behavior is influenced . . . by the social pressures applied by other participants in the school setting. More specifically . . . in those schools where academic competition, intellectualism, and subject matter competence are emphasized and rewarded by faculty and student bodies, individual students tend to conform to the scholastic norms of the majority and achieve a higher level."[19] School climate may not be as important as teaching and family background, but it appears to be significant.

One consequence of tracking in high school is that considerable numbers of young men and women of good and occasionally superior academic capability do not pursue a college-preparatory course. Since college was not part of their parents' experience and since it is still not conventional for their relatives and friends to go to college, many of these students steer clear of the academic program. But they do not know, and their counselors often fail to tell them, the long-run implications of such a decision. It may exclude them from all the preferred occupations for which a college degree is a prerequisite, since it is difficult to go to college, especially a good college, if one opts for the general, commercial, or vocational curriculum in high school. Moreover, these young people often fail to learn that the financial barriers to attending college are constantly being lowered and they tend to have an exaggerated view of the occupational value of pursuing a non-college curriculum. Guidance counselors must tread a narrow path between being responsive to their clients' desires and goals (which are often focused on entering work after completing high school) and seeking to prevent them from closing out options prematurely when they often do not know enough about themselves, the educational system, or the world of work.

It is when he is in high school that a young person is likely to have his initial contact with the world of work. The conventional route for many youths is to get part-time employment—after school, on weekends and holidays, during the summer. In general, while those who are lucky enough to find jobs may earn a sum that will help them to remain in school or even go to college, they are not likely to find their work experience helpful in clarifying their occupational aims and objectives or in adding to their skills. They are most likely to be employed in routine service jobs—delivering packages, serving as office boys, helping a gardener.

In the last few years, the Neighborhood Youth Corps has operated two programs for high school youth, one during the school year and the other during the summer, that had as their primary objective encouraging young people from poor families to remain in school and earn their diplomas. During the academic year 1968–1969 134,000 disadvantaged youth participated in the in-school program. They were paid $1.25 an hour for a maximum of fifteen hours a week. Their work consisted primarily of helping around their schools— in the library, laboratory or office, or assisting in custodial work. In the summer program of 1969, 120,000 additional boys and girls were assigned to beautification projects, maintenance of school buildings, parks and recreational facilities, and helping in various programs that provided special services to young children.[20]

The underlying assumption of both programs is that in low-income families the addition of $500 or so per year may make the difference between a young person's dropping out of or continuing in school. A recent study by Goodman and Myint offers evidence that the NYC is helping youth from poor families to stay in school. "The findings with respect to clothing, as well as those concerning the high cost of 'free' public education, are compelling testimony that the students' NYC earnings are being used for the very expenses cited by fully one-third of the out-of-school group as reasons for dropping out of school."[21]

Another tie between high school youth and the world of work exists in the limited number of work-study programs which have been in existence for many years but which enroll a relatively few students. Some programs are excellent and have carefully articulated school and job assignments which contribute to intellectual and skill development. But many others are tied to distributive education (i.e., retail selling) and contribute relatively little to the educational and occupational development of young people beyond enabling them to acquire good work habits.

Perhaps the single most important career-decision point occurs near the end of high school. We have seen that about one in four students has already dropped out of school. Of the three out of four who complete their secondary education, slightly less than half go to work or enter the Armed Services; most of the remainder go to college or enroll in a special business, technical, or trade school.[22]

While many who start junior or senior college do not finish, the majority who do stay are in a preferred position with regard to their career development. Acquisition of the baccalaureate is entrée into a wide array of desirable jobs, particularly in business, engineering, and government service. Moreover, the baccalaureate is the entrance ticket into graduate and professional schools, graduation from which provides the open sesame into the most prestigious professions.

What happens to the high school graduate who concludes or is persuaded by others that he is not "college material"? He may choose the apprenticeship route, enter trade or technical school, become an industrial trainee, or seek to benefit from one of the new government training programs.

While formal apprenticeship has never been as popular in the United States as in Western Europe as a means for training craftsmen, over 200,000 men are in apprenticeship training in this country at any one time. Almost 40,000 complete their apprenticeship annually. As with college students, there is a heavy loss between start and finish—in fact, there are more dropouts from apprenticeship programs than completions.[23] However, many who drop out of apprenticeship training after a year or so usually do so because of the high wages they can earn immediately, and eventually qualify as journeymen through other routes, primarily through skills acquired at work. They may never be formally certified, but if they are white they are likely to get and hold a skilled position and earn journeymen's wages.

Indicative of the low estate of occupational education in the United States is the fact that the U.S. Department of Labor has long counted young people who attend private vocational schools as non-students. We know relatively little about the scale, scope, and contribution of private vocational and technical training institutions. It is therefore illuminating to read in the *Vineyard Gazette* (Martha's Vineyard, Massachusetts) of the immediate plans of eighty-eight members of the high school graduating class of 1969.[24] Sixty per cent were planning to go to college or trade schools, 14 per cent were to enter the Armed Forces right away, 20 per cent were planning to find jobs, and 6 per cent were still undecided about their future. Those who were going to trade schools planned to attend the following:

    Bryant and Stratton (bookkeeping)
    Gerard's School of Hair Fashion
    East Coast Aero Technical School
    La Baron School of Hair Fashion
    Stockbridge School of Agriculture (turf management)
    Campbell School (bookkeeping)
    Northhampton Commercial College (secretarial)
    Career Academy (laboratory technology)
    De Anza College (photo journalism)
    Computer Institute
    Irene Viera (hairdressing school)

For this group, trade, technical, and business schools represent an important transitional path from formal education into the world of work.

Another important transitional setting is provided by structured training within industry. Companies select for training young people who are potential long-term employees, but since no legal arrangements can be made to insure that a trainee will enter or remain on the job, the employer runs a calculated risk. Among well-known industrial programs are the technical institutes of the large automotive companies. But training for specific employment is increasingly the pattern in many other areas—airlines, health services, utilities, certain government jobs.

Note should also be taken of the proliferation of government-sponsored training programs which today enroll several hundred thousand young people who are out of school but not established in the world of work. Such new programs have opened up skill acquisition opportunities not only for the high school dropout but also for the high school graduate. While recent emphasis has been on enrolling the disadvantaged, particularly those who have not finished high school, over 40 per cent of all persons enrolled in MDTA institutional training programs and over 45 per cent of those enrolled in MDTA on-the-job-training in 1968 and 1969 had finished twelve years or more of school.[25] Although MDTA was established in 1962, there are no follow-up data about the employment and earnings of those who complete training beyond the first job or the first year of employment. But from the scattered evidence available it appears that the skills that men and women acquire through these training programs frequently aid them not only in finding a job, but often help them to advance up the occupational and income ladder.

Guidance personnel find it difficult to stay abreast of the changing opportunities for occupational training in their own areas and almost impossible to know about opportunities in the country at large. This problem has recently been compounded by the vast proliferation of government-sponsored training programs. The systematic collection and dissemination of reliable data about occupational training continues to lag since no governmental organization is charged with its preparation and it is not a commercially attractive undertaking.

While labor-market specialists disagree about the occupational value that a man derives from serving a single tour of duty in the Armed Forces, even the skeptics admit that some men profit substantially and that all men are likely to acquire some work-associated experience in the service, such as learning to work as a member of a group, living by a schedule, learning how to function in a large organization. Since, in addition, veterans are eligible for valuable education and training benefits under the GI bill, service in the Armed Forces must be seen as one more important transitional path from school to work.

The last—and, from many points of view, the most important—path from school to work is the succession of jobs held by a young worker during his early years in the labor market. Many large organizations, especially those that are unionized, tend to hire at the lowest level and to advance workers as they gain seniority and skill. Obtaining employment in such a company more or less assures a young person that he will be able to advance at least to a level where he can eventually earn several times as much as he earned when he was hired.[26]

To whom is employment in a large organization available? Since most large companies use educational achievement as a screening device, a man without a high school diploma has little chance to be employed by one of them. Whether this criterion is sensible or not is largely beside the point as long as it is used by most large employers who believe that a man who has finished high school is a better man than one who has dropped out.

Young people tend to learn about available jobs, especially good jobs, from their relatives and friends. Hence, a young man will have the inside track when an opening occurs if his father or his father's friend is a foreman, assistant foreman, or crew leader and therefore in a strategic position to hire new workers. Moreover, most personnel departments prefer to hire the relatives of workers who have good records. Young people who are without well-placed friends, such as recent in-migrants, minority youth, and others who are disadvantaged, have a much harder time breaking the corporate barrier, even if they have the requisite educational background.

In assessing access to good job opportunities we must take into account several other factors. The first is plant location in relation to the worker's residence. Many ghetto youngsters are unable to commute to the new plants located on the perimeters of metropolitan regions. In addition, even after several years of intensified efforts to reduce discrimination in employment, many enterprises still balk at hiring young people from minority groups. When an employer insists not only on a high school diploma but also on a passing score on a hiring test, many applicants who are outside the mainstream will be kept out.

While employers have a rationale for their several screening devices, the detailed analysis by our colleague, Ivar E. Berg, of how insistence on credentials actually operates has raised many questions that supporters have found difficult to answer. Berg discovered that many managements had never analyzed their own experiences. On the basis of data made available to him, he found that reliance upon credentials frequently resulted in frustrating objectives which these companies sought to achieve, such as higher productivity and lower turnover.[27] For the past several years the nation's leadership has advised and admonished young people to remain in school, at least until they earn their high school diploma, pointing out that good opportunities are reserved for men with diplomas. Men without diplomas are handicapped. But if everybody had a diploma, what then? This question is usually skirted. The answer should be obvious: if the demand for labor is insufficient to assure satisfactory employment for all who are able and willing to work and if more applicants are able to meet prevailing hiring standards than there are jobs available, the standards will be raised to bring the two into balance. In the absence of knowledge about demand one cannot assess the suitability of workers for jobs. The relevant consideration is how well workers with particular qualifications do in relation to others who are competing for the same jobs.

The high turnover rates of many youngsters during their early years in the labor market reflect in part their efforts to find an employment situation where they will have the opportunity to advance. In part, the high turnover reflects the discharge of workers with dubious performance before such workers gain protection under the umbrella of a union contract. Usually by their late twenties and surely by their early thirties, men have settled down. Either they have found a preferred employer or they are in one of the exposed sectors of the labor market where they will have to compete with all comers.

There are other facets of the labor market that bear on the distribution of opportunities. To single out one critical institution— occupational licensing. The Manpower Administration has recently reviewed the licensing situation. During the past quarter-century, the number of occupations which require licensing has doubled. Currently some states require that workers in the following occupations be licensed: jockey, horseshoer, tattoo artist, moving picture operator, watchmaker, wild animal collector. The most recent data available (1960) indicate that about 7 million persons, roughly one out of nine employed persons, was in an occupation for which some jurisdiction required a license. A 1968 study revealed that in New York City 500,000 workers were affected by licensure. Because of shortages in training opportunities, arbitrary examinations, restricted information, high fees, and the arbitrary actions of licensing boards, the entire structure weighs heavily on those who are trying to better themselves.[28]

The key point should now be clear: the labor market itself is a major sorting mechanism—in many ways as important as the educational system. If career guidance services are to be broadened and strengthened, a better understanding of the operations of the labor market is essential for both counselors and counselees. Unless those making decisions understand its operations, they are likely to make errors in assessing their opportunities and in deciding among alternatives.

A review of pathways into work must also take note of the transitional pattern for college graduates and dropouts. About one in five college graduates goes on to graduate or professional school, after which routing into employment is often clearly delineated. Such is the case of physicians, most of whom enter internship and residency training. The graduates of other professional schools, such as law, engineering, journalism, business, also follow traditional channels—although recently some of them have begun to balk at doing so, preferring to search for what they consider more socially useful work.

Most male baccalaureate recipients enter business, often with a large corporation which facilitates their transition through an executive training program. Many female college graduates enter teaching. As is true of high school graduates, most college graduates shift around during their early years of employment as they search for a congenial working environment.

We do not know much about the paths followed by the college dropout. Many take whatever job is available; others, after dropping out of the labor force eventually return to college and complete their work for a degree. Some try to get into a corporate training program. Still others move from job to job in an effort to build their competence and expand their experience.

Several conclusions for career guidance can be precipitated from this review of the preparatory cycle through which young people pass prior to establishing themselves in the labor market. The first relates to the multiplicity of the pathways. It is this fact more than any other that underscores the need for guidance services. For we cannot expect young people, even with help from home, to know about the alternative routes or the implications of following one rather than another. The fact that the preparatory cycle is complex makes it imperative that those who offer assistance and advice be well informed about the principal educational and labor market institutions and that they know where to obtain additional information.

A second finding relates to the fact that the educational establishment has become so oppressed by the numbers of students for whom it is responsible that it has established policies and procedures more responsive to its administrative problems than to the needs of its pupils. This means that by the time students are in a position to engage in educational planning, about seventh grade, they have differential options resulting from prior sortings and assessments. At this point, guidance counselors would serve their clients best by exercising caution so as not to reinforce what may have been arbitrary earlier judgments about student potential.

The analysis also highlighted the particular dangers of a child's failing to learn to read in the early years of school, which presages his later failure in school work. If there is any role for guidance counselors in elementary school, it must be tested against this proposition: how can they contribute significantly to the educability of the child?

Although almost four out of five young people who take a college preparatory curriculum attend college, only about one out of five students who are enrolled in other curricula goes to college.[29] Guidance counselors therefore must exercise care in advising young people about their course selections. They should encourage all who are not otherwise inclined to remain on the academic track until they have had ample opportunity to test their capacities and explore their interests.

The rapid expansion of public and private training programs for high school dropouts and graduates represents a further challenge to guidance personnel. They need better sources of information about this amorphous structure and they need to become familiar with the potentialities of these several programs.

The structure and operation of the labor market is another area about which guidance personnel need more information. We have seen that it often makes a major difference in eventual vocational outcomes whether a young man obtains a job with a large company where workers advance by achieving seniority or whether he remains on the periphery, forced to work in highly competitive jobs with little or no prospect of advancement. For the majority of young people who do not go on to college it can often be a matter of the greatest importance whether they receive a helping hand into a preferred employment situation.

Career guidance has its work cut out. First, counselors must expand their knowledge of the existing pathways into work. Second, they must reduce and remove obstacles that arbitrarily impede the occupational preparation of young people. Next, they must seek to strengthen the linkages between the preparatory institutions and the world of work. Finally, they must assist young people who fall off one track to get back on it or to find another.

6

MARGINS AND

CONSTRAINTS

WE HAVE defined career guidance as structured intervention to help people realize the opportunities open to them. We have noted that from its start guidance focused its efforts on the individual and has paid only passing regard to the environment. We have called attention to the ambitious objectives for guidance, particularly in helping the disadvantaged, set by policy-makers in the 1960s. We have shown that guidance has used as its model the middle-class person with a number of options. And in the last chapter we saw how the institutional structures involved in preparation for and establishment at work, particularly the school and the labor market, open up and close out options for different groups of people.

We approach guidance within the socio-economic matrix which largely determines what alternatives people have in planning for their future. The fewer the options a person has the less scope there is for traditional guidance to be helpful; the greater the options, the less need for guidance, since the able and the wealthy can make errors and still have alternatives.

This chapter will delineate the potentialities and limitations of guidance for facilitating achievement of career goals by individuals who belong to different socio-economic groups. For analytical purposes we will set up a paradigm which uses parental income as one scale and children's career opportunities as the other.

We will approach the margins and constraints for guidance by considering the entire income distribution within the society, the whole age range, and the full panoply of the preparatory-work institutions within which Americans spend most of their waking hours. And because career guidance has been both male- and white-oriented, we will pay particular attention to women and to members of minority groups.

A word about our use of the term *option*. We see options as the alternatives from which people can choose a course of action. People attach different values to education, career accomplishment, and work satisfaction, and we will try to allow for these differences in evaluating the margins that they have to shape their future.

Family background is an important determinant of educational outcome and ultimately of occupational choice and accomplishment. The educational options available to a young person are strongly associated with the income of his parents. In 1966 over four times more high school graduates whose family income was $15,000 or more went to college than did those from families with an income of under $3,000. The proportion of graduates in the highest income group who entered college was almost twice that for all high school graduates.[1] While ability plays a part in determining college attendance, income plays a greater role. This is shown in the table on the following page from which we can make these deductions:

Among young people with top ability, those from the highest income group are almost twice as likely to attend college as those from the lowest.

In the other two ability groups, the proportion going to college from the highest-income families is more than twice that from the lowest.

A higher proportion of the third ability group from the highest-income families go to college than of the top ability students from the lowest-income families.

The educational level achieved by children is importantly affected by family income, but it is also a function of the value system that reflects parental education and occupation. The higher

ENTRANCE TO COLLEGE, BY ABILITY AND SOCIO-ECONOMIC
STATUS 1965–66[2]

Ability Group	Socio-Economic Status by Quartile		Per cent Who Enter College (within 5 Years after H.S. Grad.)
Top Ability Group	1.	High	95
	2.		79
	3.		67
	4.	Low	50
Ability Group Two	1.	High	84
	2.		63
	3.		52
	4.	Low	36
Ability Group Three	1.	High	69
	2.		46
	3.		34
	4.	Low	24

the educational attainment of one's parents, the greater the likelihood of one's attending college. Similarly, the occupational level of fathers influences college attendance: more college entrants come from white-collar homes than from families of manual, service, or farm workers.[3]

Although parental education and occupation are correlated with income, they have an independent influence on the career planning of children. Upper-income blue-collar families who have been able to achieve economic security without a college education are less likely to encourage their offspring to plan for college than are college-trained white-collar workers with similar or even lower incomes. This may be due to the disinclination of the blue-collar families to provide financial support when they know that their children can get jobs like theirs without further education. Project Talent found that among young males in the upper 10 per cent of the ability distribution whose fathers had blue-collar jobs, the proportion who did not enter college was over three times higher than white-collar sons with similar ability.[4]

Schaefer and Kaufman estimate that 40 to 60 per cent of the school-age population find school "non-relevant." These are mainly

children with working-class parents who "internalize the goal of upward occupational mobility . . . but they do not see the relevance of
traditional academic pursuits to this goal. They see fathers who have
steady jobs . . . but they never see these fathers read books, write
letters, or work problems in algebra. They ask, in effect, how will
the things which the school asks us to do make it easier for us to
get jobs?"[5]

A counselor in an upstate New York high school told us of parents
who shun the idea of college for their children so that they can
help on the farm. In addition, these parents are rarely involved
in school affairs and show little interest in their children's scholastic
progress. The counselor found that this lack of parental involvement
tends to alienate their children from school, which consequently
never becomes as central to their lives as it does to other middle-
class children.

The attitudes of students toward learning are developed before
they reach secondary school. As a Project Talent investigator
remarked, "Whatever effects background has on school achievement
don't wait until high school years to manifest themselves."[6] The
influence of values is pervasive: it affects program choices, course
selections, college plans, and commitment to and involvement in
the educational process which together have a pronounced effect
on career outcomes.

A review of research indicates that financial factors are less
significant in influencing college attendance than are motivational
factors, such as peer intentions and family aspirations. Students with
high ability and desire succeed in entering college. George Nash
concludes "that a scholarship program without a need factor which
is announced only to high school seniors will have little impact on
the college going plans of talented students. A large proportion
of less talented, poorer students are not now attending college who
could benefit from education. To get these students to college requires both counseling and careful liaison between high school and
college, in addition to financial aid."[7]

Further evidence of the need for guidance as well as for financial
support for students below the top ability level are the data collected by Willingham and Findikyan, which show that 17 per cent
of those accepted for transfer from junior to senior colleges were

"no shows." The authors report, "In large institutions only one transfer out of 10 received any form of financial aid. This is hard to reconcile with the 'model of the future' which presumes that large numbers of less affluent students will transfer to state institutions from inexpensive community colleges."[8] They recommend that counselors have detailed information about procedures governing transfers, space considerations, and financial aid if they are to facilitate continued education for those who need it.

The relationships between family income and attitudes toward higher education among middle-income groups are difficult to sort out, but the situation among the poor is clearer. Of the 70 million youngsters below the age of eighteen, one of approximately seven is in a family living in poverty.[9] Directly and indirectly, poverty closes out a great many options available to those higher on the income scale. If he is unable to support his family, a man may leave home, with the result that his son will be deprived of the model of a working father. Among Negro youth reaching the age of eighteen, only one out of two has lived his entire life with his natural parents.[10]

Low family income is also reflected in inadequate food and poor nutrition. While all the linkages have not been worked out, most experts are convinced that poor nutrition is related to prematurity at birth, retardation in physical and mental development, higher incidence of illness, lethargy, and other untoward consequences which militate against a child's developing his full potential. Since hungry children cannot learn, the recent White House Conference on Food, Nutrition, and Health emphasized the importance of the schools in providing both free breakfast and free lunch for all children from low-income homes.

Low-income families live in poor housing in deteriorating neighborhoods. When several children have to share a bed and when they cannot find a quiet nook in which to do their homework they are likely to come to school sleepy and ill-prepared. And when poor urban children go on the streets to play they are exposed to crime, drugs, prostitution, and other deviant behavior which affects how they see themselves and the world about them.

Critical as the family is in the rearing of the young, it does not carry the whole responsibility. We are increasingly dependent on government for the quality of the environment within which young people grow up, since government provides so many basic services, from schools to recreational opportunities. To compound their difficulties, poor families tend to be concentrated in states and localities where governments are unable or unwilling to provide an adequate level of services, particularly health and education.

Since direct state and local expenditures approximate annually $470 per capita, of which about half is spent on education and health, governmental outlays are only a little less than the disposable income of families living in poverty. There are proportionately twice as many low-income families in the South as in the more affluent West, yet in 1967 South Carolina spent little more than half as much per capita on these critical services as Oregon.[11]

We are rapidly becoming a metropolitan society: 130 million of our more than 200 million population live in metropolitan areas. The proportion of poor families (those with less than $4,000 annual income) who live in the central city is almost twice as high as in the suburbs. Of the approximately 250,000 poor families in the New York metropolitan area, about five out of six live in New York City and of the 150,000 poor families in Chicago the ratio is three out of four. Within the central city, poor families tend to be concentrated in what the government has designated as "poverty areas," where the poverty ratio is twice that for the city as a whole, four times that for the suburban ring.[12]

The significance of this concentration of the poor is suggested by Anthony Downs in his monograph, *Who Are the Urban Poor?* "The lowest quality schools with the least qualified teachers, and often the oldest buildings and equipment, are usually concentrated in poor neighborhoods, especially in big cities. Furthermore, wealthy suburbs spend far more per student on all aspects of education. The resulting inequality of educational opportunity tends to aggravate income inequalities."[13]

When one handicap is superimposed on another—broken families, malnutrition, inadequate housing, crime-ridden neighborhoods, poor health services, inadequate schools (disregarding for the time the additional complication of minority status so characteristic of families living in poverty)—it is not surprising that children of the poor represent a high proportion of high school dropouts and a low percentage of college students. In 1965, about three of five high school dropouts came from families with less than $5,000 annual income and only one in six from a family that earned above $7,500.[14] Of the 4.9 million students enrolled in college in October 1966, about one in eight came from a family with less than $5,000 income and one in five came from families with between $5,000 and $7,500. This means that more than two in three college students came from upper-income homes.[15]

The child of poverty is handicapped by a multitude of environmental deficiencies. It is difficult to foster a favorable attitude toward education on the part of a student in the face of adverse conditions at home, in school, and in the community which tend to generate hopelessness, alienation, and lack of faith in oneself.

Although poverty is seldom so pinching that, alone, it forces young people to drop out of high school, many youngsters are unable or unwilling to stay the course even though a high school diploma would give them an edge in the competition for jobs. High school graduates have fared consistently better than dropouts in getting jobs and in getting jobs higher on the occupational ladder. In 1967 the unemployment rate for eighteen- and nineteen-year-olds was twice as high for dropouts as for high school graduates. The youngster who has a diploma also has the edge when it comes to entering preferred training programs and in his long-term prospects for earning money. Proportionately five times as many non-high school graduates as graduates end up at the bottom of the wage scale.[16]

Guidance counselors, by encouraging young people to keep their options open, can contribute significantly to the career outcomes of many whom they counsel. The children of stable, self-supporting working-class parents warrant special attention since they have options that otherwise they may not use. Since early influences have a decisive effect on adolescent actions, efforts must be made to impress parents of young children that conformity to family patterns is not necessarily the optimal course for their offspring. Many changes are occurring on many fronts—educational, occupational, industrial, technical—which suggest that following one's parents' path may not result in comparable satisfactions.

Guidance counselors can make a contribution even to the disadvantaged who have few options. Some small percentage of this group will respond positively to their experience in school. They need to be identified, encouraged, and assisted so that they can make the leap into college. A larger proportion can be encouraged to finish high school especially if they are helped to see the value of a diploma. They need proof that continuing in school will make a difference. The poor suffer not only because they have few options, but because they have little faith that they can shape their future. There are margins here for guidance, although they are narrow. Yet Project Talent reports that "there is also some evidence that students in the lower brackets of socioeconomic status tend to have fewer contacts with a school counselor than their more privileged compeers."[17]

In our discussion thus far, we have encountered several instances of the presence of options and their non-utilization. Now we will pay special attention to two large groups for whom this problem is marked—members of minorities and females.

Minority status, because of race or ethnic background, drastically restricts opportunity. The most severely affected are the 22 million Negroes, 5 million Mexican-Americans, 1 million Puerto Ricans, 600,000 American Indians, and some smaller groups, particularly recent immigrants from Cuba, Latin America, and the Orient who have not become literate in English. About one out of every seven Americans is a member of one of these minority groups and for many this status is the most potent determinant of the shape of their lives.

Note the following comparisons between blacks, the largest minority group, and the white majority:

The percentage of black families living in poverty is more than three times the percentage of poor white families.

There are proportionately twice as many white families as there are non-white with more than the national median income of nearly $9,000.

Negroes represent 12 per cent of the labor force, but they hold only 5 per cent of professional, technical, and managerial jobs. The unemployment rate for black adults has been twice that of their white counterparts, and among teenagers it is three times as high.[18]

Discrimination prevents many members of minority groups from gaining access to the institutions and services that would help them acquire a good education and a good job. Moreover, discrimination sears the soul so that a man loses faith in himself and his ability to shape his future.

However, at long last discriminatory barriers are being lowered and removed, although not rapidly enough, and increasing numbers of blacks now have access to desirable educational and employment opportunities. While knowledge of these important changes is making its way through the various strata of the black community, many young persons still make their educational and occupational plans in terms of the earlier reality of discrimination. Sometimes this is fostered by school authorities who, as reported by Kaufman *et al.*, seek to persuade black students to avoid vocational programs which train for trades where unions have followed discriminatory policies.[19] Sometimes it is fostered by their own parents, who prefer that their children follow the traditional educational pattern and study to become teachers than prepare for fields such as engineering or business which are now increasingly receptive to youth from minority groups, or to take advantage of the recently improved access to skilled blue-collar opportunities.

Guidance should reduce the time it normally takes for old ideas and behavior patterns to give way in the face of a substantial broadening of options so that the new opportunities will be used by the maximum number.

The second instance of lack of congruence between options and their use relates to females. These are some of the critical background data:

Although about half of the males in high school pursue a college-preparatory course, only slightly more than one-third of the girls prepare for college.

More men than women with the same ability enter and graduate from college.[20]

Three times as many men as women obtain a master's degree; the ratio of men to women doctoral recipients is 8:1.

Women are heavily concentrated in a relatively few traditional fields of employment. Among managers, officials, and proprietors, males outnumber women by about 6:1.

On the average, women full-time workers earn about 60 per cent as much as men. Among persons earning $10,000 or more, men outnumber women by 19:1.[21]

The last quarter-century has seen a vast transformation in the relation of women, particularly married women, to work. Today two out of every five women of working age are in the labor force and over 60 per cent of them are married; of the female workers, 38 per cent have children under eighteen. Between 1940 and 1968 the total number of women workers increased from 14.8 million to 29.2 million.[22]

It is obvious that large numbers of housewives are making use of the option to work. But women's relative underrepresentation in higher education and their heavy concentration in low-paying jobs suggests that they are probably receiving inadequate assistance in career planning. Apparently many girls continue to make their plans for the future according to the life styles of their mothers, not in terms of new options that are opening up for them. Here is one more arena where guidance confronts a major challenge: girls must be apprised of the many alternate life styles open to them, encouraged to make realistic choices, and helped to realize them.

As we stated at the beginning of this chapter, an exploration of the margins for guidance has to go beyond the high school and consider other educational and training institutions as well as the needs of adults after they have entered employment. To these we now turn.

College attendance alone will not completely determine a person's career, but it surely is influential in shaping it. The interlocking relation between educational attainment and career outcomes can be seen in the earnings of men who have completed different levels of formal schooling. While some men value security or interesting work above high income, the generally accepted single criterion for occupational outcomes is earnings.

Most men reach their earning peak between the ages of thirty-five and forty-four, and we will therefore consider this cohort. Of the more than 11.3 million men in this age group in 1968, the median income was $8,280, the mean $9,115. The following shows the median income by level of education achieved:[23]

8th grade	$ 6,457
4 years of high school	8,521
4 years of college	12,417
5 or more years of college	13,152

Clearly education makes a difference—a big difference.

But this is not the whole of the story. We have seen that the median is slightly above $8,000. In addition,

About one out of seven men with no more than eight years of school earns above $10,000.

One in three of all college graduates earns less than $10,000.

One in three terminal high school graduates earns above $10,000.[24]

Since income depends in considerable measure on occupation, which in turn is strongly influenced but not determined by education, it is interesting to observe that about half of all professional and technical workers and salaried managers and officials, the two highest occupational groups, earn less than $10,000 annually. In contrast, about a quarter of all craftsmen earn more than $10,000.[25]

These last data suggest that while it is correct to say that, *on balance*, the more education a man has the better he will fare in the labor market, we must not overlook several important caveats. Many men with limited education do well, while others with considerable education do poorly. The personnel practices of employers, the power of trade unions, the pervasive racial discrimination that continues to characterize our economy and society, licensing regulations, locational considerations, and other factors largely unrelated to a man's educational achievement determine many job opportunities. The access of people to educational and training opportunities is without question a critical determinant of their vocational outcome. But the labor market has its own way of rationing opportunity.

Therefore, guidance counselors need to assist those who wish to go on to college, while recognizing that for some, alternative means of access to job opportunities provided in their own milieu can be satisfactory. It may be that steel workers and successful small businessmen are right when they recommend work over college *for their children*. But counselors have to search out cases where failure to continue education may constitute a serious waste of potential.

We hasten to point out that among minority groups, desirable occupational opportunities through family contact are limited. For this reason many young black people have looked to higher education as the principal route to follow to achieve upward mobility. Until now, at least, this perception has been correct. Despite the difficulties that black people have encountered in acquiring a college degree it has been easier to acquire a degree than to achieve access to such alternative opportunities as apprenticeship. Counselors must be aware, however, that changes are now under way that are lowering and removing the barriers to the occupational progress of minority groups.

We have discussed the influence of family background on the occupational choices of high school graduates. We will now consider the variety of institutions that they enter and how these influence later decisions and outcomes.

First, we will consider community colleges which provide students in large population centers with the opportunity to attend school while living at home and working part-time to cover their fees and other expenses.

Between 1960 and 1970 the number of two-year colleges doubled, and today over 1,000 institutions enroll about 2 million students. Most of the increase has occurred in state-supported community colleges, which account for almost 90 per cent of the total enrollment, less than half of which is full-time. One observer comments, "Now the community college is rapidly becoming the great distributive agency in American education. Here the student can make a fuller and perhaps more accurate inventory of his characteristics; test his aptitudes and interest in the classroom, in the laboratory, or in work-study programs. Here he can revise his vocational and educational plans by bringing them more nearly in line with his reasonable expectations."[26]

Two-year colleges are more diverse than four-year institutions in terms of both student ability and educational offerings. As one expert remarked, "The junior college student is almost as varied as humanity itself."[27] Furthermore, the age span of students is broader than in any other educational setting, ranging from recent high school dropouts at one end of the spectrum to adults of all ages. The curriculum is also more varied than that at four-year colleges, since it includes vocational and technical training as well as academic preparation for the Associate of Arts degree or for transfer to a senior college.

This heterogeneity places a heavy burden upon the two-year institution. A booklet endorsed by the American Association of Junior Colleges points with pride to the emphasis of these schools on guidance and counseling services. It quotes Dr. Robert Gordon Sproul: "One virtue of the junior college is that most of its students do what they set out to do, and cross the finish line before they have grown weary of the race!"[28] But these touted guidance services have recently been evaluated and found wanting. Only 40 per cent of the student counseling at junior colleges was given a satisfactory rating by an expert assessment team. The evaluators concluded, "This mocks the frequent citing of guidance as one of the major attributes of the junior college."[29]

High economic status is not a guarantee that children will have a comparatively easy time in negotiating the educational system. Parents can help to smooth their children's way and provide financial support but, as Conant pointed out, they can and often do preclude a sensible career resolution by insisting on academic achievement and prestigious goals beyond the desire or ability of the young.

However, young people from high-status families can afford the luxury of deferring their occupational choice. A recent study of Stanford University and San Jose City College students reveals considerable postponement of career commitment among the former whose families are predominantly upper-middle class, in contrast to early vocational decision-making among the latter whose parents are primarily lower-middle class. Levin remarks that "under advantaged conditions a different career decision timetable is likely for many. This time and opportunity is, however, not always constructively used in self and career exploration since for a college student such opportunities are not characteristically plentiful."[30]

There is considerable evidence that many college students receive little or no assistance in making their educational and occupational plans. The Stanford study noted: "Small incremental decisions along with many contingent factors determine the eventual [career] choice. The need to decide on a major, a persuasive teacher who made a particular course come alive, a job opportunity or other chance factors are likely to result in a career plan more often than a careful consideration of one's talents, interests and opportunities." It notes further that the reason that so many students do not adequately examine their career plans critically is because "nowhere are they encouraged to do so."[31]

The fact that an individual has the objective preconditions for a successful career outcome does not preclude personal indecision or failure. The affluent student may appear, at least superficially, to offer little challenge for guidance, but the fact that he is not surrounded by environmental barriers to achievement presents counselors with an excellent opportunity to intervene if, and when, help is requested.

There is irony in the fact that guidance services for the college-bound student are the central concern of the high school advisory system, but when he gets to college the student is largely on his own. While most colleges provide counseling, it tends to be directed toward personal adjustment rather than to educational and vocational goals. G. E. Hill describes it as "heavily oriented in helping young people adjust to an environment and to demands that are typically assumed by higher institutions as being 'right.' "[32] The typical college counselor is a psychologist who is concerned with students who come to him for help and who leaves educational and vocational assistance largely to the faculty or placement officials.

College entrance does not assure acquisition of a degree, since large numbers of college students drop out before they graduate. A 1962 summary of the literature on college dropouts reported that about 60 per cent of all students who enter college do not graduate at the end of a four-year period.[33] A descriptive summary of the college class of 1965 found that about half of the male college entrants in 1961 and slightly more than a third of the female students entering four-year colleges had not received baccalaureate degrees within four years.[34]

The Joint Committee on Higher Education of the California Legislature recently released its report on *The Challenge of Achievement,* which contains new data on admissions and dropouts.

—At the end of the 1950s one of every two junior college freshmen left school. Today, two out of every three drop out.

—At the highly selective University of California (Berkeley), roughly half of the freshmen entrants obtain degrees from the University within five or six years.

—Of those who leave the University, about 15 to 25 per cent obtain degrees from other institutions. This means that the attrition rate is not less than 25 per cent and may be as high as 35 per cent from among these carefully selected freshmen.

—From imprecise and limited data it may be conjectured that the eventual graduation rate for state colleges in California is below that estimated for the University.

—Of three seniors in state colleges, only two receive degrees. This proportion has been decreasing over the years.[35]

A national attrition rate considerably in excess of 50 per cent for junior colleges and approximately 50 per cent for senior colleges is probably of the right order of magnitude.

Students who transfer tend to take longer to complete their course work and many who drop out return after some years. However, a significant proportion of college dropouts never return. In 1968, almost half of the population twenty-five years or older who had had some college work had not received degrees.[36]

The reasons for dropping out are many and varied. Nash remarks, "Just as with the decision to attend college, finances are only one of a number of reasons that cause students to withdraw from college."[37] Panos and Astin found that two-thirds of the students who left college reported that they would have left even if they had had greater financial resources at their disposal. Among the most frequently cited reasons for leaving the college they first attended were dissatisfaction with the environment, changed career plans, need for time to reconsider goals, and, among girls, marriage. The authors suggest that "although great amounts of time and effort are expended annually by counselors, students and parents in deciding on the 'right' college, much more needs to be learned about the complex decision process involved in selecting a college."[38] Moreover, since only a small proportion of withdrawals appear to be due to unsatisfactory academic work, the colleges themselves should provide assistance to students who are encountering difficulty in adjusting and in accomplishing their goals.

Graduate and professional schools mirror many of these weaknesses. The problem is particularly acute for older students who have interrupted their education and training and return to school after a decade or two in the world of work or at home raising a family. They often cannot find anybody on the administrative or teaching staff who has the time or knowledge to explore with them their many questions as they contemplate a radical shift in their career. A student personnel officer indicated the problems of older students: "While older students present fewer non-academic problems to the school this does not mean that they have fewer needs. They simply have different needs which student personnel services are not set up to deal with. The university administration provides no help with the kind of problem they face."[39]

These brief comments have called attention to several points on the elongated educational system where students need career guidance and would profit from it. The training structure presents another arena with potential margins. Many individuals take some post-high school vocational training and, with minor exceptions, guidance services are not available. A 1963 government study found that only four out of ten non-college youths reported that they had received any guidance from a school or employment counselor "about the kind of training they should have or the kind of work they should look for after leaving school."[40]

During the past two decades about seven out of ten young men have had some military service. Most have served from two to four years on active duty. Although the Armed Forces have attempted to inform many secondary school counselors about the military options of young men, and although through direct contact with recruiting stations young men can learn about their alternatives, most youths enter active duty with little information and less planning. And although the Armed Forces have recently made some guidance and counseling available to those in uniform and again when men are ready to return to civilian life, most young men do not consider that their military service is linked to their former or future work or careers. In general, the guidance which the Armed Forces provide is geared primarily to their own needs of manpower recruitment and retention. Nevertheless, since they offer a large amount of technical training that is directly related to civilian work and make available a wide range of educational opportunities whereby servicemen can acquire a diploma or a degree, there is considerable reason to strengthen guidance services within the military.

The age period that until recently has been ignored or given short shrift by guidance is the long stage of adulthood after a person begins to work. Implicitly and explicitly, guidance appears to say that when a person's education and training are behind him, there is little he can do but make the best of his investment. Nevertheless, for many the early years in the labor market represent a critical period of exploration and a minority of older persons will eventually find their work unsatisfactory and feel compelled to make a shift. We are only slowly recognizing a role for guidance in providing support for young people who are attempting to establish themselves at work and in assisting adults to make better use of options that remain open to them.

Job changes and career shifts occur at all ages, although job changes decline from the high of almost 25 per cent of the male work force between the ages of twenty and twenty-four to about half that level in the ages twenty-five through forty-four, and are further reduced by half in the pre-retirement years.[41] On the average, a man at 40 can expect to make about two more job changes during his years of work.[42] As Wolfbein comments, "The time is long past when an individual could prepare for some one job and then remain in it for the rest of his working lifetime."[43]

An increasing number of middle-aged persons are changing not only jobs but also careers. Hiestand notes, "Middle-aged people increasingly have options which were not formerly available to middle-aged people as a group, and not available to them as individuals when they were young."[44] Increasing affluence has enabled many middle-aged men to leave the full-time labor force for periods of time to acquire new skills through formal education and training. In addition many individuals, such as former military personnel, acquire valuable pension rights at a relatively young age and are then able to embark on a second career.

Many mature women seek new outlets after their child-rearing responsibilities have been completed. They often require help and encouragement in finding new activities. They need guidance in evaluating their training and experience and to direct them to jobs and/or education. At last count, schools with special programs or services for adult women were located in forty-three states and the District of Columbia. These ranged from fellowship programs to enable qualified women to engage in research or creative work to orientation and training for women with limited education and skills. Often credit and non-credit courses are combined with counseling and placement services. In addition to colleges and universities, many governmental and community organizations provide guidance and counseling for mature women. Since 1965 federal funds have been available to support continuing educational programs sponsored by institutions of higher learning and these are often utilized by women.[45]

The number of older people in the United States is increasing faster than the total population; persons over sixty-five now account for one out of almost ten of all persons. People today live longer than their forebears, and the added years are usually spent in retirement rather than in work. By sixty-five, most men are retired. During 1967, two-thirds of males sixty-five or over did not work.[46] Retirement has become an accepted role, but a variety of factors affects the ways individuals prepare for and adapt to it. Riley and Foner found that "the notions of retirement held by individuals who are not yet retired appear vague." One study reported by them revealed that two-thirds of the non-retired aged thirty and over have no plans for their retirement and another study indicated that only 15 per cent of older men do considerable planning for it. In a 1963 survey of corporations, only 12 per cent reported that they offer pre-retirement counseling.[47]

Many individuals, especially in early old age, have a good deal of freedom in deciding whether and when to retire. Many retire voluntarily. The growth and liberalization of private pension plans and of Social Security permit expanding options. In the first half of the 1960s over 1.6 million retirees were below the age of sixty-five.[48] But in 1967, about 3 million males sixty-five or over worked, 41 per cent of them full-time, full year. Usually the decision to retire or not depends on health, income, attitudes toward work, and employer practices.[49]

A male who reaches sixty-five has a life expectancy of about thirteen years.[50] The increase in the number of older people and the broadening of retirement options imply that many more will confront such questions as whether to retire, when to retire, and how to spend one's old age.

We have now delineated the relationship between the life situations that people face and the potentialities of career guidance to help them. The fewer options people have, the less scope there is for guidance. But even the availability of options is often not sufficient to permit people to enjoy preferred career outcomes. They must know their options; they must be helped to circumvent barriers that tend to preclude utilization. Finally, we have indicated the many groups whose needs have been largely neglected because of guidance's overwhelming preoccupation with the high school student bound for college. Yet, while we have found many constraints, we have found many more margins.

PART II

INSTITUTIONS

7

STRATEGIES

WE HAVE NOW set forth the framework within which guidance operates and are ready to explore the strategies which direct the work of guidance counselors, the conditions governing their recruitment and training, the settings within which they carry on their work, and their key functions of client assessment and the provision of career information. This is the scope of Part Two.

It may be helpful to summarize at this point the principal findings of the preceding discussion that are relevant to the discussions that follow.

— Guidance has been centered in the high school with primary attention focused on the college-bound.

— Guidance formerly used simple *ad hoc* techniques primarily concerned with expanding information for improved vocational decision-making; contemporary guidance is committed to the ideal of psychological counseling to help the individual with all aspects of his life adjustment.

— Neither the public nor the guidance leadership has appreciated the limitations of guidance to be of constructive assistance to individuals whose lives are characterized by the absence of options.

—There are many situations where guidance services can be helpful in the career decision-making of groups who have limited
options.

—Guidance has not been fully alert to the multiple pathways
available to young people during their elongated preparation
for entrance into the work force.

These are among the important precipitations from the preceding analysis; the more general can be formulated as follows.
Guidance operates within a socio-economic structure which affects
both the range and quality of career options open to different
groups; moreover, guidance is bound by institutional structures,
particularly the school, which exercise a pronounced influence on
the career and life choices of the successive cohorts of young people
who pass through them. Nevertheless, although bound by social
realities, guidance has wide margins within which to help most
people improve their decision-making with respect to their career
objectives.

The way guidance operates depends on the goals it seeks to
realize and the strategies pursued in seeking to accomplish its
objectives. This chapter will consider these two sets of determinants.

An attempt to compress sixty years of experience into a few
categories will do violence to diversity; nevertheless, we will summarize the changing goals of the guidance movement as follows. In
its beginning, vocational guidance sought to assist a particular seg-
ment of the youthful population, underprivileged adolescents, in
their efforts to find jobs. In time, the goals of the movement expanded with respect to both the groups served and the scope of
services.

The broadened horizons of guidance now include all young people from the start until the end of their schooling as well as all
adults who have to make educational, training, or career decisions.
Logistical considerations have deterred some leaders from embracing goals which include the expansion of services to many new
population groups. They find merit in focusing the attention of the
limited number of guidance personnel upon adolescents who, it is
generally agreed, still do not receive an adequate level of services.

Initially career guidance was limited to the attempt to improve
vocational choice. But before long, its efforts had become geared to
assist with educational decision-making, particularly involving the

transition from high school to college. However, the expansion of services to an emphasis upon educational objectives was a small step compared to the next move. The guidance specialists decided that since young people, particularly during adolescence, have many developmental problems, the best support they could offer would be to respond to any request for help. Many young people avoid seeking advice from parents, teachers, and others in authority during the period in which they seek to become independent. The guidance counselor hoped to step into this breach.

This represented a major expansion in goals from career to life problems. One of the leaders of the movement, C. Gilbert Wrenn, has said that "The planning for which the vocational counselor can be held responsible is planning for work satisfactions from both employed and non-employed activity."[1]

David Tiedeman, stating that man "both remembers and imagines," sees the task of the counselor as helping the client view his educational-vocational decisions as a "means-ends chain."[2] The challenge of guidance, then, was nothing less than to help human beings develop goals which will yield them the greatest satisfaction and at the same time to help them understand their alternatives.

We have traced a substantial expansion in the aims of guidance: from helping people find jobs to helping them improve their ability to plan their lives and realize their plans. This broadening and deepening of guidance goals, of course, proceeded within the established societal framework. Recently, however, under the impetus of the racial revolution, a new set of goals has been formulated; some now contend that the thrust of guidance should be to alter the social system in order to create options for those who lack them. These activists contend that it is a mockery to talk about guidance services to people who have no options.

One leader among the activists commented at one of the conferences in 1969 as follows:

—The ills of the education system are irremediable. As long as bureaucrats are uncertain about their roles, they cannot help youngsters. Counselors should get out of their offices and learn about students' needs. Youngsters want and need to be heard. Counselors should serve as their advocates, not the advocates of the organization.

—Counselors may help build the community of which the school

is a part. It is hard for the school to educate children if the
school of the street is more powerful than the classroom.

This well-informed school administrator in a ghetto area, who
himself had served as a guidance counselor, felt that the only significant contribution that counselors can make, at least in a ghetto
environment, is to work with other leaders to help reshape the school
and the community.

We can summarize the transformation of the goals of the guidance
profession as follows:

—A substantial broadening of the clientele.

—An increase in the types of assistance provided.

—An emerging realization of the necessity to bring about institutional changes so that those without options can acquire them.

In order to reach predetermined goals, strategies must be devised;
these, in turn, require the use of certain modes of procedure. We
therefore will now consider the changing strategies designed by the
guidance movement and the tactics that have been employed in
their support.

During the first thirty years of its existence, vocational guidance
followed an *adjustive* strategy. Such a strategy is based on the
premise that a great number of people at different stages in their
lives confront reality pressures to which they must respond. They
have "a problem," "a choice," "a decision" which requires that they
act and act quickly. This was the situation of the underprivileged
children in Boston when they left school and had to make their way
into employment. It also describes young people of varying backgrounds, interests, and capacities who have to choose among alternative programs of study.

The adjustive strategy does not preclude counseling. But often
the counselor is less concerned with eliciting additional information
about the individual's strengths or preferences than with using the
opportunity to gain acquiescence to a decision that the organization
has already made for him. In a society where the doctrine of participation is valued, advisors are often willing to involve the individual
in the decision-making process, even when his involvement is more
spurious than real. The presumption is that a person will be recon-
ciled to a result if he thinks he has had some part in its determination.

The term *adjustive strategy* has a remedial connotation. It is often focused on problems that have arisen or that may arise between the individual and the organization in which he must function. Such dissonance can interfere not only with the proper functioning of the institution but also with the development of the individual. Adjustive guidance attempts to spot as early as possible students who are encountering difficulties; to single them out for conference and evaluation; and to determine on a line of action that holds a prospect of helping them to conform to institutional demands. The student may be advised by his counselor to drop one or another course in order to invest more time and effort in his other subjects. Or he may be advised to get tutorial help. If the interview reveals that the student has undertaken too many extra-curricular activities he may be urged to reduce their number.

The adjustive strategy is also used in occupational counseling. A man with seniority who has bid for a better job but who finds it difficult to master the new skills may be called in by the personnel department for a conference. As a result he may be persuaded to return to his former job; he may receive extra training; or the trial period may be extended before a decision is reached about whether he can handle his new assignment.

Advisors using the adjustive strategy have differed in the degree to which their tactics "forced" a decision or left it to the individual. Parsons wanted to engage the individual in the assessment process and to help him improve his ability to weigh alternatives. But several factors conspired to encourage the use of directive tactics whereby the counselor told his client what to do. First, there was the flowering of psychometrics, which appeared to provide a great amount of objective information about the individual. Next, most counselors had been teachers—and teachers, by temperament and training, tend to be directive. They know more and they are older. Such counselors have little hesitancy in telling children and young people what is best for them. The large numbers of pupils who have to be sorted out place a premium on approaches that stress speed. Finally, school counselors are generally expected by principals to help maintain a balance between what the school has to offer and the preferences of students. The more directive the approach the easier to maintain such a balance.

If the needs of an organization are paramount, as those of the military or a large business, directive tactics predominate. In such circumstances, it is essential to assign individuals so that they can make the greatest possible contribution to the ends of the organization. Yet even in such circumstances, when individuals have preferences for one or another kind of work or working environment, it is wiser for the organization to elicit this information and to use it in the assignment process, since proper placement is usually reflected in higher productivity.

The question may be raised whether this process of matching people and jobs is a proper concern of guidance or whether it is a function of classification and assignment. In the early decades of its development, vocational guidance definitely saw its task as bringing about a better fit between men and jobs. It was this conception of its task which led it to pursue an adjustive strategy with directive tactics.

The adjustive strategy went into partial eclipse with World War II, when personality theory came into prominence. It continues to flourish in varying degrees in different environments. For example, among the sources of discontent of college students, especially those who attend colleges or universities with large student bodies, are the restricted choices open to them. More and more class assignments are made on the basis of prior grades or first-come-first-served. Another example is the school counselor who serves as a disciplinarian: it is his task to take various actions, from class reassignments to suspension, to bring unruly students under control.

The adjustive strategy, which tends to be used with directive tactics, may prove more harmful than helpful. Consider the arena of vocational rehabilitation. It is a well-known phenomenon that the recently disabled often cannot reconcile themselves to a constrictive career goal. Most vocational rehabilitation counselors believe that one of their primary missions is to help the client develop a "realistic" view of his true situation and to make his vocational decisions on the basis of a new, if unpleasant, reality. But some counselors, because of lack of adequate knowledge of the client, the changing occupational scene, family resources, or other critical elements, reach the wrong conclusion and seek to persuade a counselee with margins to settle for employment that is unlikely to be fulfilling.

Other persons can also be adversely affected by an adjustive strategy on the part of counselors—women, minority-group members, older persons, immigrants. No person is aware of all his biases and prejudices; many counselors who follow an adjustive strategy are likely to be prisoners of their preconceptions and experiences and thereby mislead their clients.

It would have been easy for a counselor committed to an adjustive approach to tell a young German Jewish refugee with a law degree who was in London in the early 1930s that it was not sensible for him to try to become an expert in oil. The large international companies did not hire amateurs, and surely not Jewish refugees! Yet this determined young man decided to follow his own plan rather than the probability tables and within two decades he had become an advisor to presidents and kings as well as to many of the leading oil companies!

This was an exceptionally talented individual; nevertheless it illustrates the importance of allowing for the fact that a member of a disadvantaged group—a refugee, a black, an older person, a woman—may have substantial personal strengths. Moreover, the adjustive strategy is likely to lead to errors when counselors project past constraints and limitations into the future at a time when political, economic, and legal changes may be bringing about radical alterations in the environment. It was not easy to foresee, even a decade ago, that a Negro woman would be elected to the Georgia legislature. In 1940, at the onset of mobilization, some firms refused to consider a man of thirty-six for employment: he was too old. Two years later, these same firms wanted to hire men of fifty-five or even sixty!

Since few counselors have the skill or time to discover all the talents and strengths of their clients, which are often unknown to the clients themselves, and since no counselor, regardless of his skill, can be expected to foretell when major changes will occur in the body politic or economic, are likely to err if counselors indiscriminately committed to an adjustive strategy. Nevertheless, the approach has managed to survive, as suggested by the following quotation from Leo Goldman in the NVGA's authoritative overview of guidance in the 1960s: "As vocational assessors counselors tend to be describers and matchers ... and they try to find the best match between person and occupation. True, they do it with more sophistication than previously.... Present practice nonetheless retains much of the flavor of putting 'square pegs in square holes.' "³

A confluence of forces helped to weaken the use of the adjustive strategy at about the time of World War II. Many counselors grew restive because they realized that they did not know enough about their clients or the world to be sure of the answers they had been providing. The growing recognition of the role of personality factors in learning and in working checked the prior reliance on aptitude and achievement measures.

Other powerful forces operated in favor of a *developmental* strategy which, more often than not, was associated with a *non-directive* stance. We will call attention to a few of the potent transforming agents. As we noted in Chapter 3, the developmental psychology of Freud and Piaget not only came to dominate the schools of education where guidance found its home, but also won the allegiance of most of the practitioners who provided helping services to people: spychiatrists, psychologists, educators, social workers, and guidance specialists.

The elongation of the preparatory cycle played a part; children remained in school until adulthood. In fact the new style for many of them was to marry and start families before they had completed their educations and before they had begun to work. The improved performance of the economy helped. After the early postwar years, fewer and fewer of the younger generation had any difficulty in finding jobs when they were ready to work. A reaction also set in to the continued manipulation of people that was an inevitable part of the nation's military experience during World War II. The postwar period saw the beginnings of the drift to a heightened individualism which burst with full force onto the national scene in the 1960s. Finally, a deepening concern with the democratic ethos reinforced the move away from an adjustive in favor of a developmental strategy using non-directive tactics.

We have called attention to the fact that the critical stages of development—childhood, latency, puberty, adolescence, and young adulthood—now occur while the youngster is in the structured educational environment. Regardless of their preferences, school authorities had to broaden their concern from the purely pedagogical to include some awareness of and response to the stresses and strains that were part and parcel of these developmental sequences. High school principals and teaches had to contend with the fact that adolescents begin to test themselves against authority and that they are drawn into all kinds of forbidden activity.

One result of the substantial elongation of the educational cycle was that occupational concerns were pushed into the background. Many young people of fifteen still have several years before they have to worry seriously about a job. Moreover, the introduction of a variety of new curricula in secondary schools led many counselors to assume that most students would encounter little difficulty in finding jobs. Thus counselors shifted their attention from occupational concerns. During their training they had been repeatedly exposed to developmental psychology, and since they were under less pressure to concentrate on vocational or educationl problems, many counselors were strongly attracted to a strategy which involved helping young people to grow up. This led them to stress the technique rather than the substance of decision-making.

Since all young people need periodic help to sharpen their perceptions of the world around them; to become more aware of who they are and the kinds of adults they want to become; to smooth their relationships with adults in authority, particularly parents and teachers; and to approach the other sex with ease, counselors began to see their mission as helping to contribute to normal development. Effective guidance, by helping individuals to face themselves and reality, would be preventive rather than therapeutic. If the young person could make the transition from one stage of development to the next smoothly, he could cope with the new challenges he would encounter rather than be overwhelmed by them.

The guidance function was redefined as one concerned with helping all young people to make the transition from childhood to adulthood with less stress and strain. The presumption was that if they were helped to avoid emotional crises and assisted to sharpen their perceptions of reality they would be in a better position to make sound decisions about their future education and work.

Many guidance specialists who espoused the developmental approach assumed that it required them to shift attention from educational and career to life-adjustment problems. Often they leaped from career guidance to personal counseling, even to therapy. There was no need to leap that far. For example, when an adolescent counselee, in exploring certain school problems, remarks, "I am always fighting with my parents," a counselor committed to the developmental approach—recognizing that this is age-related behavior—does not have to probe further, but can turn to the issue at hand and inquire: "Yes, I understand, but how does that affect your schoolwork? You are too smart to be failing in two courses."

For the most part the developmental strategy had abandoned the directive tactics whereby the guidance specialist brings his tools of measurement and evaluation to bear on the strengths and weaknesses of the client and, after a calibrating exercise, informs him what he should and should not do. By using the non-directive approach the evolving individual is placed in the forefront of the decision-making process. It assumes that the individual alone can decide what he wants out of life, which values he holds in high esteem, which he rates lower. Nobody, not even the most skillful of counselors, should presume to take over this task of decision-making. All that the counselor should do is "help the individual attain a clear-cut sense of identity . . . helping the individual decide what kind of person he is . . . assisting an individual to find a measure of reality from which he can receive feedback against which to check his self-evaluations."[4]

The new approach held sway for all of the fifties and well into the sixties, when it came in for criticism by both theoreticians and the new activists. Halmos noted, for instance, that non-directive counseling is a myth: "No matter how much care is taken to allow people spontaneity of growth along the lines of their own choosing, it is simply not true that arbitrariness of influence on them can be avoided. The social realities of counselling—underpaid and overworked counselling staffs of statutory and voluntary bodies, too many clients in urgent need of some help, lack of co-operation by other, non-counselling services and the clients' resistance too, as well as many other factors . . . will inevitably limit the counsellor's potential of behaving nondirectively." He says, in addition, "there is not enough time for each client, and there are not enough counsellors; and if the counsellor is to help he must make some decisions. What is wrong is not that he takes [sic] them but that he may find it necessary to deny this."[5]

What the shift toward the developmental strategy and its non-directive tactics meant to many counselors, as well as writers, was the eschewal of the use of tests in counseling as not consistent with the client-centered approach. Arbuckle says that it is desirable for the client-centered counselor "to remove himself from any phase of testing if at all posible."[6] Within a few years the guidance movement shifted focus. Previously, many counselors relied exclusively on tests; now, many shunned them. To quote Patterson: vocational counseling is concerned with creating "an atmosphere of acceptance and understanding in which the client is not under pressure or threat, since threat is inhibiting to self analysis." Vocational counseling allows "the client to express his self-concept in terms of his needs, his conflicts, and anxieties, and his hopes, desires, and expectations."[7] The correct strategy, according to Leona Tyler, was to adopt "consistently an attitude of respect for what each individual client now is and lending him support and understanding while he comes to terms with this unique self of his."[8]

Whatever the limitations of the developmental approach with its non-directive bias, it still was attractive for use with middle-class clients having many options who could profit from being helped to gain more insight into themselves and thereby to make improved decisions about their future. But those who have few options need more concrete help. They need a scholarship or a job; self-insight is no substitute.

The advocates of the *activist* approach do not put primary responsibility for change and adjustment on the individual. If the system functions poorly for their clients, then changes in the system are required. Consequently they argue that the role of guidance personnel is to facilitate reforms in the system. Since guidance counselors can see where institutions fail people, they are in a strategic position to take the lead in revealing these failures, interpreting them to key groups, and encouraging those who can change the institutions to do so. At the least, they are in a position to help their clients use institutions rather than be used by them.

In its concern with the creation of new options, the activist group goes beyond the client-centered approach, although it starts with the same premise that young people should have the opportunity to find themselves and the directions that they want to follow. How-

ever, interventionist counselors believe that they are duty-bound
to modify the environment so that it becomes more responsive to
their clients' needs. Therefore they argue that the school counselor
must be actively engaged in the "development of new curricula,
development within existing curricula, administrative procedures,
and orientation and development."[9]

We are reminded of the transformations that occurred during
World War II in the role of the division psychiatrist. Initially most
psychiatrists conceived their duties to be the diagnosis and treatment of the soldier or officer who broke down. But before long the
logistical problem swamped them: too many men were breaking
down. Faced with this challenge, the abler among the psychiatrists
shifted tack. They redefined their task as that of a staff consultant
to the commanding general and helped him identify the forces in
the environment—rules, structures, duties—which were contributing to the high incidence of breakdown and which, if modified,
could contribute to a lessening of stress and strain with correspond-
ingly increased retention of manpower.

The activist counselor faces several challenges when he seeks
to bring about changes in the environment which he hopes will
contribute to the sound growth and development of his clients. The
first is the intellectual challenge to identify the dysfunctional elements of the several systems that hinder the development of his
counselees. Next, he must determine those changes which would
represent constructive alternatives. Finally, he must have the personal and political skills needed to convince those in authority that
these changes will not jeopardize what the establishment is determined to protect. To understand the difficulty of this last task,
one need only recall the likely responses of parents who are asked
by a counselor to change their child-rearing practices; those of a
principal who, believing that his first task is to maintain order, is
confronted by a counselor who suggests that order is a secondary
consideration; or of the employer who, never having hired minority-
group members, is pressed to do so in the name of humanity and
equity as well as of self-interest. The activist counselor has his
work cut out for him!

Every professional group has a reach beyond its current level of
accomplishment. And that is how it should be, for a profession has

the obligation to find new and better ways of serving the public. If it is wedded to the status quo and is concerned only with the protection of its own interests, it cannot inspire confidence and gain support. Halmos comments, "It is ... difficult to see how any professional service can be stripped of the motive or desire to be *instrumental* in bringing about a change by doing a service. The counsellor's desire to be 'instrumental' in this way is an integral part of his professional motivation. No doubt this desire may push itself forward too excessively but it is certain that far from being harmful, or even only superfluous, it is a necessary condition of effective service. A perfect non-directiveness would be a negation of this motive or desire."[10]

This thematic treatment of the changing strategies and tactics of guidance has put into sharp relief the fact that the movement has undergone important changes in goals and approaches, and there is every likelihood that it will continue to do so as its intellectual foundations are altered, new techniques are developed, and it becomes more responsive to new groups seeking services. In the chapters that follow we will look more closely at the several institutions through which guidance has operated in bringing its services to the American people.

8

COUNSELORS

ONE CRITICAL ELEMENT in any professional service is the competence of those who provide it. Key to this is the field's ability to recruit, train, and utilize capable persons. This chapter will scrutinize the characteristics of the guidance specialists who play a central role in helping people to make career decisions. Who they are; where they come from; how they are educated and trained; how much they earn; their opportunities for promotion; how many leave the field—these and similar questions are our present concern.

Logistical Overview

We will first set forth with broad brush a picture of the supply of counselors at the end of the 1960s. Throughout this chapter we will rely on the *Interagency Task Force Report,* which was released in 1967 and which is the most comprehensive treatment of guidance manpower.

The *Task Force Report* presents a loose rather than a strict definition of a counselor. It merely notes that "the supply of professionally qualified counselors in the United States is largely dependent upon the number of individuals who complete programs of counselor education at colleges and universities."[1] To this group, the *Report* adds such other professionally trained persons as graduates of a two-year program to train vocational rehabilitation counselors, and those trained in counseling psychology and clinical psychology who are engaged in guidance or counseling roles. The *Report* also includes in its estimates of current supply large numbers of less trained persons who are engaged on a full-time basis in providing guidance and counseling services in major programs. Thus, it moves away from an educational to an occupational criterion to define members of the profession.

The *Report* estimated the number of guidance personnel in three major federal-state programs, education, vocational rehabilitation, and the Employment Service, as 45,000 full-time counselors in 1966.

A more inclusive estimate would have to add guidance personnel who are self-employed and those employed by the following:

Colleges and universities
Private and parochial secondary schools
Voluntary agencies
Commercial enterprises
Special governmental programs (prisons, training centers, etc.)

A venturesome estimate would add 7,000 from these sectors. Allowing for a modest undercount of 3,000 for the entire field would bring the total to 55,000. An updated estimate for 1970 would be in the 60,000 range.

The supply of counselors has the following characteristics:

—Public programs account for most of the employment of guidance counselors.
—The overwhelming majority of counselors are in secondary education.
—Guidance services in elementary and higher education are on a modest scale.
—A small percentage, probably about one out of twenty counselors, works in a profit-making organization or is self-employed.

The distribution of the 45,000 that the *Report* counted follows:

SUPPLY OF COUNSELORS IN MAJOR PUBLIC PROGRAMS, *1966*
(ADAPTED FROM *Task Force Report*)

School Counselors		35,000
Elementary Schools	2,500	
Secondary Schools	32,200	
Junior Colleges &		
Technical Institutes	300	
Employment Counselors		4,195
Employment Service	2,630	
Neighborhood Youth Corps	300	
Job Corps	465	
Community Action Programs	800	
Rehabilitation Counselors		5,450
Vocational Rehabilitation		
Administration	4,700	
Veterans Administration	750	
Miscellaneous		355
Bureau of Indian Affairs	350	
Bureau of Prisons	5	
	Total	45,000

Recruitment and Credentials

The most striking point about school counselors is that by state law, with the one exception of Michigan, they are recruited exclusively from the ranks of those with teaching credentials. Although state requirements differ, a typical specification is that only persons with three years of teaching experience can be certified as school counselors. Some states require only one year and others as many as five. A considerable number of states also require that a school counselor have had one or more years of "work experience" outside the educational establishment.[2] It is difficult to think of any other broad field of professional endeavor where recruitment is limited to persons who have first qualified in a different profession. This means that persons must train in two fields in order to practice in one. The closest analogy perhaps is public health, which has long recruited practitioners from among the graduates of schools of medicine.

Thus, for most school counselors, guidance is a secondary, not a primary, occupational choice. For many it is only a way station. While some teachers decide on their own to shift over to guidance, others are encouraged to do so by their principals. In fact, unless one's principal is cooperative, it is difficult for a teacher to shift, since enrollment in most guidance training programs requires a letter of recommendation from one's principal and at least his tentative commitment to employ the counselor-in-training after he completes his course. There would appear to be no parallel to such a procedure in any other field of training.

Another unusual aspect of guidance recruitment is the fact that a high proportion of all school counselors begin to work in guidance, part-time or full-time, before entering training. Only later do they enroll in a graduate training program, usually at a neighboring university, in order to acquire a certificate and/or a master's degree as a school counselor.

The school principal has been the single most potent recruiter. It is he who reassigns a classroom teacher to guidance. It is he who encourages the selectee to take graduate work leading to certification. He may pick teachers who are not performing effectively in the classroom. Reassigning a poor teacher to guidance duties often results in a double gain for him, since in this way he can fill a staff vacancy with a more competent teacher. Some principals, more sympathetic to the guidance function, select teachers who appear to have a special knack with pupils and give weight to those who importune them for the opportunity to make the shift.

In recent years, more teachers have begun to study for their counselor certification on their own without a firm commitment from their principal about future employment. Prospective counselors include individuals with various characteristics and goals: the young man who sees guidance as a step toward a subsequent shift to administration; an older woman who finds classroom duties exhausting; teachers who believe that they can make a greater contribution by trading the classroom for the guidance office—who believe that they can help more as counselors than as teachers.

The method of recruiting school counselors insures that this type of work is open only to those trained and certified as teachers and who have had teaching experience. Even in the analogous field of public health which, as noted, recruits from the medical profession, entrance to training and employment seldom if ever stipulates prior clinical experience.

The requirement that school counselors be selected from among the ranks of teachers was established because most of the early school counselors were self-selected from the field of education. Teachers were considered particularly suited to helping young people select their courses and design an educational plan. Personal knowledge of the schools appeared necessary for the performance of guidance functions.

Some questions have been raised about the continued insistence on teaching experience as a prerequisite for school guidance. The critics contend that it sets school counselors apart from other counselors and that it casts doubt on whether there is a generic element to guidance and counseling apart from the setting within which it is conducted. Hence many leaders, especially among counselor educators, recommend that the teaching requirement be eliminated. But the requirement was reinforced as a result of provisions of the National Defense Education Act, which stipulated that subsidized programs for school counseling would be open only to licensed teachers. The Interagency Task Force was unable to develop a consensus recommending elimination of the requirement. It was able only to point out that the requirement introduced an additional hurdle to recruitment.[3]

Much of the support for retaining the requirement has come from the leaders of the educational establishment. We have noted the strategic role that the principal plays in controlling the flow of personnel into the field. In addition, we have noted that some teachers, particularly men, take the guidance route in the hope and expectation of speeding their upward movement within the educational hierarchy. By operating as the gatekeepers of guidance, principals are in fact exercising a major influence on the selection of future school administrators. This explains the strong preference of many of them to retain the teaching requirement.

What are the patterns of recruitment into rehabilitation and employment counseling? What factors determine the flow of people into these fields? Rehabilitation personnel come from a wide range of fields. Some were originally school or employment counselors, particularly the latter. Others move into the field from social work.

Still others have had some years of industrial experience. Many are taken into rehabilitation agencies directly after college or after a year or two of graduate work, frequently in guidance, education, or psychology. The federally subsidized special training program for rehabilitation counselors, which we will consider later, is an important source, and may account for as many as one-third of all rehabilitation counselors; the National Institute of Mental Health and the Veterans Administration programs in counseling psychology and clinical psychology at the doctorate level, or just below, are other sources.[4]

While vocational rehabilitation draws personnel from many different sources of supply, it is dependent in large measure upon its own employees for recruits to counseling. In 1963, an extensive questionnaire study was undertaken of the newly hired personnel in vocational rehabilitation agencies and four out of five of those queried cooperated. Of the approximately 2,750 counselors who were added in that year, about 16 per cent were graduates of the special training program subsidized by the Vocational Rehabilitation Administration, typically a two-year course with an internship. The single largest source of new personnel, about three out of five, were college graduates, most of whom had had an admixture of limited employment experience and graduate training. None of this large group had yet completed the requirements for a master's degree. The remainder, about one out of five, who also had had varied work experience, had a master's degree in a related field such as education, social work, or psychology.[5]

As late as 1964, about nine out of ten personnel in the Employment Service, spending half time or more in counseling, were promoted or reassigned from other positions within the agency. But about two years later the situation had altered considerably. Over half still came from within the agency, about 8 per cent entered directly from college, and 3 per cent were transfers from other counseling agencies. But, almost one in four was the product of Project CAUSE, a special governmentally financed short training program for college graduates instituted to help the Employment Service fill its newly created counseling positions for work with disadvantaged youth. This left about 12 per cent from all other sources.[6]

A few words about guidance personnel who are employed in

other programs and settings. Colleges employ two types of counselors: placement counselors, who usually have acquired a master's degree, and counseling psychologists, most of whom have their doctorate. The college campus is a preferred working environment, and these positions are competed for by counselors in other settings. Private and community agencies prefer personnel with a master's degree in counseling but are often forced to hire staff with less educational background who have had experience in other settings or in related fields such as teaching or employment interviewing. These agencies, having more elasticity as to wages and working conditions, are often able to recruit effectively from among Employment Service personnel.[7] Counselors are also employed in various programs focused on the disadvantaged, although many of them have neither formal training or prior experience in the guidance field. "For financial reasons, most [of these programs] would not have been able to operate at all if they had insisted on master's degrees in counseling or social work for their counselors."[8]

It is not easy to generalize about recruitment into guidance since the ways into it are diverse. But the following are important clues to the nature of the field.

—Few young people in college can contemplate school guidance as a career and make their plans accordingly. Instead it must be a second choice because the only route into school counseling is through teaching.

—The school principal plays a key role in determining who will be trained and employed as a school counselor. Thus entry into the field is controlled by members of a different field.

—In the three major subdivisions of career guidance—school, rehabilitation, and employment—a significant proportion of the staff work first and train later.

—There is relatively little intrafield mobility.

Since, as we have seen, most guidance counselors are employed by government agencies, their certification and hiring are subject to state laws and local administrative practices. In addition to a teaching license and between one and five years of teaching experience, the typical requirements for state certification for school counselors are: a graduate degree or an equivalent number of credits; completion of a stipulated set of courses; a practicum of supervised field experience; and periodic re-evaluation of the certificate after a decade or so, with renewal based on evidence of "professional growth."

A minority of the states have additional requirements, such as work experience outside the school; the stipulation that the degree must be in counseling or guidance; higher requirements for those who supervise or coordinate counseling activities; or specification of the school grades for which one is certified to counsel. There is, however, in most states considerable substitutability among the requirements: for instance, more outside work can be offered in lieu of some years of teaching experience, or military service can count as work experience. It is worth pointing out that states are more concerned with certifying counselors than other types of pupil personnel specialists such as psychologists, social workers, or attendance officers and that for the most part the certification requirements for counselors are more elaborate and detailed. This tighter control over the certification of school counselors reflects the willingness of the states to place more reliance on professional training for judging the qualifications of such personnel as clinical psychologists and social workers than of school counselors.

Since many school systems have had to employ school counselors who are not qualified, most states have had to issue temporary certificates. These customarily are issued to persons with teaching licenses who are engaged in guidance work, usually after they have taken a few graduate courses in guidance and counseling. When they complete their graduate work they become eligible for permanent certificates.[9]

For rehabilitation and employment counselors, the major forces governing employment are embedded in state civil service regulations which stipulate the minimum qualifications for each position. For a combination of reasons, including shortages of professionals, limitations of budget, agency salary structures, uncertainty on the part of some administrators about the value of additional training for performance on the job, there is a wide diversity of background among those who serve in these capacities.

Responding to pressure from the guidance profession, in 1964 the U.S. Employment Service sought to bring order into the inchoate structure by specifying three levels of employment in counseling positions—counselor intern, journeyman counselor, and master counselor—and detailing the qualifying education and experience and the scope for work for each level. A considerable number of the states have adopted the model. The minimum educational requirement for employment counselors is a baccalaureate degree.[10]

Since personnel regulations are written and enforced by fifty states and by hundreds of agencies, it is no wonder that the guidance field is characterized by great diversity in the requirements for certification or employment. This is one of the conclusions of the Invitational Conference on Counselors (1965): "There seems to be no general agreement among counseling specialties or among the States as to what levels or types of training or experience should be required. Each counseling specialty tends to have its own selection standards and training requirements."[11]

As this quotation suggests, the regulations mandated by the various professional groups which seek to exercise control over admission into their specialty must be considered in conjunction with the statutes of the states and the rules of the employing agency. The professional groups also are engaged in the never-ending task of specifying criteria for selection, training, certification, employment, promotion.

In many occupational fields there is a difference between what the educators insist is desirable preparation and the attitudes of employers and practitioners about what is essential for effective work performance. Nowhere is this lack of congruence greater than in the field of guidance. Without a broad consensus about the work counselors are expected to perform, it is clearly impossible to reach agreement about how they should be trained. An attempt to understand the complex forces that are agitating the field of guidance today must therefore focus on the critical training issue.

Education and Training

There are at least five important dimensions of training that warrant consideration: admission to study, curriculum specifics, type and length of the course, staffing, and student assessment.

In a 1965–1966 Inventory of Counselor Education Programs, the U.S. Office of Education found that relatively little selectivity in admission was exercised by half of the approximately 300 counselor training institutions. A successful applicant for school counselor training had to have his baccalaureate degree, a teaching license and classroom experience, and a letter of recommendation from his principal. The remaining institutions looked carefully at the candidate's intellectual abilities, his personality characteristics, and his experience.[12]

A supplemental selection device, increasingly in vogue, is faculty observation of the performance of prospective candidates in a leaderless group discussion. The faculty sets the theme and then observes the ability of individuals to meet the challenge. If a person remains mute throughout the entire session, he may not be accepted, but if he is able to participate without either domination or anxiety, he is likely to make the grade. Of course, most students know what the examiners are looking for and are able to perform accordingly.

There is a considerable body of research including, in particular, Kelly and Fiske's studies of clinical psychologists and Holt and Luborsky's research on the training of psychiatrists that points up the fragility of selection criteria at the beginning of a training program in the psychological realm to performance criteria at the end.[13] There is general agreement that one of the important tasks of a strong training program involving interpersonal competences is to assess candidates throughout the program and to encourage those who demonstrate lack of adaptability to drop out. To achieve this end, however, a training program must be constructed with an eye to its contribution to improved selection.

The present one-year master's training program is already seeking to accomplish a great deal and it is questionable whether it could take on additional tasks, particularly one as subtle as improved selection. The typical one-year program aims at providing students with some understanding of personality development, psychometrics, occupational information, and guidance as an institution. Most schools, but not all, also include at least a few hours of group guidance and some supervised field experience.

Eighty per cent of those in training to become school counselors are engaged in part-time study—that is, in the late afternoons, evenings, Saturdays, and during summer vacations. "Part-time study invariably leads to the preparation of 'technique-oriented' counselors who ... have not ... developed the understandings and skills necessary to function in helping relationships as professional counselors."[14]

Most guidance departments are located in schools of education or are closely allied with them. They frequently borrow faculty or courses from cognate departments such as psychology and sociology, and sometimes even from statistics and economics. These arrangements usually are inadequate since instructors from the major disciplines often find it difficult to adjust their offerings to students with interests in an applied field such as guidance. The guidance staff itself is likely to be composed of a small number of full-time professors and instructors, supplemented, in urban universities particularly, by part-time lecturers who often hold positions in guidance or administration in the local school system. This means that the typical guidance faculty is composed of three distinct subgroups, each with a different philosophy and outlook. The difficulties of establishing and maintaining an integrated curriculum are legion and are usually insurmountable.

There are other sources of instability and tension. As we might expect, the full-time academic staff and the adjunct faculty members drawn from the world of guidance and education tend to see the field differently. There are also differences in orientation and outlook between the full-time staff and the part-time students. The students cannot help but note gaps between the ideal system which their professors describe and the one in which they earn their living. Moreover, the adjunct staff is likely to present a third view of reality.

Counselor educators are, of course, aware that they and most of their students are on different wave-lengths. Some instructors respond by expounding ever more forcibly their "professional" point of view—that is, how a guidance system should ideally be structured and operated. If they do respond in this manner, the gap between teacher and student is further widened. Moreover, students who attend the university after a hard day's work often resist their instructors' efforts to involve them actively in the work of the class. They are likely to find certain courses such as statistics, psychological testing, and occupational information difficult and uninteresting; many never master these materials beyond the simplest level.

Students often come to practice sessions poorly prepared. They usually have not been forced to rethink their attitudes toward young people or to consider the experiences and materials they can draw on to help them in working with youth. They seldom confront in the practicum a counseling outcome which leads to a significant change in client decision-making. Whether they do well or poorly, they are likely to receive a passing grade and earn their certificate or degree. It is a rare instructor who tries and succeeds in persuading a student to drop out because of demonstrated weaknesses during training.

Many questions and many weaknesses about the present educational and training structure, particularly the one-year master's program for school counselors, can be delineated:

—There is too much stress on didactic instruction, too little on clinical experience.

—Most students study part-time, which makes it difficult for them to become fully engaged in their studies.

—The number of subjects to which students are exposed is too great relative to the time available.

—Faculty and students have a preference for dynamic psychology and there tends to be duplication among courses.

The one-year master's program for counselors has the dominant role in the training structure. The Task Force, for instance, estimated that in the quinquennium 1965–1966 through 1969–1970 there would be the following distribution of certificates and degrees awarded:

Specialist Certificates	6,500
One-year master's degrees	44,000
Two-year master's degrees	6,500
Doctorates	3,800

This means that the number who acquire a one-year master's degree will be more than four times the number who acquire a two-year master's or doctorate.[15]

In recent years, the U.S. Office of Education approved less than 20 per cent of 261 counselor training institutions as qualified to receive federal funding for programs in school counselor education.[16] It would appear that the structure of graduate training of guidance personnel in the United States must be inadequate, since government agencies are under great pressure to approve institutions as grant recipients.

Most of the training programs subsidized by the Vocational

Rehabilitation Administration now are two-year courses plus a practicum; the Veterans Administration hires for its guidance and counseling staffs only persons with doctorates or with at least sixty graduate credits plus field experience.

About one out of five Employment Service counselors is not a college graduate. The largest group consists of persons with bachelor's degrees who have accumulated some graduate credits in guidance. Only about one in nine has acquired a master's degree.[17] There are few graduate programs specifically directed toward the preparation of employment counselors. Most training is done in short-term workshops and in summer courses.

Upgrading

All training need not—in fact, cannot—take place while the candidate is studying for his certificate or degree. In every occupation skill acquisition continues to take place on the job. Experience is an important teacher, and counselors can grow in strength and understanding as they work with clients. An important consideration in professional growth is the quality of supervision. In certain work settings, the new counselor may be supervised by an experienced and knowledgeable colleague. But this is not the case in either the typical school or employment service setting. It is probably most characteristic of the guidance and counseling services of the Veterans Administration and of the well-operated community agencies.

We must also consider the opportunities for counselors to participate in continuing education and training, both formal and informal. For instance, some state employment offices hire school counselors during the summer to fill in for vacationing staff. Managers of local offices and school counselors report enthusiastically about this program. They see many advantages accruing to their own operations by the forging of new links between the local school and the Employment Service.[18] In addition, an outstanding effort at retraining school counselors has been the NDEA Summer Training Program. During the years 1960–1965, for instance, more than 8,000 school counselors had an opportunity to upgrade their skills through summer courses.[19]

Job changing is a recognized method of skill acquisition and even though, as we shall see, there is relatively little mobility among the several fields of guidance, there is considerable turnover within each field. And many who change jobs are able to add to their knowledge and experience. For instance, a school counselor who shifts the locus of employment from a rural to an urban environment, or from a high- to a low-income community, will meet students with different values and with different career alternatives. Such a counselor will be likely to reassess ways of acting and reacting to be responsive to a different type of client. This also holds for other types of guidance personnel who change jobs.

Salaries and Promotion

Salaries and career opportunities loom large in the attraction and retention of guidance personnel. The salaries of school counselors are geared closely to the salaries of teachers with equivalent years of experience and graduate study. Sometimes there may be a small differential of $500 to $1,000 in favor of the counselor, particularly if the counselor works eleven months a year, as some do. Special conditions aside, school counselors are likely to earn an average of between $8,000 to $9,000; those in school districts with a low salary scale earn less and those in high-salary locations earn more.

One of the problems school counseling confronts is the difficulty of career advancement. In a large metropolitan school district there may be a few supervisory positions in the guidance hierarchy; the director may earn $15,000 or even more, and there may be several counselors under him. But in most districts the school counselor has no way to move up except by shifting into administration. Furthermore, many states had no central guidance unit and some states had only one or two persons who supervised local school guidance operations until federal funds were provided under the NDEA in the latter 1950s to build up a capability in this area.

Given the salary spread in rehabilitation counseling between newly hired graduates with little or no training and those who have acquired a doctorate and the spread in salary levels between communities and agencies, it is not meaningful to calculate an average salary for the rehabilitation counselor. We can say that the salaries of those who have completed the two-year program tend to be higher than those of school counselors (who have a shorter work year); graduates of the two-year program are likely to earn between $10,000 and $12,000; those with a doctorate are likely to earn approximately $15,000.

Partly as a result of their lower level of educational achievement and partly as a result of the lower over-all salary levels that prevail in the Employment Service, employment counselors are the lowest paid of the three major guidance groups: the majority earn between $6,000 and $8,000; few earn more than $10,000. One reason for the low ceiling is the bureaucratic pressure that would result if a staff member earned more than the manager of the office. In actuality, however, the low ceiling has made it exceedingly difficult for the Employment Service to recruit well-trained counselors or to retain among its own staff those who acquire a higher degree.[20]

From this brief overview, the following generalizations about salaries can be ventured:

—The salaries of school and employment counselors are pegged closely to those of their colleagues.

—The average salary for a guidance counselor is below that for persons with equivalent educational background employed outside the governmental sector.

—The opportunities for advancement are limited since there are relatively few supervisory and administrative positions in the field.

—The ceiling for counselors is relatively low, about $15,000. Few counselors are able to earn more.

—If counselors want to keep their careers open, they must eventually move out of guidance into administration or other work.

Turnover

The available data for school counselors generally fail to distinguish between those who retire or die and must be replaced, those who shift out of counseling into administration and must also be replaced, and those who move from one school to another but remain in counseling. Estimates have been made of gross turnover of about

10 per cent a year; this seems reasonable. We believe that those who leave their jobs or the field are likely to be those with the least or the most training and that men are more likely than women to be among the job-changers.

Scattered studies suggest that turnover among rehabilitation counselors may be at the same general rate as among school counselors, 10 per cent per annum,

A higher turnover rate of 15 per cent among counselors in the Employment Service has been calculated. Moreover, relatively few employment counselors in the Employment Service have had more than three years' experience and few have had counseling experience in other settings. Unlike vocational rehabilitation, the Employment Service has had great difficulty in attracting counselors from other settings.[21]

What else do we know about turnover rates? Two studies in the early 1960s revealed that of the graduates of two federally subsidized programs, vocational rehabilitation and the full-year course for school counselors under NDEA, approximately one quarter were not employed in guidance the following year. Among those who were employed in guidance, only about 40 per cent of the rehabilitation counselors were employed in a state agency.[22]

The relatively high turnover rates reflect such diverse factors as movement out of the field as some seek better career opportunities, movement within the field for the same reason, and withdrawal from the field by married women.

Professionalization

The several professional societies in the field are concerned with the continuing education and professional development of their members. Within a few years of the opening of the Vocation Bureau of Boston in 1909, the National Vocational Guidance Association was organized to provide a focal point for the new movement. In 1956 the American Personnel and Guidance Association was established as a result of the merger of no less than eight professional societies whose primary concerns are suggested by their names:

American College Personnel Association, Association for Counselor Education and Supervision, National Vocational Guidance

Association, Student Personnel Association for Teacher Education, American School Counselor Association, American Rehabilitation Counseling Association, Association for Measurement and Evaluation in Guidance, and National Employment Counselors Association.

The affiliated organizations retain their basic autonomy and continue to be responsible for their own programming, research, and publications. However, the merger sought to facilitate cooperative action among these groups at the state and national level, especially with respect to the development of minimum standards, the advancement of the field, and the scheduling of meetings. The merger also facilitated the profession's dealings with legislators and administrative officials.

A recent study revealed a total APGA membership of about 27,500, roughly half of all persons working in guidance and counseling.[23] But this understates the numbers of guidance counselors who have professional affiliations, since many in rehabilitation counseling belong to the National Rehabilitation Association and others with degrees in clinical or counseling psychology are identified with the American Psychological Association or with other organizations outside the APGA.

In the context of this chapter we have a double interest in the role of these professional organizations. The first has been mentioned: By holding meetings at local, state, regional, and national levels they provide educational opportunities for their members. Through various publications, from bulletins to journals, they seek to keep their membership informed about important trends. By publishing articles on research or appraisal they provide encouragement to those members who seek to remain intellectually alert and productive.

In addition, what happens to a field such as guidance, how it is shaped and reshaped with respect to recruitment, education, utilization, frequently depends on the effectiveness with which the group can speak with a single voice for its members and give direction to their aims and ambitions. In fact, it is difficult to conceive of a field becoming a profession without the aid and assistance of a strong organizational arm.

Earlier we touched briefly on the issue of whether guidance is a profession. We believe little that is of value could emerge from our establishing or borrowing a set of criteria to delineate a profession and then measuring how guidance meets it. For example, we need to note only that nursing has long considered itself a profession and it has been generally viewed as one by the public, although most registered nurses have had little more than one year of formal post-high school education and two years' apprenticeship. While the graduates of schools of social work consider themselves professionals since most of them have earned a two-year master's degree and have served an internship, the vast majority of persons employed in this field meet neither of these two criteria, although they frequently do the same work as their better-trained colleagues and some hold supervisory or administrative positions. Most people think of engineers as professionals, and those who have graduated from an engineering school certainly consider themselves members of a profession. But a significant minority of engineers, about two in five, are not college graduates, and some of these men use higher levels of skill and receive larger salaries than many with degrees.

If medicine is considered the prototype of a profession, it is easy to place guidance at the other end of the spectrum. A physician has specialized skill; he is able to acquire it only in a highly structured and controlled education-training situation; the public recognizes the importance of this skill and permits physicians to exercise wide control over the practice of medicine; the public is willing to pay a high price for the services of physicians; and the public will accept substitutes only gingerly.

It is difficult to define the special skill of guidance counselors; it is easier to describe their goals and how they function in seeking to help people make better career decisions. While there are various courses and programs which purport to teach the skills counselors need to function effectively, we have seen that only a small number of training programs command the respect of the leadership. Probably no more than one out of five practitioners has come through a preferred route. It is difficult to generalize about the public's conception of the guidance counselor or how far it is willing to go to let him regulate his own work.

Although most guidance counselors do not meet the criteria of full-fledged professionals, those who have the title are generally assumed by the public to be qualified to help people make more effective educational and vocational decisions. As we have shown, guidance services are increasingly recognized as important to individuals and to society. It is understandable that to those directly concerned, professional status carries self-esteem, greater scope for self-determination in work, more prestige, and potential support from the public. But for the public served, the central concern must be with the several ways in which the quality of guidance services can be strengthened. In this regard the attributes and abilities of the practitioners are relevant; their formal qualifications and occupational status are less significant.

While we will leave until Part Four our recommendations to overcome many of the shortcomings noted above, it may be helpful if we now present in the words of a leader of the profession, and then in our own words, the critical dimensions of personnel trends in guidance. This is how the guidance leader sees the problem: "As the counseling profession strives for further professional recognition and status, training requirements for each specialty continually increase. . . . The variation among different groups of counselors constitutes a number of problems for the entire counseling profession. Each counseling specialty has its own unique salary scale, selection, and training requirements, and training programs. This seems to result in a semblance of competition rather than cooperation. As each group draws toward professionalization and personal identity, there seems to be proliferation of counseling activities rather than full professional cooperation."[24]

These are our tentative deductions:

—In contrast to most professionals who are strongly self-directed, school counselors enter guidance as a secondary career, often with the prompting and direction of their school principal.

—The length and quality of the training that the vast majority of guidance counselors receive is often deficient. Among the most important defects are its largely part-time nature; its limitation to the equivalent of two semesters' work; the encapsulation of the guidance faculty in schools of education; little contact with the social sciences; the overreliance on classroom instruction to the neglect of field work; and lack of congruence between course content and the realities of guidance settings.

—The field faces substantial difficulties in its attempts to retain the best of those it succeeds in attracting because of the following mutually reinforcing adverse factors: the tie of the salary level of guidance specialists to that of fellow employees in the same employment setting; the overwhelming dominance of state and local governments as the principal employers of counselors and the tendency of government agencies to lag rather than lead in wage and salary levels; the limited number of supervisory guidance positions, which means that a person who wants to move up often must move out; the absence of labor market arrangements that enable guidance counselors to move from one employing unit to another without loss of salary and seniority.

This chapter has shed light on one important aspect of the provision of guidance services, the ways in which practitioners are recruited, educated, and employed. In the next two chapters we will explore the ways in which guidance specialists perform their work.

9

SETTINGS

THE ENVIRONMENT in which people work always exerts a powerful influence on how they carry out their professional activities. Guidance personnel perform their work in a number of different settings, each of which affects the character and content of what they do. This chapter will explore the principal settings and how they serve to shape guidance practices.

The organization that hires a man determines the rules of employment. And, as we have seen, most guidance personnel tend to work for others, not for themselves. They are employees, usually responsible to a superintendent of schools and a principal, to a manager of an employment office, or to an administrator of a rehabilitation agency. Moreover, a counselor is one of many employees working to accomplish broad organizational missions, such as education, employment, or rehabilitation.

As a consequence, the functions of guidance specialists, the objectives to which they are responsive, how they act and interact with their colleagues and clients, are significantly affected by the aims of the employing organization which usually considers counseling as subsidiary to its primary mission. Moreover, in the event of conflict with their employer, guidance personnel are much less able than salaried physicians, lawyers, or architects to resign and seek their livelihood as independent practitioners. At best, they can look for a more congenial employment setting; at worst, they may decide to leave the field.

Another dimension of the employment situation relates to professional identity and career advancement, matters of critical concern to all educated persons. No matter how deeply guidance personnel are committed to a particular goal, strategy, or tactic, they must give heavy weight to their own futures.

' Reference was made in the preceding chapter to the limited opportunities for advancement that exist within guidance. In the colloquialism of management theory, the field has a broad base with little superstructure. If a man is looking for more responsibility, for more salary, for more prestige, he often finds that he must leave the field and move into another. The largest group of the upwardly mobile shift from guidance into administration in their own or into another setting. Thus, those who want to advance soon understand that the preferred way to get ahead is to be on good terms with the leaders of the organization for which they are working. Many therefore identify with their supervisors and administrative imperatives rather than with the claims of their own field or the needs of their clients. Those on the move tend to be sensitive to those in positions of power and influence. In our analysis of interactions between guidance personnel and the settings within which they work, attention will be focused on organizational objectives, on relations with colleagues and on client diversity. The present distribution of guidance personnel will determine the principal settings we will explore.

School Setting

Within the broad policy directions laid down by the school board and the superintendent of schools, the key figure in setting a school's objectives and in implementing them is the principal. Some principals who understand the potential contribution of career counselors choose them with care and permit them to determine the scope of their work. In such schools, each guidance specialist has relative freedom to decide the ways in which he will spend his time. Much of the same freedom exists for counselors when a principal is unsure of himself and uncertain about what guidance can do. Most principals are neither so sympathetic nor so unsure that they give the guidance staff a largely free hand.

Much of the advice guidance counselors provide about program and course selection is often tinged by the priorities that the principal has set with respect to student accomplishments. If the principal's emphasis is to maximize the number of students who pass, his guidance staff is likely to persuade students to take programs which offer easy courses without regard to later consequences.[1]

In many ghetto schools there appears to be an understanding between the principal and his guidance staff that they will encourage difficult students, especially troublemakers, to drop out as soon as they reach working age. This tactic is most likely to be pursued if the school is carrying an overload of students, as is frequently the case in poverty areas.[2] The guidance counselor may rationalize his action by helping the school-leaver get a job, without asking questions as to the kind of job or whether there is a likelihood that it will lead anywhere.

Another illustration of the pervasive environmental pressures under which many school counselors function relates to the college advisory system. If a principal or school board is primarily concerned with achieving a "good" college admissions record, counselors will pay more attention to facilitating a student's acceptance at some college than to his interest in and potential for further education. Moreover, they are likely to be less concerned with the suitability of the selection than with chances of admission. Guidance staff in some of the most prestigious schools in the country have followed this pattern. Often, to back up a school's claim that all, or almost all, of its college applicants are accepted, counselors advise students to set their sights lower than their potential school performance warrants; they pay little heed to outcomes beyond college entrance.[3]

This criticism may appear misplaced, since in the final analysis it is parental pressures that determine the stance of a school system, including that of its counselors, toward college admission. However, the thrust of the analysis is to make the point that the nature of the setting dominates the work of the guidance staff.

Counselors must also reckon with pressures from administrators

who see them as responsible for keeping an eye on troublesome
students and disciplining them so that they will not disturb the
functioning of the school. If the counselor accepts this definition
of his role, he may encounter little conflict with his superiors. He
has carved a niche for himself in the school hierarchy, but in the
process he has turned his back on his primary responsibility to help
young people. If he opts for being a soft-shoe policeman devoted to
keeping the institution cool, he will have his principal's support. But
the price of such success is high; his ability to help his clients will
be seriously weakened.

On the other hand, if counselors take their obligations to help
young people seriously, as many do, and if they refuse to become
detectives or disciplinarians, they may be on a collision course with
their principal. The outcome is uncertain. It depends on the way in
which guidance is structured within the school system. If counselors report to the principal but are part of a central staff division
directed from headquarters, they may be able to survive the conflict by eliciting the support of their guidance supervisors. If, however, the principal has the power to hire and fire and there is no
one to whom the counselor can appeal, it is likely that the counselor
will be responsive to the principal's demands—if only until he can
find another position where the principal may be more understanding.

Many principals want to be kept informed about any type of
deviant behavior students engage in. But the guidance counselor
has been taught that confidentiality of records is at the heart of a
professional relationship. Why should students continue to come
and discuss their problems with him if they know that he may pass
on what they say in confidence? This problem exists at all educational levels. A study by Frank A. Nugent, *Confidentiality in College Counseling Centers*, reported, on the basis of a national sample,
that 40 per cent of the institutions replying to a questionnaire indicated that information about counselees was released without client
permission.[4]

With few exceptions (which present clear and imminent danger
to society), release of confidential information is a violation of the
ethical codes promulgated by both the American Personnel and
Guidance Association and the American Psychological Association.

Since 40 per cent is probably an understatement, and since the survey included the better-staffed and -operated college counseling centers, it takes little imagination to estimate the violations of confidentiality current in the schools of this country. Small wonder that a significant number of young people, when asked whether they ever take the initiative to seek out a guidance counselor with whom to discuss their problems, immediately conclude that the inquirer must be a square—why else would he ask such a question? While educational and vocational decision-making does not have to involve client communications of a highly personal nature, the character of any counseling relationship lends itself to such revelations and it is the responsibility of the counselor to keep such information confidential.

Another constraint upon guidance activities often occurs in a one-industry town. If school and employment counselors were to advise and help a high proportion of young people to prepare for and seek jobs elsewhere, they would soon run into conflict with the local establishment. Years ago, on a tour conducted by the president of a large Southern textile concern through a company-financed school, the patron asked the class of eighth graders how many planned to be lawyers when they grew up. Several raised their hands. How many physicians? Several more. How many engineers? Five or six. Then he asked how many planned to work in the mill. Everybody raised his hand. Even at the tender age of fourteen, these youngsters knew how to respond!

In tight-laced communities a guidance staff that adopts a strategy of trying to help students with their personal problems might be accused of "coddling" them; parents would object. One school superintendent recently called our attention to the fact that the John Birch Society has regarded guidance as a Communist-inspired activity.

Those who pay the taxes that support the schools, including the salaries of guidance counselors, would consider it remiss of persons on the public payroll to broaden disagreements between them and their children. No one is hired to do that! And yet the school counselor, after learning the relevant facts, may find that a parent is making an error in pushing his offspring in one direction when the young person prefers, and is better suited, to go in another. Some

counselors may be astute enough to know how to effectuate a com-
promise between the dominating parent and the recalcitrant youngster, but many are likely to get out of the line of fire when they
realize that they will receive no credit from the principal if they
are accused by an irate parent of interfering in family matters.

So much for the possible areas of tension between the school
counselor's perception of his work and the preconceptions of those
who hire and employ him and the community to which all must be
responsive. We turn now to the counselor's co-workers. While some
counselors prefer to and do in fact carry on their work with little
or no awareness of or interference from their colleagues in other
disciplines, this is not the conventional stance. School guidance personnel in general must take into account and relate to two broad
groups of colleagues, teachers and pupil personnel specialists such
as school psychologists and social workers. Several years ago John
Darley called attention to the hostility that frequently exists between teachers and guidance counselors. Darley said that teachers
see counselors as follows:

> Counselors are administrators, and the nicest thing you can say
> about administrators is that they are a necessary evil which may
> be tolerated but, better yet, eradicated.
> Counselors provide ancillary services and are therefore expend-
> able.
> Counselors coddle and pamper those who would, and perhaps
> should, flunk out.
> Counselors' pseudo-Freudian, pseudo-psychometric jargon is the
> purest nonsense.
> Counselors' pretense of confidentiality is merely a shield to hide
> behind when the welfare of the institution is involved or their
> activities are challenged.[5]

Of course, not all teachers have such an unfavorable opinion of
the guidance staff, but we can appreciate the antagonism between
the two groups when we recall that teachers tend to be insecure
about relationships that are not explicitly structured; they believe
that students carry stories about them to their counselors; they
suspect that counselors pass on information to the principal about
what goes on in the classroom; they hear counselors assert a claim
to participate in the discussion of curriculum problems; and they

must from time to time defend to the guidance staff their behavior toward students.[6]

In theory at least, one of the important contributions that an effective guidance staff can make is to feed back to teachers their recommendations about how changes in curriculum, scheduling, grading, and other academic practices and procedures might contribute to the progress and satisfactions of the student body. But whether they are able to play this role depends on their relations with the teaching staff—and these are often strained. Many counselors realize that the principal will not support their forays into the teaching arena and, responding to the defensive-aggressive tactics of the teaching staff, they decide to stay in their own domain and opt for peace rather than conflict.

Some years ago Kenneth Hoyt argued in a much-discussed paper that the guidance staff has the responsibility to be helpful also to the teacher by "teaching units and courses in guidance . . . solving problems of teacher-pupil relations; and . . . improving academic achievement through searching actively for the causes of student behavior."[7] It is difficult to see how guidance personnel could perform these tasks unless they were invited and encouraged to by the teaching staff, but it is hard to believe that—exceptional situations aside—most teachers would welcome such efforts by the counselor.

However, teachers themselves often play important roles in providing guidance. Campbell's survey found that large numbers of students sought guidance from their teachers, and many teachers saw themselves performing a variety of guidance services and as being able to assist with even more.[8] While teachers tend to endorse guidance programs and to favor increased services, there is no evidence that they would welcome intrusions from the guidance staff into areas which they consider their own.

If the conventional relations between guidance counselors and teachers are a stand-off as the price of avoiding conflict, the relations between counselors and other staff specialists are frequently no less charged. Guidance counselors are one of a diverse group of pupil personnel specialists. These specialists provide services outside the instructional program designed to facilitate the personal and educational development of students. In addition to counselors, they include school social workers, school psychologists, attendance

workers, speech and hearing clinicians, nurses and other medical
personnel. They are expected to cooperate with each other through
referral and consultation. However, since there is considerable overlap in their preparation, duties and expectations, much conflict
ensues.

It has been noted that "In many, if not most, systems counselors
are seen as the generalist of the pupil services team who call in the
more specialized personnel as needed."[9] But, often, the latter accuse
counselors of not consulting them when necessary and of usurping
their functions. This is particularly true of social workers and psychologists, who tend to devalue the preparation and qualifications
of counselors.

In 1961 the National Institute of Mental Health made a grant
covering a five-year period to the Interprofessional Research Commission on Pupil Personnel Services in order to clarify the relationships between the various specialties. The NIMH made the
grant because of its concern that there was "unnecessary overlap,
duplication of effort, and possible working at cross purposes" since
several of the groups used the same techniques and worked with
the same clientele.[10]

It would be nice to be able to report that the study was successful, that the several groups reached agreement as to their respective
roles and responsibilities, and that state and local boards of education are now implementing their agreed-upon recommendations.
However, while interesting data were collected, some of which were
analyzed, the project never came to a definite conclusion. Confusion
continues. The school counselor is often hired, especially in an elementary school, because funds have been made available. Few
superintendents or principals are inclined to leave budget lines
open. Therefore, if they are given the money, they will add one or
two guidance counselors to their existing staff of specialists. Some
institutions are sufficiently alert and concerned to structure the assignments of their diverse group of specialists and to provide the
supervision which will insure that their efforts are mutually reinforcing and do not cancel each other out. But as the literature reports *ad nauseum,* many elementary school counselors in particular,
but often other specialists as well, complain bitterly of the confusion
about their role and consequent ineffectiveness of their work.[11]

We have already alluded in passing to the consequences of various situational pressures which affect the way guidance personnel relate to different students. To quote Hoyt again, "The counselor can and should be expected to help every pupil." In the same essay he warns against two possible dangers: that of the counselor's spending undue time with the deviant student or neglecting him completely.[12] From the vantage of this chapter, it is relevant to state that whether the counselor spends much, little, or no time with the deviant student is, in most schools, a function of the principal's desires and directives. Moreover, we know that regardless of Hoyt's dictum that the counselor should be helpful to every student, the guidance staff has consistently focused its attention on the college-bound.

Community attitudes affect the time and interest, as well as the specific advice, that guidance personnel give to members of minority groups. In the summer of 1968, some of our staff members interviewed about fifty young black men and women who had left school a short time before. The excerpts below are from these interviews. This is how the young blacks appraised the guidance services to which they had had access:

Eighteen is a bad age in high school. They try to get you out of school and they don't really encourage you to go to night school. They tell you you should enroll but give you no help. You got to be straight if you are in at eighteen—one step and you're out. . . . I was lacking in only two subjects. Some teachers did talk about college although there was no detailed description of such programs as College Discovery, etc.

My particular guidance counselor didn't take too much interest in the student. Maybe it's because they have so many students, I don't know. . . . My last class was a special class of 15 to 16 boys, all boys, in a job orientation program. It's a new tryout thing. There they feel you out to see what kind of a job you might be suited for.

I was not introduced to any guidance counselor at F. although I had met a few at W. Consequently, I was given no advice or encouragement about college prospects.

I found not only that the guidance counselor didn't have any expertise in counseling but she had no idea how to find it. My teachers were equally uninspiring.

At G.W. there are I think six guidance counselors for something like 5,000 kids. At B. I think there are ten. And that's a big goddam school. You know that school operates in three shifts. Ten counselors for what?—20,000 kids?

A particularly poignant example of the ways in which community mores influence school counselors is the way in which questions about military service are answered. For many years counselors in the majority of high schools cooperated with the recruiting staffs of the Armed Forces and distributed literature about military service, arranged assemblies in which recruiters could talk to the senior student body, enabled male students to take the Armed Services Vocational Aptitude Battery, and, when the results of the Battery became available, counseled individual students. The Department of Defense's *High School Counselors Manual* states that "it is expected that the counselors will provide test scores to the students and discuss the meaning of the results with them."[13]

In recent years, however, more and more young men have sought information about the draft not with the intent of entering military service but to learn how they can postpone or avoid it. While an increasing number of school systems, including New York City's, provide draft counseling, outside groups such as the American Friends Service Committee and various other organizations usually perform this function, if it is performed at all.

A gross generalization about high school counselors could be derived from how the guidance staff apportions its time among different functions, the students on whom it concentrates as well as those it neglects, and even the specific advice it gives or withholds. More frequently than not all this is determined by the principal. The more dominant he is the less scope the counselor has for self-determination. The major options the counselor faces are to go along or get out. Most go along. There is little that the guidance staff can do with or through teachers since they tend to stand off from and are even hostile to guidance. Without strong supervision, effective coordination between the guidance staff and other pupil personnel specialists cannot be achieved.

At higher educational levels, the classic liberal arts college has avoided vocational concerns; many do not provide any career guidance services. When I asked the dean of Columbia College in the late 1940s for permission to interview students in connection with an occupational study, his initial response was distinctly negative because the word *occupational* was anathema to him as a synonym for *vocational.* Moreover, most of the Seven Sister Colleges also neglect career guidance.[14] On the other hand, several Midwestern universities have long had a broadly based, well-staffed advisory system encompassing the whole gamut of student concerns: educational, personal, career.

College faculty members conventionally carry the responsibility for approving student programs. Many fulfill this function in a perfunctory manner once they are assured that the student is accumulating the necessary credits and course distribution to meet the requirements for his degree. In a minority of institutions a formal advisory system has been established, but even here most students are likely to seek advice and help from an interested faculty member or from their peers. Since colleges have rarely taken the task of educational and career guidance seriously, they have not staffed to meet it. Their primary concern has been to provide assistance for students who encounter emotional problems. The key staff usually consists of clinical psychologists with a consulting psychiatrist for backup. There is usually a considerable amount of informal guidance in dormitories carried out by graduate students and others who usually have little or no formal training but who often do quite well because of their empathy for and understanding of young people. In many institutions counselors are asked by the administration to report aberrant behavior that may lead to embarrassing the college or to police intervention. But once counselors are known as informers their usefulness is at an end. They are also expected to refer any student who appears to be a danger to himself or to others. This is when the psychiatric service or consulting psychiatrist is expected to take over.

While most colleges understand that it is better to separate the duties of the counselor from that of an administrator, many find this difficult to do. For instance, the man who is responsible for maintaining discipline as a dormitory supervisor or house master is often expected to act as counselor, but few can do this effectively because of their double allegiance to the administration and to the student.

Most colleges and universities have placement offices, and it is here that considerable career guidance takes place—sometimes formally, often informally. Apparently it is more acceptable to those who direct academe to place advice-giving about work in the backwater of the placement service than in close connection to educational affairs.

Since many college counselors realize that they are contributing service to only a small part of the total student body, some of them have moved out of their offices onto the campus in the hope and expectation that, through new contacts with such intermediaries as student organizations and the faculty, they will find more effective ways of aiding more students.

We have seen that the college setting is not a sympathetic environment for the provision of educational and career guidance. The presumption is that when students encounter problems in these areas the faculty is available to counsel them. But most faculty members know little about the world beyond academe. They are generally able to assist prospective graduate students, but often cannot help undergraduates who plan to enter the world of work. Colleges still have to recognize and respond to the need of many students for career guidance as a contribution both to increasing the value of the educational experience as well as to facilitating later work adjustment.

We have spoken earlier of the special problems of the community college. Thus it should suffice here to note that they, too, frequently neglect vocational guidance despite the fact that occupational training is probably the most important function they perform. Unfortunately, the prestige associated with an academic rather than a technically oriented program of studies has led many administrators and faculty to downgrade students in the latter track and to neglect their guidance needs.

Employment Offices

Most employment counselors are attached to one organizational structure, the federal-state Employment Service. They work in many settings: employment offices; schools; new outreach locations where the staff has more opportunity to come into direct contact with neighborhood jobseekers.

Among the guidance services employment counselors provide are those to high school students preparing to enter the labor market. Effective liaison between school and Employment Service is difficult to establish and maintain and often written agreements are developed by the two parties to specify the responsibilities and work of each.[15] Difficulties arise over scheduling meeting times, access of the Employment staff to school records, responsibility for interpretation of test results, and follow-up. In each of these functions there is slippage in the provision of services. However, often the core of the difficulty is the inability of the Employment Service to provide what the young person most needs—an attractive job.

The major thrust of Employment Service counseling has always been primarily job-directed, not career-oriented. The counselor often uses prescribed tests and other instruments to determine the counselee's strengths and interests. After he has learned about the counselee's special problems relating to mobility, hours of work, and health considerations if any, he tries to suggest the kinds of jobs where there are present or potential openings for which the counselee might qualify. Occasionally he may explore with the counselee his willingness to relocate to where job opportunities are better.

Within this narrowly focused context of counseling related to immediate or proximate employment, for which the specific procedures are carefully detailed in a manual, conflicts can (and frequently do) arise between the goals of the Employment Service and those of the counselee. Since the allocation of funds to the states and to the local offices is geared to past workload projected into the future, each manager is caught up in the "numbers game." Much more attention is paid to the number of applicants counseled than to the quality of the counseling. For many years counselors in the Employment Service were prevented by administrative regulations from making suggestions to a client that might entail personal financial outlays, such as that he take a course for which tuition is required. In recent years, when there has been an increasing number of new training programs for which the Employment Service has quotas to fill, many applicants have been pushed into any open program, with little regard for their interest or its value to them over the long run.

In many states the ties between the Employment Service and the dominant political party are close. The manager and his staff are careful not to cloud the political climate. One consequence of this has been the overt and pronounced discrimination against blacks, particularly in the Deep South. Recent hearings of the U.S. Civil Rights Commission provided new evidence of this well-known phenomenon; except for referrals to "Negro jobs," there is little that a Negro in the Deep South can expect from his local employment office.[16] In small communities, the Employment Service is limited both in the clientele it serves and the type of advice and help it can proffer. What it is able to do, as well as what it must avoid, depends in large measure on the attitudes of the local power structure.

Since in the past the Employment Service had no resources at its command except a modest testing and counseling capability, a mixed bag of poor job openings, and a limited tie-in to a national network of hard-to-fill jobs, its scope for follow-through was limited. If the counselee indicated a need for one or another type of remedial assistance—educational, occupational, health—there was little that the Employment Service counselor could do. Counselors seldom suggested organizations where help might be obtained. Until recently the Employment Service was a world unto itself and its staff was concerned with processing large numbers of people since only in that way could they hope to insure that their next year's appropriation would be forthcoming.

Once the federal government started to appropriate sizable sums for manpower, poverty, and work-training programs, around 1965, the Employment Service confronted for the first time large numbers of seriously disadvantaged persons, both black and white, young and middle-aged, urban and rural, who had previously been ignored. Since the scene has been in constant flux during the past five years, and since conditions differ greatly from one city to another, in fact from one neighborhood to another, the following summary statements can do no more than capture part of the atmosphere of new settings that were designed to help it meet its new responsibilities.

One of the important transformations has been the establishment of manpower service units in the heart of the ghetto. We earlier called attention to the Youth Opportunity Centers, many of which are located there. But merely to open such centers did not assure their success. Many young people were suspicious and would not go near these centers; many who went felt let down because they were not provided with jobs; and many youngsters from minority groups came away convinced that the counselors did not understand the realities of their life situations.

The last difficulty was moderated as the centers began to hire indigenous counselors, people who shared the life experience of those they were counseling. Follow-through became easier as counselors were able to refer clients to various training programs, employment opportunities, and even to supplemental services such as remedial medical care.

The exposure of the Employment Service and its rapidly proliferating adjuncts to large numbers of the poor, the black, the alienated, left its mark also on conventional guidance practices and procedures. The shortage of trained counselors helped precipitate change. It simply was not possible for the Employment Service to proceed as it had in the past. Even if there had been no staff shortages, change had to come.

The new clients were not communicative. They had little to say. Moreover, they wanted action, not talk. As a consequence, many counselors came to understand that any counseling they might be able to provide had to wait until they had helped a person get a job or enter a training program. They also discovered that since most of their clients had difficulty expressing themselves in face-to-face interchanges it was often easier to deal with them in a group setting composed of peers from the same background.

Other points surfaced. It early became clear that many of the attitudes, values, and behavior patterns characteristic of these population groups were unknown to many counselors. Their training in psychology had failed to help them to understand people with serious reality problems.

Here is a description of the operation of an experimental counseling effort for school dropouts located in the ghetto.

> The caseload consists of an intake of about 600 to 700 young people per month, most of whom are seen initially by a sub-professional who records basic information and determines eligibility. The client is then sent to a professional counselor.

Most of the young clients are routed into the Neighborhood Youth Corps. Some are sent to the Job Corps and a few with employable skills are sent to training or directly to a job. There is little or no follow-up of these referrals.

Intensive continuing counseling of the youngsters in Neighborhood Youth Corps takes place in groups. Each counselor has about 90 to 100 active cases. He goes to the job site and meets with the group but he is also available for individual consultation if the youngster asks for it.

The project arranges remediation in reading or math and it aims to move the young person into a "growth job" within six to nine months.

The director considers assignment to a job the first step in the remedial-counseling process. He does not subscribe to pre-employment counseling. "Get the kid on a job and then counsel him. Otherwise you are talking into a vacuum about promptness, responsibility, proper dress."[17]

As a result of working with the hard-to-employ the Employment Service slowly learned that many practices had to be altered, some radically. In its *Human Resources Development Concept,* the U.S. Department of Labor offers the following advice about counseling the hard-to-employ.[18]

Immediate objectives include a job or work training slot.

Follow-up while the individual is in training or on a job is essential.

Counseling and appraisal begins where the counselee is *now.*

Self-concept should be accepted as the way the applicant sees himself.

Tests should be administered *only* when they are seen as helpful assists in the decision-making process.

In brief summary, efforts to counsel the hard-to-employ suggest that:

—The conventional settings, in which the counselor sits in a downtown office and clients walk in for help or job referrals, had to give way to outreach and outstations in poverty and ghetto areas.

—The professional counselor has frequently been less able to make contact with these clients than have indigenous personnel who share their background and experiences.

—The underlying logic of developmental counseling had to be modified for these clients.

—The focus of the counseling effort had to offer concrete reality assistance first and psychological support second.

—Group methods are important as a guidance device.[19]

The radical change in the goal of the Employment Service dictated by the new monies appropriated by Congress to help the hard-to-employ led to many changes in the settings within which employment counseling is carried out, the hiring of new types of counseling personnel, and new approaches in the relations of counselors to their colleagues and clients. The Employment Service is a striking example of the interdependence of the guidance setting and counselors' work.

Rehabilitation Agencies

In contrast to that of the school counselor, the work of the rehabilitation counselor is employment-oriented. Unlike the employment counselor, the rehabilitation counselor can draw on many valuable resources to aid him in helping his client to get a job.

Given the specific objective of facilitating client employability and substantial resources to help to accomplish it, what strains or tensions exist in a vocational rehabilitation setting? The administrator of the agency is concerned with developing a good record, one that will convince the legislators to continue to appropriate funds for the program. His concern therefore is to assure that a maximum number of people are rehabilitated, although not necessarily in an optimal manner, since the latter point is not easily checked.

Although it receives strong public backing, vocational rehabilitation has problems. Despite relatively liberal funding from the states, the total capability of the rehabilitation system lags considerably behind the numbers who could profit from its services. If we disregard the backlog, which has been estimated at around 3 million, the annual number of persons rehabilitated increased from under 100,000 to over 200,000 in the 1960s, but this is still half the number added annually to the pool.[20] This means that the rehabilitation agencies must control their intake in relation to their resources. Many decisions are made with an eye to administrative necessity, such as when a counselor encourages a referral agency to speed up the training of a counselee so the case can be closed before the end of the fiscal year, or when another applicant who is ready to start training is held off until the next fiscal year when new funds become available. More pertinent, however, is the extent to which the entire selection process is geared to choosing clients who present good probability of success.

An even more critical issue relates to the criterion of "successful placement." In a Midwestern state, a successful accountant suffered a cerebral vascular accident resulting in severe aphasia. The counselor strongly urged him to accept a position as an elevator operator, although this was totally inconsistent with his education and previous level of work. Although his current condition might not permit him to do much else, a more imaginative assessment would have suggested—since family resources permitted—training for meaningful avocational activities.

Difficulties often arise from the ways in which supervisors assign cases and counselors select training agencies. If the client finds it difficult to adjust to the counselor to whom he has been assigned, he has little option but to make the best of it. In public rehabilitation counseling, as in most other counseling under government aegis, the client has little or no choice of counselor. In turn, when it comes to selecting a training agency or other resource, many counselors have strong likes and dislikes. Sometimes these prejudices work to the client's benefit; often they do not.

Even in rehabilitation counseling, which has so many advantages compared to other types of counseling, the pressures of the environment, the size of the case load, financial resources, administrative favoritism, a concern with reporting successful closures, an avoidance of difficult clients, often force the dedicated professional to make his peace with organizational goals.

There are additional facets of rehabilitation counseling that should be mentioned at least briefly. As Dimichael has pointed out, "rehabilitation is an individual process, tailor-made to each person. ... The counselor is one among a large number of professional people from various disciplines, each of whom may have skills and services to render."[21] Consequently, whether a good rehabilitation plan for a client is evolved and implemented depends in the first instance on congenial relations among the staff specialists. The rehabilitation counselor as the general coordinator has a critical role to play. The counselor also must develop job opportunities and see that placement is made. Since government monies are being expended on individuals, he must also be concerned with the financial needs of his clients. As a consequence of these and other duties, many rehabilitation counselors are so busy that they do little counseling. One way out of this "time bind" for some counselors, especially in large cities, has been their tendency to specialize by working with clients with similar disabilities. As yet there is little enthusiasm among rehabilitation counselors for the widespread use of support personnel.[22]

We have now reviewed the three major settings within which guidance personnel carry out their functions. However, at least brief consideration should be paid to three additional settings because of their potential importance for advising people with respect to their career problems: the Armed Forces, corporate enterprise, and community agencies.

As noted earlier, the Armed Forces engage both directly and through the school in pre-service counseling. Once a man is on active duty he may be encouraged to pursue additional education both to improve himself and to enhance his value to the service. But military counseling is concerned first of all with encouraging men to re-enlist. The services do not consider it incongruous to advise young men to re-enlist although they hope to be the beneficiary. They believe that if they can help to remove the hesitancies, uncertainties, and doubts an individual has about the next step in his career decision-making, both the man and the service will be better off. After all, they cannot force a man to re-enlist: they can merely delineate the benefits that will accrue to the individual.

The third focus of military counseling relates to career counseling at the end of a man's tour of duty, when he is ready to return to civilian life. In 1968, under Presidential prompting, the Department of Defense launched Project TRANSITION to provide "educational and vocational training and job counseling for enlisted personnel prior to their release from active duty to prepare them for post-service life."[23] The President acted because numbers of men, at the end of their tours of duty, were poorly prepared to find a job in civilian life.

The counseling staff, usually non-commissioned officers who have taken a short intensive course in counseling in the military, are reminded that the services want to retain as many as possible of the already trained individuals, but they are also told that they must offer important assistance to a man regardless of his career choice so that he himself makes a sound decision about his future. A report of the program, dated January 1969, emphasizes that "the counseling activity is the key to the entire TRANSITION Program." It points out that in 1968 over 275,000 service personnel received either individual or group counseling and over 50,000 of these were placed in a special training program. The goal of the Program is to provide "at least one individual counseling session per serviceman." Because of the limited opportunities available, only about one in three of the men who desired training was actually placed in a training program. While about 50 national corporations and 400 smaller companies are cooperating in providing training and placement opportunities, there remains a wide gap between potential applicants and available opportunities.[24]

The counseling staff is given a second specific assignment: "Servicemen whose home of record indicates that they may be returning to areas where economic and other problems are critical should be given special consideration in counseling and opportunities for training." A list of cities where employment problems are serious follows, and the list includes 19 of the nation's largest cities with 11 ghetto areas specifically identified. The staff is advised to encourage "mobility or movement out of such areas by counseling about job opportunities elsewhere."[25]

For most of their other counseling, the services rely primarily on civilian educational officers and non-commissioned personnel who have had a short training course. In sum, counseling by the Armed Forces is adjustive and directive and organizational objectives take precedence. The long-run career objectives of the individual are secondary.

What about the employment settings in which most men spend

the greater part of their adult lives? Do corporations provide counseling for their employees? Most large employers provide some
information and advice about job-related matters such as opportunities for training, tuition benefits, promotional ladders, retirement. Some go a little farther and provide limited assistance for
workers in such matters as health, legal affairs, transportation, and
housing which may have an important bearing on their ability to
work effectively.

But the personnel staffs of corporations do not usually counsel.
From time to time they may help an employee to be reassigned
because he does not like his work, his supervisor, or his shift, but in
general they are not involved in career guidance in the sense of
facilitating the career decision-making of employees. Such activity
might result in a worker's decision to leave the company and seek
employment elsewhere. And a staff man who adds to turnover does
not keep his job long. Many companies, probably a growing number,
have psychologists on their staffs or make use of outside consultants
for testing, evaluation, and research focused on improving assignment and promotion procedures. Some may spend a little time on
counseling, but it is surely not their principal assignment.

Corporate manpower planning is increasingly in vogue. In the
early 1960s, it was the exceptional corporation that had even a small
manpower planning staff. It will soon be exceptional if a large
company has not initiated a staff capability in this area. As companies become more and more aware of the importance of a stable
and experienced work force, they make additional investments in
training and other developmental opportunities aimed at encouraging as many men as possible to remain with them, especially
managerial personnel. This may well result in a limited amount of
career guidance, but as in the military, the primary emphasis is to
improve the manpower resources of the organization, not the life
chances of the individual.

As a consequence of industry's increased hiring of large numbers
of hard-to-employ persons, either on its own or in cooperation
with the government through a training contract, corporate staffs
are beginning to recognize the importance of counseling. In fact,
companies with training contracts have received governmental
guidelines which include the following: "Employee orientation ...

also includes preliminary assessment of the vocational and personal attitudes and potential of each individual and may include individual counseling assistance." As Karl Kunze of Lockheed (Burbank) put it: "These training programs contribute the first formal introduction of counseling into the industrial personnel system. The effectiveness of this kind of counseling is now being measured, and industry's experience with this rather specialized kind of counseling may have an influence one way or another upon the future use of counselors and career counseling programs."[26]

Disinclined to expand services which are not cost-reducing or profit-expanding and desiring to avoid potential conflicts with unions with which they have agreements, corporations are likely to tread gingerly when it comes to introducing guidance services. Only in one area are they likely to take action. Every year more and more men and women retire with a combination of assets: private savings, company benefits, Social Security. Between 25 and 30 million workers are now employed in companies which offer pension benefits. More and more companies are moving to earlier vesting and offer their employees opportunities to retire early. The decisions that a prospective retiree faces are as complex as the outcomes are critical for his later years.

Retirement, at an age when people still have some degree of freedom to choose one or another pattern for their later years, is a largely new phenomenon in American life. If more and more younger and middle-aged persons are helped to become aware of the implications of an extended period of retirement at the end of their lives, they will probably be more willing to build this fact into their career and life planning than they have in the past.

Under these circumstances, counseling for retirement may soon be redefined as counseling for the later years. The issue is not semantic but substantive. A new requirement looms ahead. Without much more experimentation it would be premature to design a pattern for retirement guidance and counseling, just as it would be to try to specify at this time the competences guidance specialists will need to assist people approaching retirement. But the direction is clear: it will be necessary to utilize the desire and obligation of large companies to be helpful to their employees in solving a wide range of problems—health, housing, finances, work—about which employees need assistance as they contemplate retirement. We may need to evolve new structures and settings whereby corporate, governmental, and community resources are combined to provide retirement counseling.

Finally we arrive at the one setting that is primarily directed to the provision of guidance services, the private and community agencies. In 1968, there were 192 APGA-approved agencies described as follows: Private (profit-making), 29 per cent; community non-profit, 24 per cent; college- and university-affiliated, 43 per cent; other (quasi-governmental), 4 per cent. As one might expect, most agencies are centered in large cities. Over half the agencies state that they provide educational and vocational counseling; others focus on such areas as marriage and family counseling, reading and speech therapy, and psychotherapy.[27]

A Midwest agency under sectarian sponsorship outlines its services as follows:

> Assistance in educational and vocational planning including scholarships and part-time jobs is available for high school and college students; vocational counseling is offered to adults; specialized job placement services are available to adults with particular problems, including older workers; a coordinated vocational rehabilitation program is offered to handicapped individuals, particularly those over 45 years of age.[28]

While the non-profit agencies accept a limited number of persons at reduced or no fees, most of them make a modest charge of about $10 an hour for counseling and $50 or so for testing and evaluation. As one would anticipate, the fee schedule of the private agencies is substantially higher—double or triple. The average staff is about eight persons, usually divided between psychologists and counselors.

These agencies gain approval by requesting the American Personnel and Guidance Association to evaluate them. Its judgment is based primarily on the nature of and conditions under which these agencies offer services to the public and the education and training of the staff.

In total these agencies represent a relatively small effort, some 2,000 professional staff out of a total that approximates 60,000. But their survival proves that some people are willing to pay for and financially support guidance services, although recently some well-established voluntary agencies have been forced to close due to lack of funds. Several points stand out. The non-profit community agencies have found it desirable, even necessary, to link their guidance and counseling services to placement activities, especially for people who are handicapped. Those which advise young people about their educational plans sometimes take the next step and seek to facilitate their entrance into college. Most agencies continue to place heavy weight on testing. Finally, the community agencies have had to be selective in accepting clients who cannot pay because their financial support is limited.

The non-profit community agency has no organizational axe to grind beyond providing the best career guidance available within its resources to clients who need its services. They must of course be responsive to their own boards of directors. The community agency does not operate under the same pressures that characterize the other settings within which guidance operates, where organizational goals and services to clients are frequently in subdued if not overt conflict. Yet the middle-class consumer in the face of tax-supported services is not generally willing to pay for guidance. This explains the slow growth to date of the community agency.

Nevertheless, the community agency has important roles to perform. It can be more innovative than government units. It can provide more intensive services for clients. Agencies under sectarian sponsorship can be responsive to the special problems of co-religionists. To the extent that the community agency is free of many constraints that confine and limit guidance in other settings, it can serve as a model for professional practice.

We have now completed our overview of the settings within which guidance services are provided. As a result we are better able to appreciate the interplay between the two. In summary, we find:

—Many administrators who hire guidance counselors, particularly in school settings, do not understand their competences, limitations, or the situational supports they require to perform effectively. Similarly, many guidance counselors have been poorly oriented to the system within which they must carry out their work.

—In almost every setting, the ability of guidance personnel to be effective depends on the establishment and maintenance of good relations with other professional staff. This is frequently difficult because of lack of administrative support and because of professional jealousies and suspicions that are accentuated by the unqualified claims that many guidance counselors make about their work and goals.

—Because guidance personnel see themselves and are seen by others as generalists in career advising in contrast to clinical psychologists, speech therapists, nurses, and other specialists, it is easy for administrators to assign a wide range of staff assignments to them and there is little the counselors can do about it.

—With the single exception of community agencies, whose prime function is guidance and counseling, administrators are usually assessed on the basis of criteria other than the quality of their guidance services. This is why many of them insist that guidance services be designed to realize organizational goals.

These distillations point up the wide gaps that continue to exist between the conditions guidance personnel consider essential for sound professional work and the environmental realities within which guidance is confined. The challenge to the guidance leadership is to find the leverages to reduce these gaps.

10

SUBURBANTOWN

THIS CHAPTER carries the analysis of settings one stage further. Here we will consider in depth school guidance as it is carried on in the junior and senior high schools of a suburban community near New York City which, according to the guidance leadership, has succeeded in developing a broad range of quality services under strong leadership. As noted in Chapter 1, we were invited to come into this community to observe and evaluate its guidance program. In carrying out our assignment we paid particular attention to the ways in which guidance services were affected by the attitudes and behavior of the following key individuals and groups: the school board, the school superintendent, the director of pupil personnel services, the principals of the several schools, the teaching staffs, parents, and students.

In every investigation, what one learns is a function of what one is sensitive to and what one is looking for. As a check on possible oversights or misinterpretations, our staff reviewed their findings with a panel of guidance, teaching, and administrative personnel in the schools and with the director of pupil personnel services. While some of our judgments may be subject to error, the value of this chapter lies in its specification of the potentialities and limitations within which a well-staffed and well-directed effort of school guidance and counseling must operate.

The relevant facts about Suburbantown can be easily summarized. It is a bedroom community that expanded rapidly after World War II. The population is almost exclusively white. The average family income is slightly below the $10,000 level. Most of the town's heads of households are not college graduates. They work at lower managerial, commercial, and skilled blue-collar jobs. The parents tend to be upwardly mobile and are seeking to provide better opportunities for their children. They are interested in and concerned about their schools and support them at a level considerably above the state's average, although local voters recently rejected the proposed school budget, signaling dissatisfaction with rapidly expanding expenditures. The community receives approximately 45 per cent of its total tax revenues from a few large corporations that are located within its limits. For the year 1968–1969, per-pupil expenditures for elementary schools were about $550; for junior high schools about $900; and for the senior high school just under $1,000. Included in these figures is a 5 per cent factor for building costs.

The school system consists of seven elementary schools (grades 1 through 6), most of which have an enrollment of between 500 and 600; two junior high schools (grades 7 through 9), with approximately 900 students each; and one comprehensive high school (grades 10 through 12) with about 1,800 pupils, which offers a college-preparatory curriculum as well as less demanding programs leading to a diploma. The superintendent of schools has served for more than thirty years and is highly respected in the community, among other reasons, because of the imagination which he showed in buying large parcels of land at a low price to allow for future school expansion. Three administrators report directly to him: an assistant superintendent; an administrator for business affairs; and a director of research, guidance, and pupil personnel services. The last has been in his post for five years having previously served in a neighboring urban system as director of guidance and vice-principal of a ghetto school. He is a man with considerable experience who has continued to broaden and deepen his knowledge as he has ascended the educational hierarchy. He has recently completed his work for a doctorate at a nearby university.

The director of pupil personnel services has direct supervision over three psychologists, one social worker, four speech therapists, one learning disability specialist, seven nurses, twelve supplemental teachers, one part-time attendance officer, six part-time physicians, including a consulting psychiatrist, in addition to the guidance staff. This staff consists of one head counselor and six other full-time counselors in the high school and four full-time counselors assigned to the two junior high schools, or a total guidance staff of eleven.

Because the salary scale is fully competitive and working conditions are considered above average, Suburbantown receives a considerable number of applications from qualified counselors for each staff opening which occurs. The director invests considerable time in interviewing prospective members for his staff, since he desires to select the better-qualified applicants in order to assure a high quality of service. In recruiting personnel he has been careful to prevent inbreeding. Since he has been in Suburbantown he has hired seven guidance counselors, only two of whom were recruited from the local teaching staff. In developing contacts with outside sources, the director relies heavily on personal acquaintance with counselor educators in whom he has trust. He never sends an announcement of an opening to be hung on departmental bulletin boards.

The director follows the policy of giving those he hires a relatively free hand. This policy is apparently followed also by the head counselor in the high school. A newly appointed counselor we interviewed told us of his satisfaction with his work setting and especially with the freedom that he had been given "to work out his own way of doing the job." When he had asked initially for close supervision, his head counselor had remarked that "both of them would know more about how he was doing at the end of three years after he had worked extensively with the same group of students."

Although the pupils in sixth grade (and their parents) receive some orientation about what to expect when they enter junior high school, formal guidance does not begin until the middle of the eighth grade, when it is directed at helping students select courses for the ninth grade (the first time students have a range of choices with regard to both subject matter and the level of instruction).

The two junior high schools, East and West, differ in some respects: the income level of the homes from which the students come; the age of the plant; and above all the personality of the principal. The principal of the West School runs a tight organization. He takes the lead in weekly sessions with teachers of the eighth grade and guidance counselors to consider one or another problem, such as identifying and providing remedial work for underachievers.

But the main thrust of guidance at West School in the eighth grade involves the students' selection of courses for the following year. The critical question is whether students select algebra and science. In fact, to insure that students do not find themselves out of their intellectual depth, many are discouraged from taking these subjects with the result that when they reach the tenth grade in high school some of them, who are headed for college, must fit them in. In the principal's view the major stress of guidance in West School should be on educational and vocational orientation. With his encouragement, and with the help of materials provided by the guidance staff, one of the teachers has built a curriculum unit around the world of work.

One of the two guidance counselors at West School also serves as the football coach, which gives him the opportunity of getting to know many seventh-graders. But he will soon have to relinquish this assignment since the director wants to relieve all of his counselors of extra duties such as coaching and supervising the lunchroom and study halls. The counselor-football coach has the reputation of encouraging students to select courses at a level of difficulty that will challenge them. He wants them to stretch, in contradiction to the school's policy, which appears to be to encourage students to play it safe and take courses which they can handle.

The other counselor at West School is a woman with strong views and an outgoing personality who does not hesitate to tell young people what they should or should not do, but we found instances where she misinterpreted test results in reaching an evaluation of a counselee's strengths and weaknesses. She alone, among the junior high school counselors, believed that the guidance staff should be actively involved in curriculum evaluation and change and sought to attend meetings at which the curriculum was under appraisal. But the academic staff did not make her welcome. The conservatism of the teachers is underscored by our finding that although the director personally sought to persuade the English staff in the senior high school to include a unit on the meaning of work, he met great resistance and failed to convince them.

Our staff interviewed four teachers in West School to elicit their views on how well the guidance function was being discharged. One strongly believed that the guidance staff should be augmented because the classroom teacher had no time to deal with guidance problems. Two others gave the kinds of answers they believed their principal would approve. They remarked in passing, however, that they had little feeling one way or the other—guidance was peripheral to their work. The fourth teacher, who had a master's degree in guidance, indicated his discontent with the quality of the guidance services. In his view, the guidance staff was spending too much time on scheduling, orientation, and testing and too little in discussions with students.

Interviews with selected students at West School indicated that they saw guidance primarily as a function related to course selection. They made it clear that they would not seek out either of the guidance counselors to discuss a personal problem. In fact, there was no adult in the school they trusted in this respect. The authoritarian style of the principal and the school's complex of rules and regulations, which led students and even some parents to talk about the school as a "concentration camp," seemed to create an impassable divide between educator and child. It appeared to us that West School was run for the security of the administration and was aimed at keeping students under control. No one in authority saw the school as an institution whose primary objective was to understand the needs of young people and respond to them.

We found conditions at East School in many respects quite different, a fact which appeared to reflect the orientation of its principal. While he is concerned about academic achievement, his primary aim is to have students use the three-year period in junior high school to learn more about themselves and explore the world about them. His emphasis is heavily on growth and development, and in this frame he sees a large role for guidance. As principal he sets the tone, and consequently many on his teaching staff consider it important to spend time with students—not only on academic concerns but also in discussions of their personal problems. As a consequence, the role of the guidance staff is minimized.

Despite the positive stance of the principal toward the developmental aspects of student life and experience, and despite the whole-hearted agreement of the two counselors with his philosophy, their performance is enigmatic. We were impressed by the reports of both teachers and students of discrepancies between theory and practice. For instance, some girls reported that one of the male counselors (who recently qualified as a school psychologist and left the district) made them cry by berating them for their academic shortcomings and warning them that, if they did not improve, they would not find husbands! We ourselves never saw either of the two counselors talking with a student, nor did we see students congregating at the guidance office. As far as we were able to judge, despite the positive orientation of the principal, contact between guidance counselor and student was largely on a formal, routinized basis. Since the teaching staff was so involved in guidance, the counselors faced the challenge of how best to relate to the classroom teacher. From the complaints we heard from teachers about the clumsy interference of the counselors, it appears that the latter fell short. Had the two counselors been more sensitive and adroit, the positive orientation of the principal and teaching staff presented preconditions for a model of effective junior high school guidance. But that was not what we found.

The Suburbantown high school is headed by a former member of the teaching staff who believes in giving his guidance counselors wide latitude in developing and carrying out their program. The head counselor had been in the public school system for twenty-five years. Her devotion to her pupils has earned her a position of respect and influence in the community at large. Both parents and students are willing to trust her and they know from experience that she will try to be helpful. Despite pressure from the director to lighten her schedule, she insists on carrying a mixed caseload of good students and students in trouble, as well as teaching an English class for handicapped children, which reduces the time available to supervise her staff of six counselors.

Each counselor is assigned responsibility for 300 students, who remain his charges throughout the three years they are in high school and who must be seen by appointment at least once each year. While there is merit in such a system in terms of continuity of relationship, it is deficient in circumstances where there is no rapport between the assigned counselee and counselor. The combination of limited counselor supervision and arbitrary student assignment carries the danger that some students will be poorly served.

Since the counseling staff is composed of individuals with different personalities, different training, and different value orientations, each tends to do what is natural for him. Some provide educational and vocational advice; others are more "therapeutically" oriented. One of the latter said that if one of his students needs help in finding a college or in preparing for a job, he would tell him "where the books are." Despite the variability in approach, the focus is definitely on the "problem case," and this is resented by some teachers, one of whom remarked that the guidance staff was "pleading too much for the student." Another teacher called the guidance office "the womb."

The relations between the teaching and the guidance staff are not what they might be. For example, some years ago, the grade of E was introduced to represent a passing mark in a course which a student wished to explore but might not otherwise have selected because of its difficulty. The E grade reflected effort without reference to level of accomplishment. As a result of personnel turnover, the original intent of the E has been lost and both teachers and counselors have forgotten how to use an imaginative grading device.

The counseling staff has relatively little rapport with the curriculum committee. What they learn from the students is often not fed back into the curriculum-making process. An even more important failing is the lack of integration between guidance in the junior high school and the high school. The junior high school students have little or no preview of the choices that will be available to them in high school, and they know less of the consequences of choosing among them.

The forward linkages are also weak. For instance, the counseling staff has given all matters of the draft and military service a wide berth, although young men who plan to enlist or will be drafted could profit from understanding their military options. Interestingly, in discussions with members of the school board, our staff found more receptiveness to introducing counseling with respect to military service than it was able to elicit from the guidance staff, who feared community criticism.

The teaching as well as the guidance staff advises students concerning college and jobs. One of the teachers, who is also a coach, informed us that he did a considerable amount of college guidance among the members of his team. He felt that he was able to give them sounder advice than they were able to obtain from their counselors. Since we encountered several complaints from parents about the quality of college guidance, the coach may have been realistic in his assessment of the situation. One parent complained that the counselor had failed to check whether her daughter had sufficient foreign language credits for college, although she had been headed for college since entering high school. Others complained about a counselor who did not mail college application blanks out on time.

A serious criticism comes from us. In our view, there was relatively little discrimination shown by the counselors about the strengths and weaknesses of the different colleges to which these students applied and among which they would eventually make a choice. The counselors often erred by encouraging able students to apply and accept admission to colleges where the quality of faculty and curriculum would be unlikely to provide the stimulation and competence necessary for professional or graduate training. Since, as we have noted, most parents were not college-educated, they tended to have little knowledge of the relative quality of different institutions and they relied on the guidance staff to make such judgments. It is important to note in this connection, however, that approximately one out of every two of the high school graduates did enter a four-year college.

A more difficult problem, which the guidance staff appeared largely to ignore, involved the almost universal desire of parents to see their children attend college, irrespective of their offsprings' interests or abilities. It is worth recalling in this connection the judgment reached by Dr. Conant after his extended evaluation of suburban high schools. In Conant's view, the first task of guidance counselors was to help parents and students alike develop a more realistic attitude toward college.[1] Only trouble will ensue if poorly motivated and poorly prepared students are encouraged to aim high in response to parental pressures. In Suburbantown, many students as they neared the end of high school had had enough of classroom instruction. They did not want to spend the next four years in the classroom, as they had during the last twelve years. Aside from a lack of interest, many could barely meet the minimum educational requirements for college admission at even the least selective of institutions; some could not even do that.

The guidance staff was well aware of the pervasive desire of parents to send their children to college, and they spent much of their time and effort facilitating this end. In addition to the 50 per cent who entered four-year colleges, another 13 per cent entered a junior or community college, and 8.5 per cent of the graduating class pursued other types of post-secondary training. The remaining 28.5 per cent either went to work, entered the Armed Forces, or married.

In this respect the facts we learned in Suburbantown are consistent with the findings of many studies, that guidance counselors tend to concentrate on the college-bound to the neglect of students who are not college-bound but who may be interested in and need assistance with respect to occupational training. This may be too critical a judgment, however, since the director of pupil personnel services has made a special effort to help young people explore their occupational interests by both encouraging a large-scale career program with outside participants and by facilitating specific contacts for students who express a particular vocational interest. It was reported to us that during one month no fewer than forty representatives of colleges, junior colleges, vocational and technical schools, large companies, the State Employment Service, and other organizations came to talk to juniors and seniors about a wide range of post-secondary school opportunities.

Through the cooperation of five civic organizations the director of guidance was able to prepare a *Vocational Resource Directory* that "provides a convenient listing of local and nearby residents who are qualified by experience—and anxious by choice—to counsel [Suburbantown] youth of high school age and older in exploring, selecting, and pursuing a vocation." In the introduction it is requested "that students do not contact resource persons directly to arrange appointments but always work through the professional worker." However, as is frequently the case, the presence of this resource does not mean that it is widely used.

The fact that a few parents feel that the school is not discharging its guidance functions effectively is reflected in their having their children tested and counseled by outside agencies. Since the college advisory system manifests weaknesses and since many of the non-college-bound are not helped to make the transition into further training or work, it is clear that the guidance and counseling juniors and seniors receive leaves considerable margin for improvement.

With regard to children with special handicaps Suburbantown gets a good mark. As already pointed out, the school system has been able to build up a sizable group of pupil personnel specialists, both full-time and part-time. This had been one of the major goals of the director and we must conclude that he had been remarkably successful within the short space of five years in assembling such a large and apparently competent staff.

While rich staff resources can be valuable for the student who needs specialized help, the presence of so many different specialists presents administrative difficulties. The social worker and psychologists complained that the guidance staff repeatedly delayed referrals to them. In turn, the guidance counselors complained that the counselee frequently had to wait too long before receiving an appointment with one of these specialists.

One arena where a conflict could have come to a head if the director had not decided to sidestep it, at least for the time being, is that of guidance in the elementary school. Currently the pupil personnel specialists act as a team in diagnosing and treating children who require special assistance. While the principals of the seven elementary schools have different opinions about how best to use the special service team—some seek to integrate it into the ongoing educational program while others treat it as an ancillary service—there is general agreement along two major axes. It is agreed that it would be desirable to make these services available to more students rather than to limit them as mandated by state law to those with the most severe disabilities. Second, there is agreement that the best way to do this would be to enlarge the number of specialists. Nobody in authority advocates that a new specialist—an elementary school guidance counselor—be added. This may be

the trend elsewhere, but Suburbantown is impressed with the
specialists they have and sees no point in adding an elementary
school guidance counselor whose contribution remains to be proved.

Reference was made earlier to the members of the school board.
We indicated that they were more receptive than the guidance staff
to the idea of introducing draft counseling. In our discussions with
these members we found that they were sympathetic to and interested in what the guidance personnel are seeking to accomplish but
have difficulty in distinguishing among ideals, goals, actions, and
results. As one of them put it, "We meet with them and listen and
after we leave we aren't any clearer as to what they are doing."

The school board continues to support the program, however,
because of its faith in the director. The members hold him in high
esteem and appreciate his sensitivity and dedication to the students.
As a result they generally approve any reasonable request he makes.
Since the director is aware of the regard in which he is held by the
school board, he may not always explain fully what he is trying to
do. There are times he may feel improved communication will not
gain or hold support for a program that cannot present hard
evidence of its accomplishments.

At the end of their field study in Suburbantown, two senior staff
members met with a panel composed of the director of pupil services, the head counselor of the high school, a second high school
counselor, one counselor from each of the two junior high schools,
a psychologist, and a nurse. As might have been anticipated, there
was no unanimity among the members of the panel in evaluating the
broad range of services provided by the school system and there
was less agreement between them and the outsiders. Yet most of the
participants were willing to subscribe to the following propositions
which emerged from the interchange:

—The operation of a guidance system is greatly influenced by the
   orientation of the principal. It remained moot, however,
   whether it is desirable or possible to develop a guidance program which would have greater autonomy.
—There is a gap between the guidance staff and other pupil personnel specialists. In part this reflects the tendency of the guidance personnel to work alone; in part it reflects the withholding
   attitudes of other specialists toward them.
—The focus of guidance in junior high school on the problem

child or on routine course selection is unfortunate. A broader developmental stance which can make a contribution to the entire student body should be encouraged.

—A problem remains in involving counselors in curriculum review, particularly in the face of opposition from the teaching staff and lack of curriculum orientation on the part of some of the counselors.

The remainder of this chapter will review the materials which have been presented so far in order to determine the directions in which they point. They should be viewed with reference to the fact that the educational and guidance system in Suburbantown is considered to be several notches above the average.

A first fact is that guidance counselors are not the only persons within the school setting who provide help to students. Coaches and teachers are involved in one or another facet of guidance. There is no evidence to suggest that these untrained persons are less successful than those who are called guidance counselors. Some of the evidence suggests the opposite.

While the two junior high school principals differed in their sensitivity to the developmental needs of their students, and while each played a major role in establishing a distinctive climate in his school, the interesting fact that emerged is that these significant environmental differences are not reflected in the over-all quality of the guidance program. It takes more than a sympathetic and interested principal to assure a strong guidance program, especially in a system where the director of pupil personnel services is in charge of hiring and assigning counseling personnel.

Every institution, and the Suburbantown school system is no exception, tends to direct its limited resources to people who cannot be ignored and to functions that cannot be postponed. Hence most guidance personnel tend to spend a disproportionate amount of their time with "problem students" who require immediate attention, and with facilitating the work of the institution by helping students to pick their courses and to plan their programs so that the school can function effectively.

In light of this emphasis, it is not surprising that many students are lost in the system since they have but brief encounters with their counselors, whom they otherwise do not seek out and who in turn do not seek them out. Many come to the end of their high school

years with little understanding of where to go next or of the implications of their taking one road rather than another. The most neglected are the non-college-bound who, at the end of high school,
seek jobs, enlist in the Armed Forces, or undertake additional
training.

Although students who did not enter college needed more help
than they perceived or received, guidance for the college-bound
also had some shortcomings. Members of the guidance staff at both
school levels appear to "play it safe." Apparently they consider it
more desirable to encourage students to take courses which they
can pass than to take a chance on more difficult subjects and risk
failure. We were not able to unravel the multiple forces which
underlie this stance; possibly it reflected what counselors thought to
be the preferences of their principal, the parents, and even the students themselves. Whatever the explanation, the results are that
many students enter colleges which fail to challenge them.

All of the responsibilty for this outcome should not be placed on
the proclivity of the guidance staff to be excessively cautious. Part
of the blame should be assessed against their lack of knowledge
about the strengths and weaknesses of various institutions and about
how they deal with criteria for admission.

Whatever the limitations of guidance counselors about the realities of the educational establishment, their shortcomings about the
world of training and work are likely to be greater. As we emphasize elsewhere, information about occupational training and the
ways in which one becomes attached to the world of work remains
among the bodies of knowledge with which most guidance counselors are unfamiliar and with which they make little effort to
become acquainted.

In addition to these specific shortcomings, guidance in Suburbantown lacked a broad developmental approach. Such an approach
would lead the guidance staff to conceive of their task as one of
encouraging the student body—all of it—to develop an educational
and occupational strategy and of providing support and information
to insure that the strategy is implemented. Too many students are
left to their own and to their families' devices. While most parents
are concerned about their children's futures, only a minority have
sufficient knowledge to help them adequately.

It may be true (although we doubt it) that with a case load of

300 students per counselor such a broad objective is too ambitious and that there simply is not enough time for the counselor to do all that is desirable. Some evidence for this may be found in the following distribution, which sets out the estimated distribution of counselor time in Suburbantown:

	Per cent
Counseling students	65
Staff meetings	5
Faculty meetings	5
Conferences with parents	10
Planning and clerical duties	10
Testing and minor administrative duties	5

While this time distribution does not seem to indicate that more hours could be shifted to counseling, we wonder whether a shift toward more group counseling might not result in marked gains in over-all effectiveness. Moreover, certain teachers engage in guidance counseling on their own. If they were asked to help, many more might cooperate, especially if the guidance staff were willing to act as consultants.

It is questionable whether we can read the experience of Suburbantown as pointing in the direction of more counselors as a precondition for strengthening the guidance services young people receive. The guidance budget in Suburbantown is about $175,000 annually, or about 7 per cent of total educational costs. Alternative patterns of utilization of these counselors would have to be explored before a strong claim could be put forward for more money and more counselors.

The tension and friction between the guidance and the teaching staffs imply that it would be difficult to supplement the guidance staff with teachers on a structured basis and that valuable feedback from the present program is being lost. Those engaged in curriculum revision are not often informed of what the counselors learn from student evaluations of courses.

While the director recognizes the importance of curriculum inputs from the guidance staff, he has not yet found a way to make them broadly possible, although he has had some success, for instance, in involving the guidance staff in the restructuring of the social science curriculum in the junior high school. Had he pursued a more active role as supervisor, he might have seen the necessity of addressing himself to this problem earlier. But he held back from expanded supervision not only because of his other administrative and planning duties, but also apparently because he believed that his staff should enjoy considerable latitude. In addition, his head counselor in the high school acted in a similar vein. As a consequence, each guidance counselor sets his own rules as long as he meets the mimimum requirements of the system—that is, to approve student programs, prepare college application blanks, and try to resolve the difficulties of those who seek their help. When this lack of supervision is put into the context of the limited field training most counselors had received, we question whether individual counselors, especially young ones, should be granted so much scope for self-determination. The fact that the director had selected them carefully is no guarantee that they do not need supervision.

In addition to extending their reach by formally involving the teaching staff, the guidance staff might tap more effectively into community resources for informational purposes. While it did elicit and receive some help from the professional and business leadership, it could find reinforcements if it looks more to the outside. It is not reasonable to expect any group of counselors, no matter how well they have been trained, to have the answers to all occupational questions that are put to them. But it is reasonable to expect them to recognize the limitations of their expertise and to know where and how to supplement it. Few school counselors, including those in Suburbantown, have yet learned how to make optimal use of resources beyond the school.

We were disturbed by the repeated statements of students that they would not discuss any personal problem with their guidance counselor because they see them as tools of the educational system. While we certainly do not want to turn guidance personnel into psychotherapists, we realize that during puberty and adolescence many "normal" children are likely to encounter problems and difficulties which, if aired, frequently dissolve or at least recede without specialized intervention. We know that some youngsters seek out a favorite teacher and make him their confidant. A forward-looking school system might consider whether students should be allowed to designate one staff member as ombudsman for the school.

Suburbantown also offers perspective on a question that has concerned the guidance field for some time—the desirability of introducing guidance counselors into the elementary school. Those in charge of the educational system in Suburbantown know that many children, especially those with handicaps, require assistance early in their school years and that specialists have a critical role to play in providing it. But they are equally clear that guidance counselors will not be able to contribute to the improved functioning of most students at this level. They want more specialists, from psychologists to remedial speech and reading teachers for the exceptional child, and prefer to rely on their regular staff for the guidance of pupils without special disabilities.

Now that the major "lessons" that we have extracted from our critical evaluation of Suburbantown are before us, what over-all judgments or conclusions can we make?

The most tantalizing fact that emerges is the difficulty of reaching a firm judgment about the quality of guidance services in Suburbantown. The director has never articulated a set of priority goals against which accomplishment can be measured. Moreover, even had he done so, it is not clear whether the staff would have accepted his goals in fact as well as in form. Even if the director and his staff could have reached agreement about the priority objectives of the program, it remains questionable whether, in light of the current state of data collection and evaluation, we could reach a judgment about whether these goals are being achieved.

However, significant gains might accrue from an effort to design and test a reporting system for program evaluation. While care would have to be taken that the staff does not become more responsive to the report than to their counselees, a system of objective information about how counselors spend their time and a follow-up of graduates would enable the administrator of a guidance program to judge its performance and to know where constructive changes might be introduced.

While we acknowledge that pitfalls lie in the path of every data collection system used for program evaluation, we still must question whether an over-all judgment about guidance in Suburbantown can be reached without hard data about day-to-day operation and about short-range outcomes.

The most important conclusion is that the total guidance effort is relatively modest despite its staff of eleven persons, plus the director who has responsibility for all pupil personnel services as well as for research. While we heard criticism by members of the school board, parents, teachers, and students about the guidance effort, we do not want to exaggerate the extent of discontent. Moreover, every person we met realized that the guidance staff is engaged in many essential and desirable functions. They play a role in the assignment of students to courses; they intervene on behalf of certain students who encounter trouble with their teachers or their studies; they assist students to select the colleges to which to apply and help them fill out the required applications; they counsel those who are not going to college and provide them with leads about alternatives that they might pursue; they occasionally hold conferences with parents; they feed back into the school system certain information about student attitudes and reactions; they refer seriously disturbed students to specialists on the staff or in the community.

The foregoing provides an overview of their tasks. The critical question that remains is how well they perform them and whether increased staff would better serve the student body.

We were disturbed to find that decisions about courses sometimes closed out options; that choice of college was not clearly based on individual potential; that the needs of the non-college group were neglected; and that there was little effective feedback from the guidance staff to those responsible for reviewing and revising the curriculum.

It must be recalled that we did not attempt to undertake a comprehensive evaluation of guidance services in Suburbantown. Our central concern was to explore the ways in which the work of school counselors is affected by the settings in which they carry it out. We learned in Suburbantown that the guidance staff was constrained by the actions of their principal, their teaching colleagues, and the parents of their clients. Significant reform would have to deal with these potent groups. But these tensions were well within limits of tolerance: a school board that had some reservations; a few dissatisfied parents; a student body that did not trust its advisors sufficiently to confide personal matters.

The more important problem was the need to define the primary goals of the guidance system. Only with clarification could there be broad agreement among the interested parties—administrators, parents, students, and the guidance staff—about what to expect and what not to expect from a school guidance advisory effort. Without it, every possible reaction from favorable to unfavorable can be justified. It all depends on the criteria that are brought to bear and the experiences of the individual.

11

INFORMATIONAL PROCESSES:

PERSONAL ASSESSMENT

EDUCATIONAL and career decisions require that the individual learn about himself and about the world of school and work, and integrate these two types of knowledge in making his plans. Guidance can help the individual evaluate the relevance of the information he has accumulated about himself in the context of what he has learned about the opportunities and options available in the educational and occupational world.

In guidance, personal assessment has traditionally relied on psychometric methods and findings; career information has relied on occupational publications. In the training of guidance personnel, functions of assessment and information have conventionally been treated separately although they are inextricably interwoven. For example, the young boy who learns that he is not as competent at sports as his peers acquires at one and the same time an assessment of himself and a knowledge that certain work—professional athletics—is an unlikely avenue for him.

Our recognition of the interrelatedness of these two areas has led us to deal with personal assessment and career information as a single theme, although we have divided the materials into two chapters as a matter of convenience. We also realize that the acquisition of information about oneself as well as the acquisition of information about the outside world is a dynamic process that starts at birth.

It is the realization that self-assessment and information about the world of work frequently occur as one experience that leads us first to outline the developmental experiences that affect both personal assessment and knowledge of the world of work. We shall then proceed to examine the approaches to assessment and occupational information that are characteristic of guidance practices. We shall then suggest some of the critical problems of information utilization that must be faced if individuals are to improve their educational and career decisions.

The process of learning about oneself and the world in which one lives takes place largely without formal guidance. We shall note the informal aspects of information acquisition, but we shall focus on the role of guidance services in helping the individual to assess himself and the objective reality within which he lives and works.

The transformation of the child into an adult is a slow process of exposure and response to diverse forces, including the judgments that others make about him. The first inputs into the process of discovering one's identity are from one's parents. It is they who smile, compliment, encourage, inhibit, scold, reward, and punish the young child for the actions he takes and those he avoids. The whole of his early existence is an exposure to evaluation by parents and by others in his immediate environment.

In the home a boy not only begins to learn about himself but also about the world of work. He early senses whether his father likes his work, merely endures it, or is frustrated by it. And a girl learns about her mother's attitudes toward housework and jobs.

Further, the child is exposed to additional formative influences from other adults, peers, books, and television. Many images about work come through. The preschool child, even though he cannot sort out and verbalize about the subject of work, has probably started to understand that work is of critical importance in life and that he will soon have to begin to deal with its prototype— by going to school.

By the time a child enters the first grade he has developed a style for dealing with matters familiar and unfamiliar. Children differ from one another in their curiosity, initiative, trust, self-confidence, relaxation with strangers, ease of adjusting to other children, and all of the other dimensions that mark their relations to people and things.

At another level, their cognitive and other abilities differ: some have begun to read, others know how to count; some have a good ear for music, others have a knowledge of the ways of animals; some have traveled and seen strange things; others can run fast or hit a ball well. Teachers vary in their interest and response to different abilities and skills.

Another kind of learning that affects one's self-image takes place in the early school years. A child becomes conscious, often for the first time, of the ways in which his family's style of life parallels or differs from that of his classmates. He may sense, again often for the first time, whether he comes from a rich or a poor family; whether his father's work is respected or not; whether he belongs to the religion or race of the majority. In school, the child is likely to become aware of what the sociologists call ascriptive qualities—those that set him in social space.

Thus the early years of the child's experience in school contribute a great deal to his growing perception of himself. The school is the second powerful environment, after the home, to which he is exposed. Moreover, the school is the first formally structured competitive environment where he is repeatedly assessed. Young children usually receive grades or other evaluations and they soon learn whether they fall into an advanced, an average, or a backward group. Despite efforts to disguise whether they are on a fast or slow track, the facts soon become known to them through the inadvertence of teachers or administrators or from what they pick up from the conversations of their parents or peers. Where there is no formal tracking, teachers frequently arrange to distinguish between those who are bright and those who are slow through a seating plan, reading groups, or other device, and their judgment soon becomes known to all the members of the class.

While the ability to absorb instruction is the principal criterion used by the school to differentiate among students, it is not the only one. The children's conduct is important. Those who do not conform to the teacher's standards are singled out for ridicule and punishment. Many whose behavior is disruptive are poor students who find it difficult to follow the work, but some are good students who become bored and restless. Some of them, both poor and good students, will soon become known to the teaching staff as problem children, having been labeled by information one faculty member passes to the next.

A considerable amount of information accompanies the child as he moves from one grade to the next; prior teacher judgments are often confirmed because the child lives up to expectations. At some point an unruly child may be referred to a pupil personnel specialist or to an assistant principal or principal who is likely to regard a record of negative comments as evidence of deviance and to handle the child accordingly. The administrator's judgment of the child may then become his own self-judgment and what may have been an easily remedial condition becomes a self-fulfilling prophecy.

As we noted in Chapter 5, the school offers a second cue to the child and his parents about who he is and who he is likely to become in the form of different tests of learning ability, which for many years have been assumed to be predictive of future achievement. While there is now more awareness of the limitations of many test instruments, of the impact of school environment on test scores, and of the limited predictive value of tests with regard to adult performance, they continue to be widely used.

The schools offer a third cue. Classroom learning is focused primarily on language, numbers, and abstract thinking. These are the essential elements of the development of cognitive competence. However the school does relatively little to assist students in appraising their abilities in such areas as the artistic, the political, the interpersonal, the manual, where accomplishment tends to be downgraded when it does not coincide with academic attainment. Yet a great many people eventually earn their livelihood through competence in one of these areas.

The educational system is twice remiss in this respect. It does not provide adequate opportunities for young people to explore their interests in these fields and it does not give them an indication of their potential or competence in these fields. The outstanding exception is athletic prowess. Most schools place considerable emphasis on competitive sports and the young man who demonstrates superior performance on the gridiron, the baseball diamond, the basketball court is likely to be singled out, encouraged, and helped to go on to college. The substantial neglect of the non-cognitive areas can be traced more to the traditional criteria that colleges use for admission than to the preferences of schools at lower levels. A narrow focus on cognitive skills leads to restricted and therefore faulty evaluations, which limit the opportunity of the young person to learn more about himself. He is assessed and reassessed according to his ability in mathematics, English, history, science. But the school places little or no value on non-academic achievement.[1]

There are further limitations built into the school's assessment process that help to confound rather than clarify the individual's self-image. While grading systems purport to evaluate the effort which young people devote to their studies, most assessments are based on results—particularly on conformance to teacher expectations —not on the process of learning. But we know from adult experience that much of the difference in performance is a function of characterological factors, such as ambition, imagination, risk-taking, energy, tolerance for routine, ability to encapsulate defeat, which reflect the importance that a man attaches to his work and the ways in which he goes about performing it.

Aptitude and skill are important, but so are determination and energy. It is difficult to challenge the generalization that most marks students receive reflect aptitude and prior opportunity more than current effort and progress. Teachers and principals use grades to measure the progress students make. But there are gross differences in the ability and prior achievements of students at the same grade level. For instance in 1969, in District 5, Manhattan, fourth graders in different schools had reading scores ranging from an average of 1.2 years below the national norm of 4.7 years to 1.4 years above the norm. An educational system with so great a degree of variability in performance will find it difficult to use test data effectively.[2]

In addition, the grading system may offer to a young person the wrong indications about himself and his abilities. When a student gets good marks in school, it is not always clear what they connote. Does it mean that he ranks near the top of his class, his school, his community, his region, or the country? Marks that indicate that a youngster is a "top student" are often ambiguous. In fact, the ambiguity that attaches to school grades as an index of performance capability is such that many colleges, the Armed Forces, and large employers have had to resort to special testing for a better assessment of what a person knows or can learn.

Only a small minority of students are able to do outstanding work in all subjects—English, mathematics, science, and history. Is it sensible to tell a young man who is interested in becoming a chemist that he has a bleak future because he is doing badly in German and his marks in history and English are undistinguished? Yet as an administrative convenience, schools tend to average the marks that students receive. In college, selection for the dean's list, election to Phi Beta Kappa, and other distinctions and honors are usually awarded on the basis of the student's over-all score. And the U.S. Civil Service Commission provides a bonus when it appoints students who have maintained a 3.5 or better average (out of a maximum of 4.0) while in college.

It may not be possible to operate a mass educational system without making gross differentiations among applicants and students. But caution is needed if the evaluation devices are not to be credited with more than they are capable of doing. Young people must learn that the options that will eventually be open to them will depend in part, possibly in large part, on the competitive grades that they are able to attain. But it should also be made clear to them that the pursuit of grades for their own sake carries significant costs. When able students avoid taking "hard courses" for fear that they will receive low marks and thereby reduce their chances of gaining the next rung on the ladder, it is a perversion of the educational process. For example, engineering enrollments have not increased in recent years. One hypothesis is that many able students, faced with the danger of the draft, do not want to run the risk of getting low marks or flunking out and therefore opt for an easier curriculum.[3]

We have seen that the schools often provide cues which confuse rather than which aid a young person and his parents correctly to assess his strengths and weaknesses. Nevertheless, often the school's message is loud, clear, and important. This is the case when young people who come from low-income families find that they are doing well in their courses and begin to contemplate going to college and pursuing a professional career, a course which had not been part of their parents' or their own planning. An opposite example is when a student and his successful professional father agreed initially that he should study medicine, but an undistinguished school record in the sciences and mathematics leads the young man to reconsider and to select an alternative more consistent with his aptitudes and achievements. Here are two instances where the signals from school performance are important.

But problems may, and often do, arise when students have a mixture of strengths and weaknesses; when those who receive passing or slightly better grades show no special strengths; and particularly when students show a discrepancy between their aptitudes and their achievements. In these instances it is often unclear what conclusions the young person and his parents are to draw about his educational plans and his occupational orientation. For them the school is not a good testing ground. It sends back confused signals. At best it helps the young man decide what he should *not* do.

From the time the young child enters kindergarten until he graduates from high school he is constantly assessed. But the assessment has less to do with who he is and who he might become than with how well he does on the assignments that the school sets. Moreover, in his later years in the school system he is likely to receive little help in increasing his understanding of the post-high school educational and training institutions and of the labor market. He will receive even less help in putting the two bodies of information together.

The fact that the school leaves so many students unclear about who they are and who they would like to become helps to explain why many young people begin to clarify their career objectives only after they have worked for a few years, had a tour of duty in the Armed Forces, or served in the Peace Corps. Part of the clarification comes as a result of more time, more experience, and more reflection. Part of it comes from less equivocal signals about what they like and can do well.

We have outlined the many ways in which the young person may be confused or misled about himself. His parents may be at fault; the school may have sent him incorrect signals; he may lack the experience he needs to resolve his doubts about the strength of alternative interests, capacities and values. In the light of so many misleading indicators, there is much that guidance counselors can do. Let us first note their current role in assessment and then consider how it might be strengthened.

We have seen that the educational system continually makes judgments about the students who pass through its hands, partly to see how well the system is performing, partly to have information to pass on to others within the system who, it is assumed, will be in a better position to handle a student if they know more about him, and partly because other institutions such as colleges, mental health clinics, or the courts may request an evaluation. Guidance personnel usually play a major role in these assessment procedures although they offer little help to the student in clarifying his career plans.

Let us review briefly the different ways in which guidance personnel are involved in student assessment. The educational establishment has long used group testing for a wide variety of purposes: to assess the progress of students; to identify those who do very well or very poorly in order to provide special services either of enrichment or remediation; to determine the ranking of pupils or schools in relation to others in the locality, region, or nation.

In many systems, especially smaller ones, guidance personnel often have sole responsibility for administering and scoring such tests. They are also responsible for administering and interpreting group tests such as interest inventories which are used to help students in their occupational planning. In addition, guidance counselors, in and out of school settings, are likely to resort to individual testing when they are confronted by counselees who are uncertain about their abilities or interests.

The counselor is also likely to be the one in the school hierarchy who has the task of making an on-balance evaluation of a student when needed for internal or external purposes. In all of these ways the counselor is involved in personal assessment. Let us consider each in turn.

Schools make extensive use of group tests; according to Thorndike and Hagen, in recent years several versions of different types of tests have been widely used by school systems:[4]

Type of Test	Number of Versions
Intelligence	15
Aptitude	7
Reading	14
Elementary School Achievement	6
High School Achievement	5
Interest Inventories	9
Adjustment and Temperament Inventories	14

When the U.S. Office of Education sought Congressional support for the training of guidance and counseling personnel in the late 1950s, it stressed the need for more testing, particularly in smaller schools. The implicit logic was that tests would reveal the hidden strengths of students which had not been revealed by classroom performance. Once the "talented" students had been identified, they could be singled out for special attention. Teachers, guidance specialists, and principals would then be able to encourage them— and their parents—to formulate their career plans so as to take full advantage of their intellectual gifts. The expressed sentiment was the conviction that through testing and guidance more able young persons would be encouraged to go to college and eventually to enter one of the shortage occupations important to the nation's defense.

At the time the conventional pattern of group testing in schools involved the use of standardized intelligence and achievement tests. Scores were entered on the pupils' records and were rarely communicated to the student or to his parents. In recent years parents in some states have taken court action to force disclosure of their children's scores. Yet few parents insist on being informed and the scores tend to remain privileged data to the school personnel, of little or no use to the student. Essentially, the test scores merely become one more input into the student's cumulative record, together with his grades, teachers' comments, and family data. Since guidance counselors usually must approve student course selections they often use the test scores, together with the other available data, as a basis for approval or disapproval. If the student's plan is congruent with his previous classroom performance and with his test scores the counselor will usually approve his program without further exploration or probing of interests and plans. There are other students waiting and some may have problems which require detailed attention.

Given the usual discrepancy between counselor availability and counselee need for service, a practice that is geared to identify glaring non-fits between a counselee's record and his plans seems practical. While it would be desirable for the counselor to explore with each student his emerging career strategy, the priority task for the counselor must be to spot clear discrepancies between a student's record and his plans.

One important potential gain from mass testing and cumulative records would be derived from the guidance specialist's consideration of the scores and class standings of individual students in search of leads that might be used in educational decision-making. The simplest case is that of a young person who scores much higher on intelligence than on achievement tests. In the jargon of the trade, he is an "underachiever," but it is easier to affix the label than to follow up such leads and to look for the causes of under-achievement. It is even more difficult to help bring about changes in the school and home environment that might prevent it.

Occasionally the reverse situation occurs; young people are informed that their test scores show that they have limited ability although they have been performing well in class. A guidance specialist must weigh the possible causes of discrepancies in order to avoid improperly discouraging a student from continuing in his chosen field. After all, the discrepancy might reflect nothing more than a block in dealing effectively with short-answer questions, and even if it signifies more it is questionable whether test performance should take precedence over classroom work.

As we noted in Chapter 5, in recent years the whole testing effort has come under heavy attack from representatives of minority groups who claim that the instruments, particularly those used to assess intelligence, are biased in favor of children who come from middle-class backgrounds and whose life experiences and vocabulary make it easier to cope with the test questions. Moreover, there has been a slow accretion of research findings which indicate that, with orientation or after a relatively short exposure to a new environment, many young people from minority groups are able to show a significant improvement in their scores.[5] Guidance counselors have the responsibility to exercise extreme caution in making use of test scores validated for one population group and used to assess the performance of another. Unless they exercise such caution in interpreting test data they will add to the difficulties of self-appraisal and career planning of minority groups. Vocational rehabilitation counselors have long known that people with physical handicaps must not be assessed on the basis of the scores of a non-handicapped population. But apparently the moral of this lesson is being learned only slowly by many who are involved in testing and assessing members of groups who are handicapped by language, by education, or by economic factors.

We have noted that most large school systems use standardized tests to sort and evaluate students. Counselors should be concerned with the appropriateness of the instruments; with the conditions under which the tests are given; with discrepancies between test scores and other evidences of performance; and with significant changes in test scores over time. Most importantly, they must not join any attempt on the part of the administration or the teaching staff to use low scores to blame young people rather than the school for lack of progress in learning. Otherwise, they are lending their professional standing to efforts to use test results to justify student failure. By so doing, they show disregard for meaningful revision of curriculum and teaching methods.

Although testing in school is centered on intelligence, aptitude, and achievement batteries, the citation from Thorndike and Hagen called attention to the widespread use of interest and personality inventories. In many schools where the principal and the counseling staff use testing as a basic tool in guidance, all students are likely to be subjected to these inventories and many take them more than once during their junior and senior high school years. The question is how much can be extracted from these inventories that is relevant for career guidance.[6]

The use of personality tests is predicated on the assumption that if a counselor can learn more about his client's motivational system and his emotional dispositions, he will be better able to advise him about lines of work that will be congruent with his needs and desires. Through an interest inventory, the guidance counselor hopes to ascertain the areas and fields to which his client is likely to respond positively as well as those to which he is not attracted. While adults are usually able to answer a question about their interests, many adolescents say, "I don't really know." Consequently, counselors resort to a battery of tests in the hope of eliciting information about the interests of their clients.

Among the interest inventories, the two major instruments are the Strong Vocational Interest Blank and the Kuder Preference Record. As sympathetic a critic as Leona Tyler has pointed out that the Strong test has limitations for use with high school students because it is difficult to score and has little relevance for the large non-college group. Kuder's vocational battery was developed from an inadequate sample and follow-up.[7]

Interest inventories are complex psychometric devices. Separate scores communicate little, for it is the analysis of the total profile of preferences and dislikes that cues the individual. Another difficulty stems from the use of occupational titles in the Strong. For example, an individual reviewing his profile without careful discussion with a counselor might well react with strong negative feelings to a high score on the "mortician" scale. The test does not suggest that he has necrophiliac interests, but that he has some interest in occupations characterized by small, independent business operations.

There is clearly a need to restrict the use of interest testing to situations where the counselee can be adequately prepared for the test and informed what he can or cannot expect to learn from it. The test profile offers a basis for *exploration* of self-image in the context of occupational images and a chance to link these impressions to information about actual work situations. Interest inventory interpretation separated from career information inputs is meaningless.

As the Bixlers pointed out as early as 1946, personality tests are equally limited because of the uncertainty about what they are measuring and their lack of predictive value.[8] In the context of career guidance the paucity of information linking personality test scores to personal characteristics needed in a variety of occupations makes personality testing even less justifiable. But these and other criticisms have not reduced the widespread use by schools of the whole array of testing instruments.

There are, then, many test results, only some of which are directly related to career guidance, filed away and available to counselors but often not to counselees. It is not surprising that many school counselors want to use test results when they advise pupils. When a junior high school student draws up a program which includes algebra and the counselor has some doubts about his being able to handle it, he can look at the student's mathematical achievement and aptitude scores to help him decide. The danger is that the counselor will place excessive weight on group norms and overlook important individual factors such as the student's interest in the subject and his classroom performance.[9] A blatant example was a young Negro student who reported at the Superintendents' Conference at Teachers College in the summer of 1969 that a counselor in a high school on Long Island recently rezoned to admit minority youth, after glancing at a new student's papers, remarked, "With a record like that, you'll never make it here!"

One rationale for passing along detailed student records and making them available to all authorized persons (and sometimes unauthorized persons such as prospective employers) is to facilitate course assignments. But as we have seen, the costs are high. Students who get into trouble with the system and accumulate a record filled with negative comments are unlikely to have a second chance.

Students and parents approach guidance counselors according to whether they think the counselors can help them. The knowledge that the guidance staff must approve their programs and can assist them to get into college leads most middle-class youngsters to ingratiate themselves with their school counselors. Many parents, from both low- and middle-income homes, are so impressed with the guidance mystique that they follow the recommendations and decisions made by the staff even when they question whether the prescription fits their offspring.

Yet the fact that guidance counselors are part of the school's organizational complex and are responsible for providing evaluations of young people to outsiders, such as college admissions officers, conflicts with their primary role of being helpful to the individual student. This helps to explain why a recent Massachusetts study of pupil services recommended that guidance counselors no longer accept the responsibility for writing evaluations to colleges about students they have counseled.[10]

In any event it is difficult for a school counselor to make a sound assessment of students, especially adolescents who are wary of adults. Young people from upper-income homes usually seek advice elsewhere.[11] Those from low-income homes often do not like the advice their friends have received from the counseling office and therefore stay away. Many who seek help find that their counselors are pressed for time. But the heart of the difficulty relates to cues. The student's marks and test scores are available. He provides some details about his family. And he can report about his educational and work experiences and what he likes to do. A perspicacious counselor may be able to find a great deal in a student's record and recital. For instance, the counselor may note that the student has had an uneven school record both over time and among subjects. After discussion, the student may understand that unless he is willing to close out important options he must try to earn at least passing grades even in subjects in which he has little interest.

A frequently encountered counselee is one who says that he has no interests and who looks to the counselor to help him formulate a career plan. To such students many counselors recommend a battery of tests in the hope that the results will reveal previously hidden strengths or interests. But as we have seen, it is unlikely that the tests will provide useful cues.

A skillful counselor may decide that a limited amount of additional testing may help an individual over an impasse, especially if there is prior agreement about how the test results will be used. But, frequently, a recommendation that the student take a series of tests is the easy way out. Many counselors go along with their clients' verbalized hopes that the tests will provide definitive answers to their questions, but they rarely do. In recent decades, many guidance leaders have warned that tests have a limited role to play in the process of career guidance, but harried practitioners tend to overlook this warning and continue to resort to psychometrics as an answer.[12]

Recognizing that many of their counselees are in search of definitive answers and forgetting the cautions that attach to test interpretation, many counselors use scores in absolute rather than in probable terms. No test score alone can predict an outcome for any individual. Nevertheless, it is more common for a guidance counselor to say to a high school senior that "with a combined SAT score below 1400 you had better not apply to Harvard" than to explain to the young man that the fact that he comes from a small town in Ohio, that he has been the editor of the school paper, and that he has shown initiative in getting interesting summer jobs may be sufficient to tip the balance in his favor. A more reasonable statement would be: "In any case, I think you should apply as long as you realize that your chances of being accepted are not high, but they surely are not hopeless." In a world characterized by uncertainty, many counselors convey the impression that they have more knowledge than they, or anybody else, actually have.

How can we explain that when faced with a guidance problem so many counselors resort to testing and then seek to link the results to a specific educational or career plan rather than follow a more open, looser, and less directive approach? Part of the answer lies in the time pressures under which so many counselors work. Often guidance specialists are able to call on colleagues who specialize in psychometrics to oversee and score tests. And even if they have to do it themselves, the time cost for many tests is quite low. Moreover, many counselors have been fairly uncritical of what tests can and cannot do and have tended to overvalue them. Others tend to follow an authoritarian style and like "hard" test results. They make their recommendations sound more scientific by interlarding them with esoteric references to percentiles, norms, standard deviations, and the like.

What are the essential elements of a sound framework for personal assessment? Personal assessment is a process in which a counselee, seeking clarification of his career goals, reviews with his counselor his strengths and weaknesses and explores the answers to questions about which he is uncertain. Both counselee and counselor start with a fair amount of information about the counselee's personality, background, and performance to date. As the counselee interprets his own characteristics, the counselor has an opportunity to judge whether the interpretations are reasonable or to suggest alternative interpretations. Occasionally the counselee is encouraged to take a test to get some additional clues about his capacities or interest, and this becomes one more input. The counselor must interpret test results in terms of their incremental input, knowing that the new information will be relevant only if the counselee is helped to assimilate it into his decision-making. It is the counselee, not the counselor, who needs to become self-conscious in developing and implementing a career plan.

This is a time-consuming undertaking and one which requires a predisposition on the part of the counselee to work toward clarification; and it requires a counselor with understanding and skills that will enable him to assist his client in broadening and deepening his self-understanding. This approach is difficult to institutionalize; nevertheless, the following dangers should be avoided:

—The presumption that grades in school are indicative of performance in the adult world.
—The broad-scale recourse to testing on the assumption that the results will provide a sound basis for career planning.
—The danger of closing out specific choices solely or primarily on the basis of test results.
—The failure to recognize that school evaluations (including tests) are limited primarily to cognitive functions and do not record the strengths and weaknesses of students in many other critical areas of performance.
—The dangers of indiscriminately passing along damaging information about students as they proceed through the school system, thereby preventing them from getting a second chance.
—The preoccupation of guidance specialists with using data for student evaluations to the relative neglect of its possible use in career planning.

While it is easy to justify concentration on school guidance in evaluating one or another aspect of contemporary guidance because of the focus of most guidance effort on adolescents, some attention must be paid to other guidance settings, particularly with respect to personal assessment. As we have seen, school counselors are more heavily engaged in evaluating students than in working with them to deepen their self-perception and to help them in their career decision-making.

A more sophisticated approach to assessment is likely to be made under the following conditions: where counselors have the opportunity to spend considerable time with each client, and where, in the face of sparsity of information, additional inputs from tests and other sources provide a sounder basis for career planning. Given these preconditions it is not surprising to find that personal assessment as an integral part of career counseling is more widely practiced in community agencies, the Veterans Administration, and vocational rehabilitation agencies than in the schools. The staffs in these agencies tend to have had more training in psychometrics, have more clients who have special handicaps, and are usually able to spend more time with each of them to develop a career plan.

Pursuing what can best be described as a clinical approach, they tend to resort to widespread testing among other reasons because of the need to discover the type of specialized training or employment that the client requires to build a career. But some of the difficulties that develop in the process of personal assessment in school settings are also found here—as when vocational rehabilitation counselors are overly directive and try to push their clients in a particular direction rather than help them make their own decisions. Moreover, the finding that only about half of all rehabilitation clients receive counseling indicates that the clinical approach, with test results and test interpretations woven into the making of a career plan, may be the preferred but is surely not the usual pattern.[13]

As noted earlier with regard to minority groups, one of the difficulties that counselors of the handicapped face is to know what allowances to make when interpreting the results from tests that have been standardized on populations free of disabilities.

Brief note should also be taken in the present context of the General Aptitude Test Battery (G.A.T.B.), which the Employment Service has used for many years as a major adjunct to its counseling and placement services. This battery consists of twelve tests which measure nine aptitudes; eight of the tests require paper and pencil, and four use apparatus. The battery takes about two and a half hours. The Employment Service has grouped over 600 occupations in a limited number of Occupational Aptitude Patterns and has established norms with different cutoff points for specific aptitudes. Through testing, particularly of new workers without experience, the counselor is able to suggest fields where the applicant is likely to do well.[14] In recent years, as the Employment Service was confronted for the first time with large numbers of persons from minority groups, many with low levels of literacy, it discovered that the G.A.T.B. is not a well-honed instrument to evaluate the aptitudes of everyone. One tester remarked, "This test is fine if you can read at a sixth grade level ... but we have kids who can strip a car in 10 minutes who cannot pass the mechanics aptitude test."[15] While the Service has endeavored to modify the G.A.T.B., its success to date has been limited.

One interesting effort to improve assessment procedures for the hard-to-employ has been the development of a "work sample" approach, an outgrowth of the experience with the physically handicapped in sheltered workshops, to determine what clients are able to do, both initially and after they acquire some experience and confidence. "Work samples" comprise a group of increasingly difficult and varied work tasks. The literature suggests considerable success with this approach, particularly when the work samples are part of a larger process of moving disadvantaged persons into paid employment after they have been assessed and have had a period of vestibule training.[16]

What general findings and conclusions can be precipitated from this discussion of the role of personal assessment in career guidance? The first, and perhaps most important, observation is that guidance counselors have a distinctive role to play in helping people acquire more self-insight so that they will be in a better position to formulate their career plans. This is not the only task that guidance specialists perform, but it is surely one that should be at the center of their work.

We have found that for a variety of reasons, including lack of time, lack of client interest, lack of adequate counselor training, preoccupation with evaluations for institutional purposes, many guidance specialists, particularly within the school setting, do not conduct personal assessment in a manner that is conducive to helping individuals develop improved career plans. They frequently overemphasize testing and frequently misinterpret test results, thereby misleading their clients as to their options.

We know from our earlier discussion that most guidance counselors have a psychological bias. They are preconditioned to see the problem of career decision-making primarily in psychological dimensions. While heavy work loads generally limit their attempts to explore the psychodynamics of the decision-making process, they prefer psychological techniques, and their frequent use of tests is one manifestation of this.

Moreover, economics reinforces ideology. Most tests are sold by aggressive publishers who constantly strive to enlarge their market. Many publishers make extravagant claims for their instruments, thereby heightening the receptiveness of counselors who must handle large numbers of clients. As Gustad complained, "The only cure for the ills of testing is more testing."[17]

C. H. Patterson summarized the thrust of this chapter when he stated, "If the client is to use the results of tests he must (1) understand them and (2) be able to accept them."[18] Faced with the need to assess large numbers, counselors have understandingly looked for short cuts. Testing appeared to be a way out. But as we have sought to make clear, personal assessment is a much more complex undertaking, including a joint probing and evaluation of the individual's strengths and weaknesses. This is the first of a two-stage process. The second involves the individual in gaining more insight into the world within which he must seek to realize his goals.

12

INFORMATIONAL PROCESSES:

THE WORLD OF WORK

THE PROPOSITION was advanced at the beginning of the last chapter that critical to career decision-making is the individual's knowledge of himself and the world in which he must eventually find a job and pursue a career. We stated, in addition, that guidance has seen the enhancement of such knowledge as its central function. In this chapter we will explore how the individual acquires information about external reality and what the specialized role of guidance is in this regard. Since the collection, dissemination, interpretation, and use of information involves costs to the individual as well as to society, a blanket recommendation of more and better information is not a responsive answer.

Sound decision-making implies that an individual has reliable information about his alternatives and some indication of the consequences of opting for one over another. There are several implicit assumptions that should be made overt. The individual may be unaware that he does in fact confront a choice. Even if he is aware, he may simply be uninterested in the difficult task of weighing alternatives and acting on them; he may prefer to follow his buddies and drop out of school and take the first available job. He may not know how to learn the pertinent facts which would enable him to make a better decision. Finally, he may be unable to distill from the information that is available the facts he needs for an informed judgment.

The implicit challenge to the guidance specialist is to use information to help his clients increase their awareness of their options, to demonstrate and encourage them to explore their alternatives, and to assist in interpreting the information to which they have access.

Each of us continually acquires information about his environment, although it is not always correct and in many instances it is insufficient for the purposes at hand. Few individuals have all the experience and data they need to reach informed judgments about their alternatives. Adequate decision-making requires a capacity to recognize the additional information one needs and knowledge of where to obtain it and how to evaluate it.

Another dimension of the informational problem relates to the different ways in which information about the world of work is communicated. Most persons grow up and live in an environment in which work has significance. Every day a young person learns a little more about the complex structure of work that plays so large a part in the shaping of this world. Much of the "transfer of information" takes place without his seeking it and without the awareness of those who are transmitting it. But neither fact diminishes the reality of the transmission. By way of shorthand, we will call this unstructured learning "exposure."

Even in megalopolis, where many children reach adulthood without having visited their father's place of work and without a clear idea of how he spends his hours when he is away from home, the young person is directly exposed to many different workers. The following is a list of occupations which an urban twelve-year-old daughter of professional parents was able to record:

Doctor	Dermatologist
Dental hygienist	Principal
Teacher	Fireman
Dentist	Caretaker
Lawyer	Librarian
Writer	Vender
Artist	Stockbroker

Maid	Building Superintendent
Conductor (bus)	Fuller Brush Man
Handyman	Elevator Operator
Repairman	Policeman
Secretary	Interior Decorator
Stewardess	Scientist
Milkman	Life Guard
Counselor (camp)	Rabbi
Optometrist	Conductor (music)
Storeowner	Waiter
Musician	Runner
Actor	Orthodontist
Clerk	Matron
Butcher	Operator (telephone)
Fisherman	

People also increase their knowledge about the world of work through direct experience—that is, by working. In earlier times boys growing up on farms learned about work by helping their fathers in the fields just as girls learned about domestic arts by helping their mothers around the house. Even today youngsters get their first introduction to work by helping their parents. This is still the pattern on the farm. It is also the pattern in many small towns where children help out in the store, the gas station, or the bakery. And it is by no means unknown in the large city, where many of them do odd chores, from delivering parcels to copying accounts.

By the age of seventeen, many young men and women are likely to have had some experience with part-time or even full-time jobs. While most of these jobs involve little more than the simple routines of arranging inventories, waiting on customers, or cleaning a store, they provide youngsters with a firsthand view of a work place and, in the process, they also learn about the necessity of reporting regularly to work, of remaining at work for a stipulated number of hours, and of adjusting to the employer's hierarchy by accepting and following orders. Even if their specific job experiences are constricted, they learn about the environment of work.

Another method of information transmission is through formal communications, which were formerly restricted to the printed word but which increasingly encompass a variety of media including film-strips, movies, and television. As jobs and careers have proliferated and as the routes into them have become more diverse, employers, government, schools, and guidance specialists have realized that sole reliance on work exposure and experience would not provide most individuals with sufficient information for sound career decisions. As a result there have been steadily expanding efforts to increase the amount and variety of information about careers and jobs and about education and training opportunities to help the individual extend his horizon and to provide him with information relevant to his choices.

We will not discuss at this point whether, and to what extent, it is possible to commit to paper, to computer tapes, or to film significant information about the world of work in a manner that will enable people to see their options more clearly and how they can take advantage of them. But since there are scores of junior and senior colleges, hundreds of training opportunities, and thousands of beginning jobs in every large metropolitan area, it becomes evident that there must be a place in career decision-making for non-experiential knowledge about the world of work. If young people believe that their job opportunities are limited to what they have learned from direct exposure and experience their perceptions will be restricted indeed.

In the pages that follow we will be concerned seriatim with the types of information that people need to improve their career decision-making: with the experiential sources on which they draw; and with the nature, range, and quality of formal career information. We will then review the informational role of the guidance counselor and present some evaluative judgments.

The first kind of information that young people need is a clear description of the high school curricula available to them, the conditions governing admission to various programs, and the implications for future career development that attach to completing one or another of these programs. Although school systems differ, until recently many did not encourage parents to become involved in their children's course selection on the assumption that parental involvement would hamper the school operations. As a consequence many parents, particularly those from low-income homes, have only a vague idea of the range of offerings provided by the school system or the implications attached to various alternatives. At a minimum, the educational authorities should provide information to pupils and their parents about the structure and operations of their schools and their curricula, the requirements governing entrance into various programs and the occupational outcomes of graduates who pursued various routes. A strong guidance system might help reduce the barriers that stand in the way of improved communication among the school, parents, and the pupils.

Many changes are occurring in the occupational arena, and these in turn are altering the established opportunity structure. For instance, many fields are opening up to minority groups for the first time. Women are being hired and promoted in new areas. Significant changes are occurring in long-established wage patterns and career opportunities. Unless the schools draw attention to these important changes, young people and their parents are likely to remain ignorant of them or to minimize them. Parents are likely to project their own experiences in planning for their children, not realizing that important changes have in fact occurred and that more are on their way.

For example, it was conventional in the black community for the academically able to prepare for teaching, in which there were opportunities for an attractive if segregated career. Today, however, the door of opportunity for the college-educated Negro has swung wide open. But many blacks are skeptical that a new day of widened opportunities has actually dawned. They know that hopes raised in the past were later dashed by white reaction. They do not believe that they do, in fact, have improved educational and employment opportunities. Therefore it is necessary that knowledge of new trends in minority employment become known to parents and young people who are today deciding about their future, and the school must speed this process.

A third type of informational need relates to the financing of higher education. Comparatively few parents with low incomes encourage their children to set high educational goals largely because they see little or no prospect of being able to help them finance a college education. However, the range and types of financial assistance for qualified students have been vastly expanded in recent years and additional assistance looms on the horizon. But many parents learn about the availability of loans and scholarships too late, if they learn of them at all.

The past few years have been characterized by a proliferation of new programs directed to helping members of disadvantaged groups qualify for admission to college, and by the establishment and expansion of many new types of training opportunities for the non-college population. However, many young people have little or no knowledge of these newly established programs; they do not know how to get into them or the advantages they can derive from them. Their family and friends, and often their counselors as well, cannot give them the information that might stimulate them to action.

Reliable and relevant information about colleges is not easily available. To some extent this is a reflection of inadequate college guides and catalogues; many catalogues omit critical information about such things as the ambience of the institution; its intellectual orientation; relations between students and faculty; and campus political activity. Moreover, information about the numbers, proportions, and characteristics of the students who transfer or drop out is rarely available.

But even if all this information were disseminated and if it were thoughtfully perused by the prospective college student, it might still be of limited value. Most young people have never lived away from home; they have not had to manage their own time and money; nor have they been permitted to cut classes at will. The boy who reads about different colleges and makes a choice at seventeen is never the same young man who returns home at the end of a freshman year of independence and exploration.

Profiles and descriptions of colleges, like profiles and descriptions of jobs, cannot provide the quality and depth of information that people require or desire. Moreover, visits to campuses, like visits to work places (even when they include opportunities to talk with those enrolled or working) cannot fill in all the lacunae. The young person who must decide whether to go to college and what college to attend frequently does not have enough knowledge about himself or about college to know the questions to which he should seek answers. The early years at college, like the early years at work, are for many a period of trial and error. While this fact does not mean that improved materials are irrelevant, it does imply that the guidance counselor can perhaps be most helpful in regard to college by suggesting how students might incorporate uncertainty and trial into their planning and how to cope effectively with the pressures and challenges they are likely to encounter.

Even wider is the gap in information about the types of post-high school training opportunities that are available, the conditions governing entrance, and the potential rewards from completing one or another course. Many profit-making institutions advertise and employ drummers on a commission basis to attract students, and the information they make available exaggerates the quality of the programs and the jobs open to those who complete them. At the opposite extreme are many unions which, at least until recently, made information about their apprenticeship programs available only to their own members and their friends. It was only after repeated failures that the Workers Defense League in New York City in the mid-1960s was able to obtain a list of apprenticeship programs in the construction trades. It was only a decade or so ago that Harold Clark of Teachers College had to resort to the yellow pages of the telephone book to compile a listing of the trade and business schools in the principal cities of the United States. While the last years have seen a growing interest in this arena on the part of both governmental and non-governmental organizations and while some progress has been made to collect, codify, and disseminate information about training opportunities, the fact remains that it is a major challenge to a high school senior or, for that matter, an adult to obtain an overview of the range of training programs in his immediate environs and such pertinent details as tuition costs, entrance requirements, length of the course, placement opportunities.

We have noted the difficulties that many young men encounter in obtaining reliable information about the draft, particularly their options about how to avoid military service or to delay induction. This is a subject that most high schools have avoided for fear that it would involve them in political controversy. Moreover, unless a high school student seeks out a recruiting sergeant he is not likely to have too much of an idea of his alternatives with respect to military service until he reaches his senior year, when there is usually an assembly directed to this subject. The Department of

Defense does publish a considerable amount of reliable information, but it is available only to those who seek it.

So far our emphasis has been on the needs of young people who are in the educational-training cycle and who intend to remain in it for some further period prior to entering full-time employment. What about the informational needs of the significant proportion who before or immediately after earning their high school diplomas become job seekers? What do they need to know?

Relevant information is seldom available to young job seekers because of the slow growth of labor market research, the preoccupation of high school guidance staffs with the college-bound, and the traditionalism of the government agencies that produce most of the occupational information.

First, these youths need information about the ways in which to look for a job. Particularly they require access to information about where employers are currently hiring new workers. Since most employers have screening standards, it would be both time-saving and psychologically protective if they could learn of the places where they are likely to meet the employment requirements. Moreover, it is important for them to know whether past employment practices which might have ruled them out, such as discriminatory hiring, have been altered so that they do not cut themselves off from opportunities that are now available.

There are marked differences in the conditions under which work is carried on: inside or outdoors, individually or as a member of a group, under tight or loose supervision, with more or less necessity to work overtime. However, information about these matters is not always available to the worker-to-be.

There are even more critical matters that are likely to be unknown to a prospective worker. It is reasonably easy for the job seeker to ascertain the going wage, but he is less likely to know about company policy with respect to in-service training and promotional opportunities. Even more elusive is information about how to progress up the occupational and income ladder by moving from one job to another in a planned effort to acquire skills and capitalize on them. Despite the widespread belief that most skilled workers in the United States have acquired journeyman status through apprenticeships or through a formal training program, the fact is that most have added one piece of experience and competence to another through a succession of jobs.

Employed workers require information, also. For instance, a man of thirty who is dissatisfied with his routine job often does not know whether there are better jobs available; if so, how to go about getting one; or whether his chances would be improved if he took some special training. Although a great amount of job changing, both voluntary and involuntary, takes place, there is little reliable information available to those involved in the process.

Similarly, although millions of mature women return to the labor force—six out of ten women employed in 1968 were over thirty-five years of age—many find it difficult to learn about the jobs that are available, whether they need additional education or training to qualify for better-paying positions, and where such training opportunities are available.[1]

And as we have pointed out, the transition out of the labor market into retirement is still largely *terra incognita* except for a limited amount of factual information that the government and other large employers make available about Social Security and pension rights.

Having outlined some of the types of information different groups need prior to and after their entrance into the labor market to improve their decision-making, let us briefly consider the sources on which people rely to help them find their way through this complex arena.

As we have noted, a considerable amount of information is absorbed by young people as they hear their parents, elder siblings, other relatives, and friends discuss their jobs and the jobs that others have. Such subjects as work, income, opportunity are staples in the conversation of most adults. Unlike sex and crime, they are usually discussed freely in the presence of young people.

In addition, youths receive cues about work from their immediate community. Youngsters growing up in poverty or low-income neighborhoods may have no models that relate hard work to a preferred style of life. In fact the only person with money whom they recognize or know is often a racketeer or a numbers man. In upper-income areas, many youngsters see their fathers working hard but getting little pleasure from their high earnings. Both groups need help to understand the linkages that exist in our society between orientation to work and styles of life, and the opportunities that different persons have to enter and succeed in occupations that will be meaningful to them.

Other important sources of information and misinformation are popular magazines and books and, especially, movies and television. While an occasional magazine such as *Ebony* has made a specialty of printing interesting crisp accounts of blacks who have achieved success in various occupations, and while an occasional TV program such as *Opportunity Line,* presented in cooperation with the State Employment Services, offers a realistic picture of current job openings and of people who have been recently hired, much of what is transmitted through the popular media is distorted.

Most movies or TV presentations that portray occupations concentrate on such esoteric ones as cowboy, neurosurgeon, or detective. When they focus on mundane workers such as bus drivers, assembly line operators, repairmen, they usually provide caricatures rather than the truth. Rare indeed is such a documentary as "Hospital," a presentation of the workings of a municipal institution incidentally depicting a range of health occupations, which when shown in New York City early in 1970 was deliberately scheduled for an hour when few schoolchildren would be likely to see it!

Every day all sorts of messages are received by people about jobs, wages, opportunities, but much of the information that comes through is distorted. As Seymour Wolfbein noted at a Conservation conference, everybody who uses his eyes and ears is constantly exposed to occupational information. The critical question is its relevance and reliability.

Another source of occupational information is that which young people absorb from their experiences in school, both indirectly from the curriculum and from specially designed efforts to provide them with career orientation and information. From kindergarten on, many schools present information about work and occupations in connection with instruction in English, history, social studies, but most curricula have not been structured to provide systematic knowledge about the world of work, occupations, and incomes. It has been estimated that "less than 5 percent of the instructional time of the first six years of schooling could be described as related to the study of work in some direct or indirect association."[2]

The lack of tangency between the regular curriculum and orientation to work has led some schools to experiment with approaches aimed at overcoming this shortcoming. One approach introduces quite young children to materials that relate to the world of work. Some educators believe that kindergarten offers a first opportunity to discuss occupational roles. Other educators make a strong plea in favor of having an occupational unit built into the curriculum sometime between the third and sixth year. A fourth-grade project entitled "Investigating Jobs in Our Community" includes such topics as the number of workers employed in each occupation, whether particular jobs are expanding or declining, requirements for entrance, earnings, union membership, opportunities for advancement, seasonality. The teacher reported that the project helped the children learn "something about the value of work and the right attitudes toward work."[3] The basis for her conclusion remained unexplained.

Another effort to provide occupational information and orientation to students is the result of the mandated requirement in a considerable number of states that every junior or senior high school provide a formal course in occupations as part of its regular curriculum. In many other states, local educational authorities provide such instruction either as a unit within social studies or English or as a separate course. A detailed review in the early 1960s of the situation in New York State, where the course is not required, revealed considerable dissatisfaction by school superintendents, directors of guidance, and teachers, because the materials were usually presented as a unit within a course rather than as a separate course; most of the teaching staff were inadequately prepared; there was no agreement as to objectives or controls; the course or unit was usually offered at the ninth-grade level, which proved too early perhaps to elicit an enthusiastic response from the students, who reported that the classes were dull and that they did not profit from the exposure.[4]

Large-scale dissatisfaction with ways of bringing the world of work into the curriculum does not mean that the task is unimportant or impossible. It does suggest, however, especially in light of the charge of so many students that the curriculum is not relevant, that more experimentation is called for before the effort is reinforced or abandoned. The difficulties of providing a satisfactory solution derive in large measure from the opposition among most leaders of

American education to a vocational emphasis within the basic curriculum.

Since there is no easy way to construct the curriculum to include an orientation to work in general and to jobs in particular, many high schools have decided that the most feasible alternative is to move beyond the classroom. This helps to explain the popularity of the Career Days, career fairs, assemblies when representatives of various employers and occupational groups are brought into the school so that upperclassmen can listen to the outsiders describe their fields and ask questions. There are many variations, often aimed at scheduling the presentations over a semester or the school year to avoid the confusion that is likely to follow successive hours of lectures. These efforts are likely to be constructive to those young people who participate, especially if the speakers cover a wide spectrum of occupations, if they are interesting, and if they are well-informed and convincing. Often, however, they are deficient on one or more grounds.

Another approach followed by many school systems is to arrange plant visits, usually in the elementary grades but also in junior and senior high schools. Often, however, the time allotted for these visits is too short and the preparatory and follow-up discussion so brief that young people learn little other than what they can glean about work and the working environment from a hurried walk through the plant. Recently, certain school systems, such as Detroit's, have sought to use periodic plant visits to assist in easing the transition of pupils from school to work. In Detroit, various large employers have "adopted" certain ghetto schools; they help young people from these schools to explore work and working conditions in their plants with an aim of facilitating their eventual employment.

How valuable are these efforts at bringing representatives from the world of work into the school or taking students from the school into the world of work? If the effort is limited to one or two trips a semester to the local airport, a factory, or occasionally to a company headquarters, the excursion is likely to be just that and little else. One or two youngsters may see a new aspect of work, such as when they see blacks or women in executive positions. But brief random exposures rarely have much impact on a young person's career planning.

Some have been impressed with the Swedish program, in which students leave the classroom for three weeks in the ninth grade (sixteen-year-olds) and are placed in different employment settings so that they can learn at first hand about the world of work. It is assumed that this period of exposure to a work environment contributes to curriculum choice and to directing and raising occupational objectives, as well as to supplementing knowledge about the nature of and preparation for work.

In addition to career programs and occasional plant visits by American students, representatives of the local employment office and of the Armed Forces visit a large number of high schools. Aptitude tests are often given to prospective job entrants and some are counseled about work possibilities. This is an additional informational effort, but it usually comes too late in the student's high school experience to permit prolonged consideration of alternative choices and is more in the nature of a placement than a guidance service for those who will need jobs soon.

As we have pointed out, the linkages between schools and the Employment Service are tenuous. Frequently, the student's only contact with the Employment Service is when he takes the G.A.T.B., the basic evaluation instrument used to measure aptitudes by the Employment Service. For follow-up, counseling, and placement a student usually must take the initiative to go to the local office of the Employment Service. If the Employment Service has useful information about job openings and job prospects, which most school guidance staffs lack, the information is usually not readily available to the students who need it, surely not in school. They must seek it out.

Some high schools are visited by college recruiters who are looking for certain types of students, often athletes. Recently these recruiting efforts have been broadened. For instance, the National Scholarship Services and Fund for Negro students has been seeking able black students for more than a decade to encourage them to apply to colleges with promises of financial and other assistance. Many young people have changed their plans as a result of such encounters.

In the light of the growing estrangement between the generations and the critical attitudes of many young people toward whatever they are told by adults, some principals and guidance counselors invite recent alumni who have made good adjustments in college, in the Armed Forces, or at work to speak to students. The objective of such interaction is both motivational and informational. Young people are more likely to trust their peers than their elders.

Because of the difficulties of revising the curriculum to include the occupational orientation they believe many students need and want, a growing number of educators and guidance counselors have become attracted to the idea of work experience as a developmental opportunity for young people.

There is considerable support for work experience for high school students that relates what is taught in school during the half-day or the alternate week that they spend in the classroom to the solution of problems that they encounter at work during the other half of their schedule. Experiences in and out of school are considered an integrated learning experience.

High school work-study programs have existed for some time in various cities, but most of them have been restricted to juniors and seniors, often to those enrolled in selected commercial and vocational programs. Currently experimental programs have been designed for a younger group (fourteen- and fifteen-year-olds). All work-study programs are seeking answers to the challenge of how secondary education can be made more responsive to the needs of the many young people who find book learning and classroom procedures so unstimulating that they remain passive or even hostile toward school. The new approaches are exploring how education can be made more relevant and useful to the non-bookish person, many of whom must currently remain in high school until their seventeenth or eighteenth year although they learn little.

Renewed emphasis is also being placed on cooperative programs at the college level. Here work experience is seen as a boon to students from low-income homes who must meet rising educational costs; as a counterpoise to many students who are disturbed by lack of relevance in the conventional curriculum; and as a potent way to help individuals expand their occupational horizons.

Are exploratory work experiences an effective device for conveying realistic information about the world of work? Most students work part-time or during the summer. As pointed out earlier, jobs help to give young people some "feel" for the discipline and rewards of the work place. But many of these jobs, such as delivering newspapers or running a mimeograph machine, are routine and seldom require more than simple physical energy. There are many reasons to expand the opportunities available to young people for employment, especially during their long summer vacations, such as their need to occupy their time, to earn money, and to associate with adults. In general, American employers do not seek to hire young persons, especially for brief periods. If it were possible to elicit more employer cooperation (recently there have been some favorable signs such as expanded summer programs for young people still enrolled in school) and if school counselors played a more active role in student placements related to interests and goals, young people might be encouraged to use even limited work experiences to test their perceptions of themselves in the world of work and, where appropriate, to formulate new choices.

In these kinds of ways, some educators and school counselors have been seeking to add breadth and depth to the informational base available to young people to help them clarify their career decisions. But the major effort to broaden their perspective has not been through curriculum offerings, occupational exposures, or work-study programs, but has centered on making available to them specially prepared occupational information, primarily in printed form. This has been and continues to be the major approach used to help people learn more about the world of work. It seeks to familiarize them with a range of occupations, requirements for admission and advancement, conditions under which work is carried on, in order to provide them with a better idea about vocational options and how to realize them.

In the early days of vocational guidance, several leaders in the movement, such as Harry Kitson of Teachers College, wrote books which sought to organize information about occupations and jobs in a manner that would be helpful to counselors and counselees. By the 1930s it was clear that the varied and dynamic nature of the American occupational structure could not be effectively organized and analyzed by academics working alone. Only government could collect and sift the large amount of information. Consequently, the U.S. Department of Labor began the systematic study of occupations and in the ensuing years published two basic compendia which have since been revised several times: *The Dictionary of Occupational Titles* and *The Occupational Outlook Handbook.*

The most recent edition of the *DOT* is an ambitious undertaking; it defines over 30,000 distinct job titles and organizes them according to various types of classification, such as by industry, by technology, by worker traits and functions, as well as by job requirements.[5] *The Dictionary of Occupational Titles,* as its name indicates, is a dictionary. The reader cannot learn from the *DOT* about such things as wage levels, union requirements, and opportunities for advancement. And there is little information about the nature of settings within which these jobs are available. With such basic aspects of work ignored, the *DOT* has limited value for guidance. It may help a counselor put a man on a useful track, but the client must search elsewhere to learn what he needs to know before choosing among alternative jobs. In fairness, we must state that the *DOT* was not constructed as a guidance tool but was developed largely to help placement and training specialists.

The *Occupational Outlook Handbook,* first published in 1949 by the Department of Labor and now in its eighth edition, is specifically guidance-oriented.[6] The *Handbook* provides broad information about 700 occupations and 30 major industries which is supplemented by the *Occupational Outlook Quarterly.* It includes information about the full gamut of jobs: blue-collar, white-collar, and service. As the term *outlook* suggests, the emphasis is on present conditions and future trends in the demand for labor. Information is presented about access to different occupations and about where additional knowledge of a field can be obtained. It contains numerous illustrations of workers on jobs. It is a major resource for counselors who need career information. Since the *Outlook* is written in the stilted style of governmental prose, commercial publishers have undertaken profitable ventures by adapting its materials and rewriting and illustrating them. Among firms specializing in such efforts are Careers, Chronicle Guidance, and Science Research Associates.

In 1967, Ferguson published its *Encyclopedia of Careers and Vocational Guidance* in two volumes, priced at $30.[7] Most of its articles are more readable rewrites of materials that appeared in the

1966–1967 edition of the *Handbook,* which sold for $4.95. While there is great variation in what schools spend on occupational information, a 1967 survey showed that the average high school budget was $178.[8] An expenditure of $30 for one item thus represents one-sixth of the annual budget for occupational materials. And when the new edition of the *Handbook* appeared in 1968, the *Encyclopedia* became out of date in many critical regards—a year after publication.

Recently there have been local efforts to provide occupational guides for terminal high school students. For example, *The World of Work on Long Island* describes 156 entry-level jobs in major fields of employment in Nassau county. This book was based on the experience of counselors who spent six weeks working for twelve different local employers in a project financed by the County Youth Board. It contains not only specific information on individual employers but also includes descriptions of the personal experiences of counselors as employees of these companies.[9] Since few of the non-college-bound in metropolitan labor markets relocate, a guide that stresses local information has particular pertinence. If it involves counselor cooperation in its preparation it is likely to be even more effective because of counselors' broadened perceptions about the world of work.

Occupational materials are also published and distributed by a variety of other organizations such as magazine publishers, some state governments, nonprofit organizations such as the B'nai B'rith, trade and professional associations, business firms as a form of institutional advertising, and by school systems. Many professional organizations, trade associations, labor unions, and large corporations publish occupational materials as recruitment devices. While they often provide some information about an area of employment, it is sometimes difficult for the potential job seeker to get realistic data from these sources since many of them tend to stress the favorable aspects and ignore the disadvantages of the job.

We have said relatively little about the role of the guidance counselor in making information available to students and in helping them interpret it. While most individuals acquire the bulk of their occupational information from informal experiences and exposures, the counselor can play an important role in the communication of information. Many young people are referred by their counselors to occupational source material in the form of handbooks, books, and pamphlets, some of which are purchased by the school and others received free. These are part of the resources of almost every counselor. When a high school junior or senior with no strong vocational preference appears, the counselor may suggest that the counselee skim through certain materials and that they talk again. If the student has a tentative field in mind but would like to learn more about it, the counselor may have materials to lend him or he may offer to obtain them or suggest to the student several sources that he might pursue on his own.

However, the availability of a large body of occupational materials, even if well indexed and attractively displayed, does not necessarily indicate that the informational function is being performed satisfactorily. A student needs an opportunity to discuss the materials with his counselor in order to sort out what he has learned for use in his career decision-making.

Over the years the American Personnel and Guidance Association has sought to upgrade the quality of available occupational information by evaluating new publications and audio-visual materials submitted for assessment. But, as with many grading systems, most items receive a passing mark. Moreover, the evaluators are constrained to select the best from what is available.

The *Occupational Outlook Handbook* and other government and private publications have high sales: approximately 80,000 copies of each edition of the *Handbook* are sold, which makes it a best-seller among government publications. Little is known, however, about the use to which these materials are put after they have been purchased. Various surveys reveal that counselors think well of the *Handbook* and related materials that the federal government publishes, but they fail to reveal much about how they are used in guidance.[10]

In Perrone's survey of counselor appraisal of occupational information, he found that the *Handbook* was the most frequently mentioned information source and was regarded as the most authoritative source of outlook data. Most of the counselors surveyed stated that the available occupational materials are congruent with student need despite agreement that only one-fourth of these resources are directed toward terminal high school graduates and that the poorest quality of information is aimed at those entering work or work preparatory programs immediately after high school. Yet, as Perrone notes, this group constitutes more than half of the country's high school graduates.[11]

We are constrained to question the judgment of these counselors. To recognize that students who are not planning to enter college are poorly served by available informational resources and to discount this shortcoming appears to reflect a grave misconception of the informational needs of many clients.

Campbell recently elicited student reactions to occupational information and found that over half felt that the materials are "quite helpful." The major complaints were that the materials are "too general," "they do not answer my questions," and "they do not give the real picture." Others commented that they are boring, out of date, difficult to read.[12]

At a conference on Occupational Information in Vocational Guidance, Gysbers summarized his review of occupational information as follows: there is a concern with the increasing quantities of information and with quality, coverage, reading level; the materials are unidimensional and fail to deal with psycho-social aspects of work; finally, they are too general. He adds a quotation from Viteles to emphasize the meaning of "too general"; a 1923 description of the characteristics of a librarian was:

A love of reading is not a major qualification since a librarian has little time for reading. She needs accuracy, quickness, neatness, a pleasing appearance, and application necessary to do much routine work. All of these qualities must be founded upon a sincere and active enthusiasm for library work.

He noted that if one substitutes *celery scraper* for *librarian* the description fits equally well![13]

A drawback we have noted is that many young persons who are most at sea about what they might do if they drop out of high school or remain only for diplomas are poor readers. Unless an occupational brochure is put together in an attractive fashion with many illustrations and unless the writing is simple, they will not read it. Much of the occupational material fails to meet these standards and as a consequence many who most need information cannot use what is available.

Although films are expensive to produce and relatively difficult to distribute and use, their potential contribution to guidance has probably been underestimated, especially in terms of the opportunities they present for group participation with question-and-answer periods following the showing, and as an alternative for the poor reader.

We deal briefly with the computer as an informational device elsewhere, but it should be noted here that one of the claims that might be made for placing reliance on it in the future is that it may engage the attention of more poor readers. They might be more willing to turn dials than to turn pages. But if the computer is to hold their interest it will need to be programmed with highly relevant information, largely of a local and immediate nature— and that is likely to prove impractical.

The relevance and usefulness of much of the occupational materials that are prepared and distributed raise additional questions. There is little point in making printed materials available to young people in the hope of increasing their understanding about the occupational structure unless they seek it. Unless they have questions to which they are seeking answers, they usually will not take the time and effort required to read informational publications; even if they do, their reading is not likely to have significant impact on their thinking and acting. These preconditions also influence the usefulness of alternative audio-visual and computer devices. Unless the student wants information and will take the time and effort to seek it, no medium will prove successful in arousing more than fleeting interest.

Some criticism has been levied against guidance counselors on the score that they are poorly informed about economic and occupational trends and that they are little interested in this dimension of career development; they prefer to deal with aspects of career choice that are more directly related to personality. A 1966 survey of school counselors in New York State revealed that they considered themselves less prepared in occupational information than in any other aspect of their work.[14] Hoppock has stated that "the weak counselor pools his own ignorance of occupations with the ignorance of the client and from this shallow pool tries to help the client select an appropriate occupation."[15] We are not inclined to contest either of these criticisms, that many counselors know relatively little about the world of work and that they are not interested in this phase of guidance. In fact, we can add a third. In the preceding chapter we pointed out that personal information has little significance for the counselee except as the counselor helps his client to use it in developing his career strategy and tactics. Similarly, the key to occupational information in a counseling setting is whether the counselor helps the counselee use informational inputs in clarifying his goals. The more the counselor knows about the world of work, the better he will be able to assume this role, but even if he knows a great deal it will be of relatively little value to his client unless the client is helped to incorporate it into his own decision-making. Yet Perrone's report indicated that there is little attempt on the part of most school counselors to do this. He states: "It seems possible to conclude that counselors dutifully make reading materials available to students and hope the materials contain valid data and students can glean relevant information for their personal use."[16]

So far we have considered almost exclusively the informational needs of young people in high school. We should note that even for this group there is an imbalance: the concentration has been on occupational information with relatively little attention paid to labor-market information which bears more directly on helping young people get a job. Many people, especially from low-income groups, need local labor market information more than occupational descriptions.

We must note briefly the absence of readily available information about the transition from higher education into different types of jobs and specific work settings and the opportunities that different employers and fields offer for further skill acquisition and advancement. For instance, the student who majors in English or sociology needs to know in what fields he might find a job; whether it is sensible to consider graduate work in his specialty or at a professional school; and the organizations that have good training programs for new employees.

Others also need improved information. Many adults are beset by special problems. Consider the needs of mature women who are entering or re-entering the labor force; of recently discharged prisoners or mental patients; of the physically handicapped; of the middle-aged worker who has unexpectedly been laid off. All of these people need specific information, such as the availability and usefulness of transitional arrangements such as special training and educational opportunities; the location of employment and counseling offices where they can receive help in assessing themselves and in learning about placement opportunities; and specific leads to employers who may be willing to employ them.

We will leave until Part Four our suggestions about the ways in which improvements in occupational information, including the use of new mechanisms such as computers, might contribute to strengthening the career-decision process. At this point we will simply summarize the major findings and open questions which have emerged from this survey of the present state of the available information:

—Occupational information is an essential ingredient for improved career decisions.

—Every individual obtains considerable occupational information from his family, the community in which he lives, and from the popular media to which he is exposed. However, much of this is misinformation.

—The schools, particularly secondary schools, have been experimenting with different types of structured exposures to increase knowledge about occupations. Through their own efforts and through experimental programs under the auspices of their schools, many teenagers obtain jobs and thereby add to their knowledge of the world of work. This exposure is seldom used by counselors in helping their clients improve their career decision-making. While some of the leads are promising, there are objective obstacles to the expansion of work-school cooperative programs which hold the key potential.

—A considerable body of occupational information is published and distributed for the use of counselor and counselees. However, much of it is too general or too abstruse to be directly helpful, particularly to the high school dropouts and terminal graduates who often have the greatest need for it.

—Most of the written materials deal with specific occupations.

Few are focused on such matters as how to get a job and how to advance thereafter.

—By training and inclination many guidance counselors place a low value on occupational information. Few have the time or desire to deal with it in a manner that would help their counselees incorporate it effectively into their career planning.

There are, however, correctives built into the maturing process and work experience which assure that many people will acquire critical types of occupational information when they can still build on them to improve their career planning.

During the first years of full-time work young people, the non-college group in particular, frequently move from one job to another and thus learn more about work, wages, opportunities for advancement. This is a corrective to the limited information with which they enter the labor market. Many college students avoid making definitive commitments about their future work and careers until late in college, and many delay until beyond college. This often prevents the college student from optimizing his educational opportunities, but this is a cost he may be able to pay.

Young men ending a tour of military service are in their mid-twenties before they make a work choice. At this age a person has usually learned substantially about the world about him. He will be better able to sort out and assess the wealth of information about career possibilities.

These correctives must not obscure the fact, however, that many young people could profit if they had access to improved information at an earlier time in their development. We have also noted that different groups of adults could profit from improved information and from the better use of that which is available. The responsibilities for meeting these needs rest in the first instance with government, who must garner and distribute information and, second, with guidance, who must interpret it.

The following are some of the major challenges that confront guidance personnel in the area of career information:

—They must learn more about the structure and operation of the labor market and about how to keep abreast of its major changes.

—They should adopt a more critical approach to the informational sources available and feed back to the producers, particularly the federal government, the limitations and shortcomings of the available information. They should also take the lead in pointing out to state and local governments the adaptations of national data which would be helpful in their work.

—They should attempt to elicit assistance from community leaders in broadening opportunities for secondary school pupils to become better informed about the world of work through work experience that is integrated into a program of structured learning.

—They should pay more attention to the uses their clients make of various informational sources and make recommendations to the producers based on what they learn.

—They need to explore how occupational information can be integrated more effectively into the guidance process, especially via group discussions.

—They should study critically the advantages and disadvantages that attach to using mechanisms other than the printed word in conveying information to clients that would help improve career decision-making.

—They might participate profitably in the collection and evaluation of local employment-market information in order to deepen their knowledge and understanding of the training and work options that their counselees face.

We noted at the beginning of the last chapter that personal assessment and career information should be treated as a feedback system in which the individual has the open-ended task of learning more about himself at the same time that he is learning about the reality of work. The critical challenge is to put the two bodies of information together to clarify goals and the means to accomplish them.

Whether an individual succeeds in this task depends in large measure on the effectiveness of the information utilization process. Among the key determinants of effectiveness are:

—Presentation in a way that makes sense to the client. Thus, reading the *Occupational Outlook Handbook* is more useful to the able than to the poor reader. Similarly, the presentation of test data in statistical terms has limited value to a student who is inept in dealing with numbers. Improved guidance requires continuing experimentation in the informational realm to test client use and comprehension. If group procedures for guidance are to be more generally employed, similar requirements should be set and met. Groups must be so constituted that the members can utilize the information presented and the presenter must consider the approaches most likely to engage and hold attention.

—Assuring that new inputs lead to new decisions. It is not enough for the counselor to check that the information presented is understood by the client; it is essential to follow through and see what the client does with it. For example, if the client is told that despite erratic performance his teachers consider him to be of college caliber, the critical question is what the student does with this new informational input.

—Setting the stage for the next level of information and exchange. Once a student decides on his next course of action, he will have a new set of questions about himself and about the world of education and work. A major challenge to guidance personnel is to help clients formulate questions that can assist them in moving ahead in their decision-making. At this point in the process, the guidance counselor must see that the client is exploring anew both himself and the external realities. A neglect of either may lead to a faulty decision.

An adequate informational process consists of structured inputs, a check by the counselor that the information is understood, discussion of the alternatives that the client is considering, assistance in formulating new questions, and the introduction of additional information to assure improved educational and vocational decision-making.

We believe it is essential to end the present dichotomy whereby most guidance counselors are concerned with refining the instruments used in personal assessment and the informational specialists are concerned with improving the quantity and quality of occupational inputs. It is necessary to improve both. But the critical challenge is to improve the informational *process* by facilitating both the exploration of self and of external reality in order to assure more effective career decision-making.

PART III

GUIDEPOSTS

13

TRIAL BALANCE

WE HAVE NOW reviewed the broad settings within which guidance operates, its various goals, and the means utilized to realize them. Our judgments about the extent to which present guidance services contribute to the educational and vocational needs of individuals and groups are implicit in the foregoing chapters and will be made explicit in Part Four.

As we noted at the outset, we did not undertake a systematic evaluation of guidance services. We did, however, consider a large number of evaluative studies, and in this chapter we will review and assess them. Specifically, we will discuss the knotty methodological issues involved in evaluation and the findings that can be extracted from a sample of evaluative efforts, and we will assess whether such studies hold promise of yielding useful information for policy determinations about the future scale and direction of career guidance.

To evaluate any service is difficult. Take the service closest to guidance—education. Despite the large sums the American people spend on education, we know little about the long-run impact of educational services. Many of the key facts essential for critical judgments are not available and it is difficult to evaluate the facts that are available, among other reasons because there is no broad agreement among leaders of education, any more than among guidance leaders, about the goals to be accomplished. Some educators stress character-building, some the attainment of knowledge, some the acquisition of marketable skills. Even when there is a consensus about goals, there are often disagreements about how to judge whether they have been achieved. In addition, it is necessary to take into account the character of the student body, the training and competence of the teachers, the ambience of the school, and the influence of home and community as they affect the success of the educational effort.

Because of problems of goal definition, selection of criteria and the variability of inputs, the task of evaluating personal services such as education, health, or guidance must be approached with modest expectations. However, if improved judgments are desired, it is reasonable to attempt to identify the critical issues in evaluation.

Evaluation of guidance services, especially guidance in school settings, has engaged the interest of a considerable number of researchers for a long time. Most of them have directed their attention to one of two aspects of the guidance process. Some researchers have been concerned with studying the quantity and quality of guidance services available to different segments of the population. They have centered their attention on the inputs into the system and the ways in which they have been used. Others have been concerned with measuring results from access to guidance services; they have concentrated on the outcomes of the process.

As we have noted, prior to any attempt at evaluating a service, the investigator must define the goal of the service, and there is considerable disagreement within and outside the field about what guidance should attempt to accomplish and how program performance should be measured. If there is disagreement about goals, there can be no agreement about the results of an evaluative effort. For instance, for one investigator guidance services in a high school can best be measured by the pupil-retention rate, while for another it is judged by the proportion who enter college. Yet the same school, in comparison with other schools, may have a high proportion of both dropouts and college entrants. How then would one evaluate its guidance services?

In assessing guidance services, the predilections of appraisers are critical: one evaluator may use time spent in individual counseling as a measure of quality; another may concentrate on informational resources, the testing program, or counselor preparation. In assessing outcomes, one must be cautious about attempting to measure such vague goals as "improved decision-making," "work satisfaction," and "personal happiness" which the guidance leadership has selected as worthy ends of their effort. Merely to list these goals is to illustrate the difficulty of using them in any evaluative endeavor. Since it is not sensible to inquire into the effectiveness of a service unless one can specify ahead of time what it is expected to accomplish in terms that can be measured, the selection of goals is critical.

Selection of goals is one major hurdle to evaluation; the second is the difficulty of selecting criteria to measure the objectives. Let us say that work satisfaction is a desirable goal of career guidance. To measure this outcome we must have criteria which will assess this subtle concept. Yet to date nobody has been able to arrive at a generally acceptable yardstick with which to measure something so subjective as "satisfaction."

If career guidance is seen in terms of providing assistance to individuals to accomplish specific objective ends, such as admission to college or promotion to a better job, the outcome is the criterion. But in recent decades more and more stress has been placed upon vague and long-range goals such as the optimal use of one's education and training, personal adjustment, improved decision-making, and good citizenship. If the goals of guidance are subjectively grounded, there is little prospect of assessing the guidance process. Then the problem of criteria becomes literally insoluble. The authors of an outstanding evaluation of guidance, Tammimen and Miller (*Guidance Programs and Their Impact on Students*), make the important point that if objectives are defined in behavioral terms and measures of that behavior are viewed as criteria, the problem would be half solved. But, they add, "the difficult task of developing sensitive, valid measures of the specified behavior would remain."[1]

A great deal of the evaluation of guidance services has concentrated on the assessment of the effectiveness of only one facet of the larger process. Most evaluation studies have sought to appraise the effectiveness of "counseling." Even those who grant that counseling plays a dominant role in most guidance programs do not argue that it is the only function that should be performed. Yet, few attempts have been made to evaluate other guidance services, and even fewer have assessed a guidance program as a whole.

So far we have noted three problems in evaluating guidance services: the difficulty of defining goals; the difficulty of specifying criteria; and the inclination of most investigators to focus on one facet rather than on the process as a whole. There are additional difficulties that we must consider.

There is the matter of differences in clientele who seek and use guidance services. We know that people in upper income groups tend to have access to more and better services. The children of those who are high on the income scale also have many other advantages—they attend better schools, they are more likely to remain in school, they get better jobs. While some careful studies of the impact of guidance have sought to control for socio-economic factors, others have not, and others have done so inadequately—as when, in measuring outcomes, they fail to take account not only of family income but also of differential availability of such services as free higher education. It is for these, among other, reasons that Rothney, who has been deeply concerned with the evaluation of guidance for several decades, has concluded that it simply is not practical to design a study project in which both the experimental and the control groups are properly matched.[2]

For example, it is accepted that the Harvard Business School is the outstanding institution of its kind in the country, perhaps in the world. The usual evidence presented is the higher occupational achievement of its graduates compared to the graduates of other business schools. If entering students at Harvard have grades and scores not substantially different from its major competitors, one might conclude that Harvard is superior. But it would be necessary to determine in advance whether Harvard attracts many of the sons of the nation's business elite who are certain to have the edge in the struggle up the occupational ladder. Or if this hypothesis were proved incorrect, one would still have to explore alternative explanations such as whether the alumni of the school are strongly entrenched in corporations which offer young graduates preferential opportunities for achievement.

Since there are substantial differences in background, circumstances, and expectations among clients of guidance counselors, it is not feasible to structure inquiries into the effectiveness of guidance without taking account of the multitude of factors that determine both the opportunities and barriers that clients face. There is little meaning to the question of whether guidance *per se* is effective or not.

Another critical dimension is the variability in the resources involved in providing guidance services. We know that there are substantial differences in the ratio of counselors to students in the secondary schools in the different regions of the country. But in addition, there are qualitative differences among those who counsel. A meaningful evaluation of guidance must assess differentials in inputs in relation to differentials in outcomes. The conventional method of assessing counselor competence in terms of certification is inadequate. As James Lister has demonstrated, much finer reading are required.[3] In addition, studies that purport to measure inputs must establish program standards. Yet such standards are arbitrary until proof has been adduced of the effectiveness of specific interventions.

An additional parameter which must be considered in an attempt at meaningful assessment is the larger socio-economic environment within which are embedded both opportunities and barriers for those who look forward to further education or to work. A guidance program in a high school in a rural non-farm community in Georgia or Alabama should not have the same goals as one in a school serving a low-income group in Pittsburgh or San Francisco. The presence or absence of tuition-free post-secondary educational and training opportunities, the scale of the labor market, the availability of specialized service programs and a great many other "facts of life" must be considered by an effective counselor. Consequently studies which deal in gross outcomes, such as the proportion of high school graduates who go to college, must be responsive to the variability that characterizes our social and economic environment; evaluations which disregard this variability will be erroneous.

A further consideration relates to the expectation that guidance efforts by themselves can result in changed outcomes. Weighty and cumulative influences shape a person's life—his family, school, and the labor market—and guidance alone is likely to be impotent in the face of powerful counter forces. A young person who enters the labor force for the first time at the end of high school or at the end of college has been through a formal preparatory process of twelve or sixteen years following about six years at home. Throughout this entire period he has been exposed to models, information, and experiences which shape his view of both the world of school and work. A recent calculation for one of the nation's largest school systems indicates that a student receives an average of about one hour per year of individualized counseling in junior high school and two hours per year in senior high school, making a total of nine hours over the six-year span.[4] If we disregard all the inputs prior to entrance into junior high school and stipulate that he is exposed to about 1,200 hours of school a year, we find nine hours of guidance to 7,200 hours of total school exposures during this period, or a ratio of roughly 1:800.

It is difficult to find a rationale that would justify giving a unique weight to guidance unless it is directly focused on critical decisions. When guidance is associated with a specific educational or occupational outcome, such as admission to college, placement in a job, acceptance into an apprenticeship program, then indeed it may take on special significance. But without a direct and concrete outcome how can much lasting significance be attached to even the most open and supportive interchange between counselor and counselee? In light of the personal and experiential factors involved in shaping an individual's life, the short exposure to guidance is unlikely to prove determining. If an aspect of one's life changes because of guidance, it is likely to be in the arena of expectations, of a sharpened strategy, of possible improvement in tactics to achieve a particular goal. But the external reality will not be altered. Political, economic, and social determinants will be as operative tomorrow as yesterday. We need not denigrate the possible contribution guidance can make to a young person's career decision-making to point to its fragility in the face of potent environmental and personal constraints.

There is one more consideration that bears on the evaluation process. This can be described as the changes that time introduces into both the evaluative process and its outcomes. As time passes, findings from earlier evaluative efforts become less relevant. For example, there would be little reason to apply findings drawn from the experiences of counselees in the 1930s to the tight labor market of the 1960s. Similarly, as we have noted earlier, when opportunities begin to open up, as they have for women and blacks, it is wrong to use findings that stem from a period when discrimination was more intense. Consider the implications for evaluation of making no allowance for the changes in the training of counselors. Earlier, many counselors had little more than a few graduate courses; today, a significant minority are graduates of a two-year full-time graduate program. If the time span covered by an evaluative study is long, it is likely that the findings will have little relevance for the present and less for the future.

We have now reviewed briefly the difficulties of evaluative research, even where there is agreement about the goals to be assessed and the criteria to be used. In summary, we noted the following obstacles to evaluating guidance: variability among clients; differences in the quantity and quality of the guidance services to which counselees have access; the fragility of guidance versus other determinants of career outcomes; the non-comparability of the services available over time.

These conceptual difficulties in evaluation were not evident to the research community at the outset. In fact, they surfaced as a result of the problems confronted by investigators and their critics as they attempted to frame the recalcitrant materials. Research is a process and, in the effort to add to the store of knowledge, investigators became increasingly aware of the difficulties that stood in their way. At this point we will look more carefully at some of the evaluative studies of guidance that have been conducted in recent years.

The studies that we will review can be ordered as follows: evaluations of services, of outcomes, of total guidance impact, and of guidance as a social process. As frequently happens with attempts at typologies, certain studies can be placed in more than one category, but since the schema has rhetorical rather than analytical significance this is not a serious matter.

One large-scale effort to evaluate vocational guidance services provided in a large number of similar institutions (high schools) was undertaken by Robert Campbell of Ohio State University in

1966.[5] He sought to describe "the present status of guidance in public secondary schools ... and to compare the viewpoints of school administrators, counselors, teachers, students and parents on guidance issues." Questionnaires were mailed to a representative group of 738 high schools of all types and usable replies were received from 353. Each cooperating principal was asked to distribute questions to one counselor, five teachers, five parents, and ten students.

Despite the bias that might be present in a sample selected in this manner in light of the stake principals have in the operation of their schools' guidance programs, some of Campbell's findings are revealing. He found that how counselors spend their time depends in large measure on the type and location of the school—academic, comprehensive, vocational; rural or urban. Students in all types of schools agree that aid in choosing an occupation is the most important guidance service; the availability of guidance services far exceeds their use even in schools where students indicate a favorable attitude toward guidance. Although counselors in every type of school spend the largest block of their time in individual counseling, they generally agree that the time thus spent is insufficient. In a large number of schools the needs of pre-vocational students were neglected; less than one-quarter of all counselors concentrated on serving this group.

Variation in expectations for guidance programs among different groups—pupils, parents, teachers, and administrators—underscores the amorphous character of the field. Campbell concludes that "if guidance programs are to be effective in meeting service needs with limited resources, they must be designed systematically and realistically to achieve a set of clearly stated objectives selected from a much larger set of possible objectives." The challenge, as his study indicates, is to arrive at agreement on goals among the various groups in the school and then to encourage utilization of the service by students.

In 1960, Project Talent, in its broad-scale, long-range assessment of high school students, sought to learn about the state of guidance in American high schools.[6] Among its preliminary findings about guidance were: a significant minority of schools (27 per cent) had no regularly assigned staff member whose principal function was guidance; the proportion of trained counselors was small; the major activities in which counselors engaged were test administration, course selection, and college advising, with a heavy bias in the direction of services to the college-bound.

David Armor, using data collected by the U.S. Office of Education in the mid-1960s in connection with its large-scale inquiry into educational opportunity (Coleman Report) and supplementing them with findings from a questionnaire conducted in the Boston area, presents his conclusions in *The American School Counselor*.[7] Armor finds that there is a marked variation in student-counselor ratio among regions. For instance, in the metropolitan areas of the Great Lakes a ratio of 1:481 prevails in contrast to 1:695 in the Mid-Atlantic states. Variability in counseling utilization among regions, between urban and semi-rural settings, and from school to school is a matter of concern to Armor, who believes that the key to the "institutionalization of the program and its proposed commitment to students was the average percentage of time counselors devote to counseling students on an individual basis."

Armor does not justify the criterion of individual counseling, nor does he prove its effectiveness. In fact, he himself presents data from several upper-income schools in his Boston sample which indicate that students in these schools still get most of their advice about colleges from their families. Nevertheless, he finds that counselors see more of such students than of others. He remarks that "the students who may require assistance most may be using the facilities least."

Another recent evaluation is *Pupil Services for Massachusetts Schools* by Gordon P. Liddle and Arthur M. Kroll.[8] This study of pupil personnel services including guidance was based on interviews, questionnaire surveys, and regional conferences of practitioners and other informed persons. Among the important findings are:

1. School principals dominate the entire pupil services structure. Guidance counselors "often seem to represent the final dumping ground for tasks that are not handled by the principal or the assistant principal."
2. Counselors in secondary schools appear to have a better understanding of post-high school educational opportunities than of broad employment trends and local employment opportunities.
3. A counselor may see the typical high school student two or

three times a year for a thirty-minute interview. Students
state that they do not think counselors have a significant influence on their educational or occupational plans.

4. There is an apparent uniformity in guidance programs throughout the state, and there is almost no evidence that existing
   practice is effective practice. "At present, it seems difficult to
   distinguish between a halo effect and genuine impact of
   services."

All of these studies have a common trend. Their aim is to
measure guidance services in a group of related institutions in
terms of a generally accepted standard, such as the formal qualifications of the guidance staff, the ratio of counselors to counselees,
or the range of services provided. Such survey data can yield useful informational data, although we must not exaggerate what can
be learned from them about the significance of guidance services
to the user.

A related approach, focused on a retrospective view of whether
particular groups received guidance and on their assessment of its
significance for their career decision-making, is exemplified by the
work of Franke and Sobel in their study of how people entered
shortage occupations and by Horowitz and Herrnstadt's investigation of the paths into tool- and die-making in the Boston area.[9]
In both instances the assessment of guidance services was incidental
to the primary concern of the researchers, but they uncovered important facts about guidance. A careful reading of the two research
studies points up that few among those queried had had access to or
had made use of guidance services. Moreover, the guidance that
was received by a small number was rarely influential in their
career outcomes. Most of these workers had learned about career
opportunities from friends or acquaintances or through their own
labor-market exposure.

Jacob Kaufman and his associates at Pennsylvania State University conducted two major evaluative studies of vocational education for the U.S. Office of Education in the mid-1960s.[10] In the
process they focused considerable attention on the guidance services
that were available to students pursuing different curricula. They
found that over half the vocational students, but less than one-third
of those who followed an academic or general program, reported

that they had never discussed their course choices with a counselor; of those who reported that they had had some formal guidance, three-quarters had a favorable estimate but vocational students were less likely to report favorably; over two-thirds of the girls and more than three-fourths of the boys who were planning to work after high school reported that they had never discussed their occupational plans with a guidance counselor; counselors rarely encourage black youths to attend vocational schools or to prepare for non-traditional occupations; black students are overrepresented in the general curriculum and underrepresented in academic and vocational courses of study.

The following quotations reveal some of the author's conclusions:

> By any criterion, guidance, as currently carried out, was one of the major weaknesses found in this study of vocational education.
>
> As a general rule very little effective vocational counseling takes place in high school. In the junior high school, the counselor's role is to slot students into tracks.... In the senior high school most of the counselor's time is spent with those seniors who plan to go to college.
>
> An evaluation of the effectiveness of vocational guidance was impossible because so little of it is being conducted.

While we must not ascribe undue importance to what people relate about the services to which they have had access and have used, we must not ignore the consumer. We were pleased to gain access through Morgan Lewis to 200 replies of respondents in one study to questions about their reactions to the guidance services which they had received. The wide range of their comments suggests the difficulties of evaluation better than most statistical material:

Positive Comments

At the time not as helpful as they seem now.

Helpful—directed into aptitude areas from test results.

They were helpful. Our school held regular guidance meetings. They would bring in employers to talk with us.

Mr. —— discussed Shop and brought a book about it. I read it, and decided to take machine shop.

They forced you into taking things you didn't want. This was good.

Very helpful. Kept after me. Introduced me to many influential people.

Very helpful. Counselor helped by talking to my English and Math teachers to help me when I was low. She helped me to understand the importance of an interview for jobs.

Often helpful. They brought out things I had never considered before; and helped in making decisions.

They really helped me "unjumble" my thoughts.

Went to counselor every day practically. She was definitely a big help.

Very helpful because he didn't try to change my mind. Encouraged my ambitions.

Negative Comments

Not too helpful. They went strictly by grades, not interest.

Worked mainly with college prep people.

No, because we were both confused as to what I wanted to do.

Only *ill-prepared* teachers functioned in guidance.

I never saw him. I think these people are a waste of taxpayers' money.

I discussed problems with parents, not counselor. Counselor was always too busy.

Not at all. Counselor told me I was too dumb to go to nursing school.

He said nothing; merely asked me what I wanted.

Not very helpful. Too busy with other students. Too few counselors.

The discussions were of no help since the counselors made the choices arbitrarily.

Not too helpful. Wanted me to go to college. I knew I couldn't go—expenses—didn't give me assistance for business world.

Not helpful—one-sided—went by the test, too strict, did not wish to listen to what you wanted.

None, they did not have any depth in vocational information.

One really messed me up.

Even the best of the studies which evaluate the range and quality of guidance services are inadequate since the crux of the issue is whether, after receiving guidance, an individual's career outcome is better than it otherwise might have been. A few researchers have sought to use classic experimental designs to develop definitive answers to this question.

David Campbell, in *The Results of Counseling: Twenty-five Years Later,* published in 1965, followed up 731 counseled and non-counseled college students who had been found to exhibit some differences in a study of matched pairs by Williamson and Bordin in 1940.[11] The experimental group had sought counseling as freshmen while the others had not. The twenty-five-year follow-up revealed that the counseled group demonstrated better academic achievement and accomplishment and that it did slightly better than the control group in terms of occupational achievement, income, and social contribution. The difference between the two groups was greater in their academic than in their career performance. However, the two are not independent: we would expect that a man with a baccalaureate or an advanced degree would have better occupational accomplishments than one who has lesser credentials. The nub of Campbell's follow-up study may well be that even minor assistance and support at a strategic point in college may tip the scale in favor of completion of studies which, in turn, will tip the scale in favor of a higher level of occupational achievement.

A few notes of caution about Campbell's study are in order. The college aptitude scores of the counseled group with graduate degrees were higher than those of the non-counseled; despite their demonstrated accomplishment, the counseled were less satisfied with themselves and their lives; they are more likely to seek professional help than the non-counseled. We must guard against drawing broad conclusions about the long-range effectiveness of guidance when the results are equivocal, and when there is reason to suspect inherent differences between persons who actively seek help and those who do not.

Professor J. W. M. Rothney has been concerned with evaluations of school guidance for many years and has contributed extensively to the field. In two follow-up studies of high school students, he produced positive findings with respect to those counseled in a specially designed guidance program, and found that counseled students were more likely to complete post-secondary training and to manifest greater vocational achievement and satisfaction than were the non-counseled.[12] The differences were small but some were suggestive.

In their 1960 survey of evaluation studies, Rothney and Farwell exhibited little enthusiasm about the quantity and quality of the evaluation research which they had carefully reviewed.[13] At our Conference on Guidance Theory and Practice in 1969, Rothney summarized his position as follows:

> The question of evaluation is a tricky one. We still do not know how to evaluate guidance if it can be evaluated at all. We must go beyond client satisfaction. We do not know what is important in evaluation. Control groups are no good for this purpose. Humans are simply too complex. If you add guidance people, schools are more likely to accomplish their purposes. Evaluation data are bad because of the problem of criteria. Guidance is effective only with those who accept intervention.

Since Rothney has been more concerned than any other academician with the problem of evaluation, his summary judgment must be given weight.

Another approach aimed at discovering whether counseling makes a difference in later behavior and outcomes was that of Lister and Church, who undertook a review of research, unpublished, "School Counseling Effectiveness: A Search for Evidence," in which they critically appraised twelve published studies of counseling of secondary school students.[14] In the opinion of the authors, these twelve were the best of the much larger number that had been published in terms of scientific rigor and scholarly reporting.

According to a variety of short-run counseling criteria, the guidance interventions reviewed by them appeared to have been effective. But this favorable assessment must be read against the following background: the counselors were better prepared than the average; the counseling in which they engaged was more intensive and systematic than that customarily available to high school students; and most of the counselors whose work was reported on were not members of the regular staff of the schools where they engaged in the counseling.

In a related and also unpublished study, "School Counseling: For Better or For Worse," James L. Lister reviews a group of research studies for evidence on the critical question of whether the school counselor facilitates and enriches "the personal development of the students with whom he works."[15] Among the important facts which Lister extracted from the research literature were:

Unless the counselor has empathic understanding and respect for the counselee and makes genuine responses, the outcome will be negative. The counselee will function less effectively.

Whether a counselor is able to help his counselee depends on his ability to function relative to the level at which the counselee is functioning. The average counselor would impede the development of most of his counselees.

A study of 30 counselors with master's degrees near the end of their counseling practicum indicated that "these counselors would have been either minimally helpful or harmful to students in a continuing counseling relationship.

At the beginning of graduate preparation, graduate students in the helping professions are functioning at the highest level at which, on the average, they will ever function.... The level of formal preparation bears little relation to the helper's level of functioning.... It is fair to conclude that at least half of the counseling relationships in which the typical school counselor participates are apt to have harmful consequences to the student who comes for help.

Lister emphasizes in his concluding observations that the research studies he reviewed relate specifically to the counseling relationship and are not concerned with the effects of other guidance services. He suggests that the equivocal responses to school counseling that have been reported may be grounded in the realization that many counselors are not able to provide useful help. His final sentence is "School counseling *can* be for better or for worse."

While there are many differences in these studies in terms of time perspective, the use of controls, the designs utilized, reassessment of prior research, they all share a common bias. Each investigator raised difficult questions about the nature of career outcomes, the selection of criteria to measure them, and the scientific methods employed to collect and analyze the data. The burden of their findings can be expressed in Rothney's words that "the elaborate claims of members of our profession for the efficacy of counseling and guidance . . . [are] not proven."[16]

A third type of evaluative study can be described as one which seeks to determine "total impact" of guidance services. It seeks to take account of and be responsive to the whole range of guidance inputs, including the intellectual and social background of the counselees and the character of the school as well as the entire range of possible outcomes. Such a study further recognizes that no one outcome, such as high school graduation or entrance into college, can be used to assess the effectiveness of a composite of guidance services provided to a heterogeneous population. The outstanding example of a study of "total impact" is the recent report sponsored by the U.S. Office of Education and the Minnesota Department of Education, *Guidance Programs and Their Impact on Students*.[17] The authors were concerned with evaluating the impact on outcomes of *all* inputs of the school guidance program. Thus they included not only the various activities performed by guidance counselors, but also all other measurable characteristics that might have affected outcomes. Moreover, they sought to take into account in their design the ways in which factors in the school and external environment unrelated to guidance might also influence results. These are some of their important findings about 479 public high schools in the state of Minnesota that graduated one or more pupils in 1964:

> —The best guidance programs tend to be in schools where they
> are least needed—that is, where the students have good ability,
> come from advantaged homes, and where the school climate
> encourages scholastic excellence.

—In schools with less able students and an anti-academic climate, counselors tend to spend more time on "problem students."

—The one guidance "input" that has an effect on hoped-for outcomes is the personality of the counselor as perceived by students and observers. "The counselor as a human being, rather than any specified guidance function he performs, affects the lives of students most." This factor is strongly associated with satisfaction with guidance, holding power, continued education, less underachievement, less unrealistic vocational aspirations, etc.

—Guidance programs contribute little, if anything, to stronger self-concept. "If anything, self perceptions seem better where there is less contact with counselors."

—There is no evidence that guidance programs help to improve instructional deficiencies in schools where there is a great deal of underachievement, or to change unrealistic vocational aspirations, or to contribute to the pursuit of continued training.

On the basis of their findings the authors recommended that "counselors . . . consider spending less time and effort with individual students in attempting to ameliorate problems brought about by negative influences in the school environment . . . and more effort in doing what they can to bring about changes which will facilitate healthy growth."

Recognizing the difficulties which have beset efforts at scientific evaluation, the U.S. Office of Education is supporting an ambitious long-term project under the direction of Professor Frank Wellman of the University of Missouri.[18] Wellman is developing a taxonomy of guidance objectives which will specify the measurable actions which can be considered the legitimate outgrowths and outcomes of guidance. In addition to this taxonomy of objectives, he hopes to provide a classification scheme of student and environmental variables which presumably affect outcomes. The design further provides for measures of counselor characteristics and counseling practices and procedures.

Wellman has gone a fair distance toward making explicit the multiple variables that must be defined and measured if meaningful results are to be obtained in assessing whether and how much of a difference guidance makes with respect to educational, occupational, and related outcomes. The scale of the effort precludes even tentative findings becoming available for about five years and it is estimated that another ten to fifteen years will have to be spent before broad-scale findings emerge.

The extended period required to carry out this inquiry increases the risks. Large-scale follow-up studies are difficult to complete. Even if this hurdle is surmounted, the researcher may stumble on one or more of the following barriers: developing valid measures of outcomes; sorting out the relative importance of a vast number of interacting inputs; avoiding the contamination of forces from outside guidance which affect outcomes. If these difficulties are surmounted, will it be possible to apply the results reflecting conditions in one point of time to a changed environment in which clients, settings, staff, and goals are perhaps substantially different?

Consider the consequences if Abraham Flexner had used such a design in his evaluation of American medicine at the end of the first decade of this century.[19] If he had decided to wait for the mortality and morbidity data from the Census of 1920; if he had carefully assessed the existing range of differences in the education and training of the members of the medical profession; if he had paid attention to the variations in hospital plant and equipment, he might have learned much about the inadequacies of medical care in 1910 but he would have contributed little to improving it by 1920! Flexner started with both faith and knowledge: faith that improvement in the education and training of physicians would be beneficial; knowledge that many of those currently in practice had inadequate competence and skill. No schema of evaluation should ever start from scratch or fail to ask ahead of time the purposes to which the results can be put.

This brings us to the last of the approaches that have been employed in evaluation, that which sees guidance as a social process and which raises questions about the services it provides and about how these are related or should be related to the larger environment to which people are exposed and to which they must respond. We consider that the present book is such an effort at evaluation.

Educational Decision-Makers by Cicourel and Kitsuse opened an important new dimension in the evaluation of school guidance.[20] The authors looked at a high school located in a high-income

suburban community in the Midwest which had a total of 22 full-
time and part-time counselors with a counselor-student ratio, depending on grade and curriculum, of between 1:100 and 1:225.
About three out of four of the graduates of the school went on to
college.

The major thrust of the authors' analyses and findings is that
one cannot blithely assume that an improved ratio of counselors
to students and corresponding improvements in counselors' training
will necessarily benefit all students. The authors present considerable material which suggests that children from low-income homes
whose parents have had relatively little formal education are likely
to be assessed and guided not in terms of their capacities, interests,
or potential opportunities but in terms of the preconceptions and
prejudices of the guidance personnel who tend to divide young
people into the college-bound and the non-college-bound according
to their family background. The authors levy two serious indict-
ments. The counselors misapply clinical terms and diagnoses to
young people from lower-income families and in so doing find a
rationale for dealing with them as problem cases, rather than as
students who require more assistance than their classmates from
more affluent homes. Among the deleterious consequences of this
type of guidance is that such youth are steered away from the
academic track and from broad participation in school activities.

Here is an important piece of evidence that school guidance
can be a disservice to certain young people. Although there is no
way of knowing how pervasive are the practices that Cicourel and
Kitsuse uncovered, their study is disturbing in its description of
the margins for manipulation that counselors have to control the
sluices that determine the opportunity channels for different groups
of pupils. The diffuse restiveness that characterizes many black
communities reflects in part their growing awareness that the
educational hierarchy often does not provide constructive advice
to their children. Some counselors are prejudiced; many are in-
sensitive to the emerging values and goals that are helping to trans-
form ghetto residents; many more are poorly informed about vocational opportunities; and almost all are subservient to their principals
and to a system which often deals unfairly with minorities.

Another study that treats guidance as a social process was undertaken by Jesse Gordon of the University of Michigan, who assessed thirty-five experimental and demonstration programs funded by the U.S. Department of Labor.[21] His report, "Testing, Counseling and Supportive Services for Disadvantaged Youth," is full of revealing insights although the demonstration projects he reviewed had not been designed in consonance with the canons of research and evaluation. His most important findings about guidance follow:

—Many counselors erred in postulating that the joblessness of the young men in these programs reflected primarily psychic weaknesses rather than environmental barriers.

—These clients were unresponsive to non-directive counseling but responded well to counselors who sought to intervene on their behalf and to help them be admitted to a training program or find a job.

—Counseling was most successful when linked to a direct service, such as job placement. In fact, until his objective situation was improved the counselee was largely impervious to help.

—Counseling a man after he got a job was more important than counseling prior to his beginning to work. Crew leaders and others were often able to provide important support.

—The clients needed fast results; they were responsive to money incentives and they gained confidence when counselors were able to break their problems down so that they could master one at a time.

—Paraprofessionals and indigenous workers proved to be effective counselors.

—Group counseling proved highly successful because of the ways in which peer pressures could be used as reinforcement.

Since the counselor plays so strategic a part in the guidance process it is relevant to mention in this review of evaluation studies an investigation into the results of a special program to train counselors to serve the disadvantaged.

John Dailey's evaluation of the CAUSE Projects confirms several of Gordon's findings.[22] It will be recalled these Projects trained a large number of college graduates in a short program of eight weeks and then assigned them as counselors to Youth Opportunity Centers. Here are some of Dailey's illuminating findings:

—According to peer ratings, counselors who had taken the short course had better counseling ability than other counseling staff, and they showed better rapport with their disadvantaged clientele.

—The greatest weakness in the performance of these short-termers was their failure to understand the operations of the Employment Service within which they were counseling.

—There was no evidence that race or age made a difference in the ability to counsel. However, women made better counselors than men.

—In the judgment of trainees who completed the course the so-called non-elite universities offered better training, and the survival rate was higher from these institutions.

Until more definitive information becomes available, Gordon's and Dailey's findings should be used as a check on the conventional wisdom about the ability of counseling to be helpful to different groups and the extent of training necessary for counselor effectiveness.

The burden of this chapter underscores our conviction that while guidance personnel are not major producers of perfect solutions, they are not necessarily inadequate as helpers. We believe that guidance as a total effort is not to be dismissed as irrelevant, but it should not be looked to as the cure for the multiple difficulties that people face in developing and implementing their career goals.

We have been aware from the start of our inquiry that there is a non-congruence among what guidance personnel do, what clients expect them to do, what the leadership of the profession has established as goals, and what society expects of the field. In our view, a great many people experience difficulty in formulating and implementing their educational and career objectives. Some of them need and can make constructive use of assistance from competent counselors who can help them understand themselves, the reality they confront, and to relate the one to the other.

Moreover, we believe that while each person is unique, many individuals face similar problems which derive from the institutions to which they are exposed, and that the solutions to these problems often require institutional reform. Hence a further challenge to guidance is to specify where institutional changes might contribute to the broadening and realization of options, and to utilize their skills to contribute to such reforms.

It is doubtless true, as Rothney has stated, that evaluation has not received the attention it deserves and that the elaborate claims made by the guidance leadership are not a substitute. But we have seen the great difficulties of designing and carrying out evaluative studies. Some observers believe that in a society characterized by increasing competition for public revenues, unless the challenge of evaluation is met, guidance runs a risk of losing out. But that is questionable. Our society spends one hundred times as much on education and on medical care as it does on guidance without any evidence that all, or even most, of these expenditures are productive.

The results of evaluation are desirable as evidence when the protagonists of any service are challenged by critics. And it is essential that opinions be buttressed with facts, wherever possible. But if progress can be validated only by facts, progress would cease, since many programs, including guidance, do not lend themselves to definitive evaluations. This does not mean that a society cannot determine whether a particular effort should be expanded, contracted, or modified. There is always some ascertainable knowledge about the effectiveness of a service. In a rapidly changing world, the challenge is to increase that knowledge by any and all approaches, by theory, history, comparative analysis, case studies, even if we must forgo, at least for the time being, empirically validated evaluations.

There is a middle ground between the ideal evaluation which cannot be designed and carried through for the many reasons we have reviewed and a decision to accept many irrelevant assessments of limited facets of a total program as a substitute. Even in this imperfect world, we can do much better than we have by a concentrated effort to collect, analyze, and evaluate the specific short-run outcomes that follow upon the provision of guidance services to different groups.

14

CAREER PATTERNS

THIS CHAPTER will attempt to distill from our ongoing research certain findings about jobs and careers, to order them into a schema, and to point out how knowledge about the career patterns that comprise the schema can be used by career guidance specialists.

Scholars in guidance and related fields have studied the objective parameters of employment as they have sought further understanding of the ways in which jobs, careers, and the world of work are structured. Donald Super, for example, proposed a three-dimensional classification of occupations in *The Psychology of Careers*.[1] To Anne Roe's classification of jobs by level and field,[2] Super added an industrial dimension, "enterprise," to distinguish the organizational aspects of different kinds of work settings. By and large, however, such schemata have been used mainly as a framework for assessing the psychological aspects of work and the satisfactions of individuals. Super has suggested that "with this kind of classification in mind, and with some understanding of the person with whom he is dealing, the counselor may then have some notion of where the individual fits into the scheme of things."

In contrast to this approach to individuals, much of the work of the Conservation staff during the past two decades has been concerned with the ways in which different *groups* explore, become established, and progress in their work and careers. In some of our studies, we included personality determinants in career outcomes, but our primary concern has been with the way in which the job market structures the options that people confront and shapes the decisions they make.

In 1969, approximately 90 million persons worked at some time during the course of the year. Any attempt to order the work and career experiences of so large and heterogeneous a population cannot capture the full range of variation. The categories that we have designed are intended to be an analytical device only, as a means of encapsulating variabilities in career outcomes. Among the principal precipitants are:

—The careers that people have are a function of the skills and competences they acquire during the preparatory process, the work and life goals that inform their adult years, and the strategies they pursue with respect to the labor market in terms of the opportunities that they confront.

—As a result of work experience, most workers are able to add to their competences and skills and thereby improve their positions.

—Cumulative work experience, which is concomitant with aging, also often leads to changes in career expectations and options.

—Some people encounter broadened opportunities. Others discover that they will be unable to realize their original goals and change them. Still others, having reached their initial goals, may become dissatisfied and look to new fields.

The individual reveals his career values and goals in the ways in which he responds to the options he confronts at different stages of his life. Because work in our advanced technological society tends to be structured, the interactions between what an individual seeks to accomplish at and through work and the available employment opportunities result in a limited number of basic work relationships of the following types:

—*Individualistic*—The individual is largely responsible for determining the conditions of his work.

—*Organizational*—The individual holds a position in an organization which largely determines the work he does and the rewards he earns.

—*Market*—The individual's employment is continuous but its terms are set by conditions of supply and demand in the labor market.

—*Peripheral*—Here, too, the conditions of work are set by the market but there is no continuity of employment. Because of personal desire or social rejection, the individual is loosely attached to the labor force.

These four relationships to work can be considered as stations in career progression. Their ordering, however, is not sequential. At various stages of his life—the preparatory process, the period of establishment at work, or in the mature years—a person may move from one category to another. In the discussion that follows, we will identify those most likely to fall into each category, those who may move into it, and those who will probably move out of it. The shifts that people make as they move from one employment relationship to another may be said to constitute a series of loosely delineated career patterns. Throughout, we shall distinguish between major patterns, characteristic of large numbers of workers, and minor patterns, shifts that are possible in an open society but which occur with far less frequency.

The Peripheral Group

The peripheral group includes those whose attachment to work is less than full-time, full-year. Most young people begin their encounter with the world of work in this group. While still in school, many hold part-time jobs during the school year and full-time jobs during vacations.

High school dropouts and some graduates are often in the peripheral group, either because of desire or necessity. Many young people under eighteen cannot obtain full-time jobs; some are still too unsettled by the turmoil of adolescence to work regularly, day after day; and others are unwilling to work regularly at the full-time jobs available to them. They find a job, work for a few days or a few months, and then leave, knowing that they will usually be able to find a similar job.

The largest group among peripheral workers are married women whose commitments at home lead them to seek part-time jobs. Of the 30 million women in the labor force, roughly 60 per cent fall into this group at any one time.

A third type of peripheral worker is recruited from among the vulnerable members of the labor force—the released prisoner, the ex-mental-hospital patient, the recent migrant from the farm, the discouraged adult. Personal handicaps or society's prejudices prevent them from being accepted as regular workers. They must take whatever jobs are available to them and many are unable to find more than temporary employment. Their work experience therefore is a series of short-term jobs between periods of unemployment.

The fourth type of worker in this group is composed of older persons who are on the periphery because of limited demand for their labor or because they want to work only part-time. Those on Social Security have a financial disincentive to earn more than a stipulated amount.

We see, then, that a peripheral attachment to work is characteristic of the following major groups: people who are entering or who are in the process of withdrawing from the labor force and women who prefer to work part-time. It also includes men who cannot find or keep a regular job. In absolute terms, those on the periphery account for slightly less than half of all persons with work experience during the course of a year.

It is the younger workers in this group who are most likely to shift to another group as their careers progress. By the time they reach their middle twenties and are able and willing to make a more permanent attachment to the labor force, young men are likely to be distributed among our categories as follows: those with the most education and training will be found in the individualistic or organizational group, those with less education in the organizational or the market group. Only the most disadvantaged or disorganized will remain permanently on the periphery.

Some middle-aged handicapped persons—the ex-patients, the ex-prisoners, the recent migrants—will move over to a market relationship and a few may even be able to join an organization where they will be able to look forward not only to continuity of employment but also to job progression.

A considerable proportion of married women, the majority of whom are among the peripheral workers at any given time, are able to become full-time workers as their children become older. Most of these women become attached to the market or organizational group; a few join the individualistic group, such as a woman physician who returns to full-time practice or a former part-time sales woman who opens a boutique.

We have followed those who move out of the periphery; who moves into it? Most of these people once had a market relationship to work, although some may have had an organizational or individualistic attachment, but because of adverse employment conditions or personal misfortune, they have lost their footing and have not been able to find another regular position in the economy. They are able to find only part-time or intermittent work.

In summary, there are few people who during the course of their working careers are not at some time on the periphery.

The Market Group

The *market* relationship to work is characterized by people in full-time jobs who have little opportunity for advancement and limited job security and other perquisites. Job tenure is subject to general labor market conditions rather than to organizational relationships.

Large numbers of full-time female workers are in this category. These include many who are employed in small offices and retail establishments or as unskilled and semi-skilled factory workers. Because of marital expectations young women often view work as of short duration and are willing to serve in jobs that hold few prospects of substantial advancement. They are loath to enter long periods of specialized training and employers are disinclined to risk investing in them.

Many men fall within this same pattern, also. If a man comes through the preparatory process with modest educational achievement and without having acquired any specialized skill, and if he fails during the period of establishment to acquire skill or to secure employment in an organizational structure where he will be advanced as a result of seniority, then he too will be at the mercy of the market. His adjustment to the world of work is conditioned by the fact that since he has no special skills to offer an employer he has to accept whatever job is available. It may be a steady job—as a doorman or a hospital attendant—but it holds little promise for the future. His employer can get a replacement easily and that means that the job will pay relatively little, today or next year. Moreover, such a job offers little opportunity for advancement.

However, a small percentage of those whose employment is initially tied to market conditions, especially men, may shift over to the individualistic, the organizational, or the peripheral groups. Many men want to go into business for themselves, and some, who are initially unable to, succeed after a time through a combination of savings, bank loans, and help from relatives. This is the situation of the taxi driver who buys his own cab or the waiter who opens a franchised diner.

Many people who belong to the market group, recognizing their vulnerability and the limited prospect of improving themselves, try to shift to an organization where their job will be more secure and the likelihood of advancement greater. Whether they succeed depends on the conditions of the labor market, their age, and their circumstances.

A third possible shift for men who originally were part of the market system is to the peripheral group. This may reflect disability due to illness, injury, or aging that reduces their ability to compete with others. It may be psychologically grounded: a man who realizes that his future includes only a low-paying job may finally decide that it is sensible for him to work only when he needs money and not otherwise.

There are smaller numbers who are likely to shift from other work relationships into the market group. We noted earlier that this may characterize women who previously were on the periphery but who wish to work full-time. The other inflow consists of men who have failed at self-employment or have lost their footing in an organization and are forced to settle for what the market offers.

The Organizational Group

By far the largest category in the adult male population is the *organizational* group. A wide array of employment structures are involved in this relationship: government, business firms, non-profit enterprises, structured labor markets, particularly in construction, transportation, and manufacturing.

Organizational attachment involves employees at every skill level.

At each level the same broad principles apply: jobs tend to be regular; promotions are usually made from among the existing work force; seniority plays a large part in advancement.

A few words about the paths into organizations. Most men make the transition in their early or middle twenties, shortly after completing their formal education or training. One of the implicit and explicit goals of their search to become established in work is to find a satisfactory position which includes career opportunities. Although most large corporations make an effort to smooth the path for baccalaureate and higher-degree recipients at the managerial and professional level, the evidence shows that many young people do not remain with their original choice of employer and shift after a few years to another organizational relationship.

Much the same pattern holds for the less educated and trained— the white- and blue-collar work force. Here too there is considerable moving around in the early twenties as young men try themselves out and at the same time add to their knowledge of the organizational world. But by their middle or late twenties, they make a long-term commitment. Only in that way can they gain the advantages that are offered by an internal labor market with built-in protections.

The dominance of organizational forms of attachment grows out of the important and increasing role of large units in the American economy and the limited number of desirable alternatives to working for such organizations. Large American employers, initially in manufacturing but recently in other sectors as well, have preferred to hire entry workers without specific occupational preparation and to indoctrinate and train them in company procedures and practices, in the hope that most would remain with the company for a long time, if not for the whole of their working lives. Trade unions have placed major stress on seniority: promotions to better jobs, with or without additional specialized training, are available to the workers with the longest satisfactory service regardless of employer preference. This principle also operates with respect to layoffs, overtime, or any other options that affect workers' income and perquisites.

Finally, most Americans, having noted the advantages that accrue to men whose jobs are almost immune to the vagaries of the market, who are promoted regularly, who have fringe benefits and deferred income through private pension plans, have opted overwhelmingly

for positions in organizations which can best be defined as "structured" markets. The organizational pattern has a great deal in its
favor: employers, trade unions, and workers all tend to prefer it.

Nevertheless, there is a small but steady shift out of organizations,
primarily to the individualistic group. There is the corporate executive who, when his children are in college, decides not to spend the
last two decades of his working life in the same setting but starts a
business of his own. He sees little point in waiting to be promoted
from assistant vice-president to vice-president and prefers to take
a cut, sometimes even a large cut, in salary and emoluments and
have more autonomy over his work and more opportunity to shape
the remainder of his career.

In addition, men who complete apprenticeships, particularly in
the construction trades, often become contractors, hoping to gain
control of their careers, to make more money, and to enjoy more
satisfactions.

Brief note should also be taken of the fact that if a large organization encounters difficulties as a result of a reduction in government
expenditures, disturbed market conditions, or mergers which result
in staff reductions or plant shutdowns, many men and women may
have to shift to the market or the peripheral group. This is more likely
to be true of those in the upper age groups, who have limited mobility
and who have no skill that is in demand in other large units.

The Individualistic Group

The individualistic group, like the organizational, contains several
distinct components. There are self-employed professionals—physicians, lawyers, architects—as well as such professionals as research
scholars who, though employed by a university, are able to determine the direction of their own work. This category also includes
an assortment of independent businessmen including the cab owner,
the small retailer, and those in a mixed status such as holders of
franchises. The majority of farm owners also fall into this category.

This group also includes a number of persons with varying orders
of talent and skill who build their work and career around their
competences and who are able to direct their work by controlling
their services. Examples are independent commercial artists, cabinet-

makers, television actors, electricians. Despite differences in background, in type of work, and in the circumstances governing their relations to the market, their common characteristic is the fact that they are largely in control of their own work, subject to the extent of the demand for their services. As with all people who must earn money by selling their labor or the product of their labor, they are not able to operate solely out of inner determination, but they can do so to a much greater extent than most other workers.

The vulnerability that attaches to being on one's own helps to explain one of the characteristic shifts in career patterns that takes place. A considerable number of young people in their late teens and twenties aim high: they look forward to becoming successful authors, to breaking through on the New York stage, to becoming important research scientists. But after years of application, they begin to read the returns and realize the desirability of shifting. Many of them opt for an organizational attachment: the unsuccessful researcher enters a government agency; the unsuccessful writer joins the public relations department of a trade association; the unsuccessful actress joins the training staff of a large utility.

Others who are forced out of individualistic enterprise, particularly small businessmen, often can do no better than look to the market for a full-time job; and some, especially those who have had to sell their businesses, may be so vulnerable that they are able to exist only on the periphery.

In addition, certain professional men, particularly physicians, give up private practice and accept bureaucratic assignments in a structured situation such as public health or join a hospital staff as full-time employees. This usually represents a permanent career shift.

On the other hand, when a distinguished academician leaves the university for government service or a lawyer who has been in private practice does likewise, one cannot be sure whether their move is a change in pattern or whether it represents a temporary shift. It depends on what happens next. If the academician returns to the university within a few years there is no change. If he decides to remain in the government, there is.

The self-employed farmer, businessman, professional still has a place in the American economy, but such opportunities have been shrinking for many decades, and there is little likelihood of a reversal in the years ahead. A more subtle development is that managerial and professional persons employed in large organizations now insist on a higher degree of self-determination in their work.

The following conclusions can be distilled from this analysis of career patterns:

—The dominant career pattern in our contemporary society culminates in an organizational relationship. This provides most men and some women with basic employment security, reasonable income, and opportunities for advancement.

—To exercise significant control over one's work (the individualistic relationship) requires either professional education, a specialized talent or skill, or the ability and willingness to take risks involving the potential loss of one's life's savings.

—There are options for mature workers to shift from one situation to another as personal and market conditions change.

—Some men and many women workers are never able to make a stable attachment to work. In career terms, they are left behind with only a marginal relationship to the economy.

We have described career patterns and the shifting that occurs among different groups of workers to provide guidance theoreticians and practitioners with some additional knowledge about the strategically important environment of adult work—which is, after all, the arena where men and women must deal with their occupational problems. We will now seek to make explicit some of the major linkages between these patterns and career guidance.

If the career patterns which have just been delineated represent a reasonable model of the American economy at the present time and in the near future, it behooves the guidance specialist to use the model as he counsels his clients—young, mature, and older. For advice-givers must always take account of reality even when a client is willing to challenge it.

To make the linkages between this model of career patterns and guidance practice as sharp as possible, we will outline below selected areas where counselors can best make use of it:

—Guidance counselors have long known and stressed the importance for young men of acquiring education and training as a prerequisite for expanding their career options and work satisfaction. They have been much less attuned to the consequences that flow from the fact that many girls and young women fail to be concerned while in high school, junior, and senior college with acquiring the foundations on which to build a career. This underinvestment is one reason that so many women later make limited progress in the world of work.

—Guidance counselors must recognize the importance of the period of establishment (the early and middle twenties) when many young men, through a combination of military service, diversified work experience, and additional education and training, are first able to build a foundation for a career.

—A considerable number of young people start out with the hope of succeeding as self-employed professionals or businessmen. Some make it; many others do not. Guidance counselors should point out to young people the lines of retreat that are open to them if they try and fail.

—The poorly educated or otherwise disadvantaged young person is usually handicapped when it comes to getting a job with opportunity for advancement. Guidance specialists who are able to steer these young people in the right direction—and particularly if they are able to help them obtain employment with a large organization—may make a critically important contribution to their work lives and over-all social adjustment.

—While the majority of women workers at one point are interested in part-time jobs rather than full-time employment with career prospects, many eventually want to trade their peripheral status for more secure jobs with opportunities for advancement. Guidance counselors should be alert to the probability of this shift for many women and encourage and help them prepare for and make it.

—Guidance counselors should recognize that many men, after a period of years at work, voluntarily or involuntarily change their career goals. Knowledge of the paths that are available and the potentialities of a successful outcome can assist guidance specialists to improve their career advising.

The foregoing links are suggestive rather than exhaustive. The principal object of our formulation of career patterns is to call the attention of guidance specialists to the major channels into which the work experience of adults is directed. We must explicate one additional point, possibly the most important of all. We emphasized that most people have limited control over their own work. They must respond to the dictates of the organization or the market. They are told what to do, in a great many instances how to do it, and when and for how long. The conditions under which they work and the wages and benefits they receive may be satisfactory, and they may find gratification in interpersonal relations on the job. If these elements are present, workers may derive satisfaction from working. However, many workers are restive about the conditions under which they work and the rewards they receive. Moreover, inability to determine the nature of one's work often results in failure to derive satisfaction from it.

Since the opportunity to pursue an individualistic career pattern is circumscribed by the nature of our society and economy, the prospect for major gains in intrinsic satisfaction through that avenue is bleak. Guidance counselors must recognize this. While some experiments have sought to expand the worker's interest in his job, in general, more satisfaction for workers will derive from a relaxation of rigid standards of behavior and a more permissive atmosphere in many work places. Meanwhile, many workers, from corporate vice-presidents to elevator operators, seek their satisfactions off the job. As our society becomes more affluent, there will be more opportunities and more options for workers to have additional time in which to pursue avocational interests. Guidance counselors must deal with this reality as with others. They need not worry; most of their clients are realists.

15

THE PROFESSION'S

STANCE

MANY OF the difficulties in providing effective guidance services to the American people outlined in the earlier chapters are known to the guidance leaders and they have attempted to find answers to them, both ameliorative reforms and long-run basic transformations. This is not to say that there is general agreement among the leadership with respect to either diagnosis or therapy, but there are broad areas of agreement despite the persistence of continuing differences.

We believe that it is important to preface our conclusions with a description of the profession's current position with respect to reform and reconstruction. This will enable us to indicate those of its views we share and those with which we differ, the reasons for our disagreement, and our alternative recommendations.

For delineating the profession's self-image and its plans for the future, we will place primary reliance on the *Report of the Interagency Task Force on Counseling* of 1967, which was concerned with a solution to the problem of providing counseling and related services to all those in need of such assistance.[1] The membership of this task force was widely representative of the leadership in counselor education, the professional guidance organizations, allied professional groups, and of guidance practitioners from various settings.

The ten recommendations put forward in the *Report* had substantial support from the group as a whole.

Our additional sources included *Man in a World of Work*, edited by Henry Borow, to which we have referred in earlier chapters and to which we now return because, as its Foreword remarks, "This publication represents the profession's best current thinking on the nature of vocational guidance, the meaning of the human work experience, the relationship of the individual to the labor force, and research and practice in vocational guidance. . . . As a vehicle for professional upgrading, as a progress report to the members of the Association, as an overview of the vocational guidance·movement, and as a literary milestone, this volume is presented by the officers and trustees on the occasion of the NVGA's Golden Anniversary."[2]

Early in 1970 Van Hoose and Pietrofesa's compendium *Counseling and Guidance in the Twentieth Century* was published. This volume contains the reflections and formulations of twenty-two persons who had been chosen by a special panel of the American Personnel and Guidance Association "as representative of the field of counseling and guidance." It supplements the Borow volume and provides the most contemporary statements of the positions of persons the editors refer to as "the fathers of the current guidance and counseling movement."[3]

Another source was the detailed record of the three conferences called in 1969 by the Conservation of Human Resources staff, prior to formulating its own conclusions and recommendations, to inform itself of the current views of leaders of the guidance and allied professions.

We have also used the testimony relating to guidance presented to the U.S. Senate Committee on Appropriations dealing with the Departments of Labor and Health, Education and Welfare at the end of 1969.[4]

To keep this review within bounds we will consider a relatively small number of issues affecting goals, strategies and methods which the leadership has identified as of critical importance as it looks to the future.

Guidance and counseling remain centered on the developmental problems of the individual. One of the major propositions advanced by Arthur Traxler in the Van Hoose and Pietrofesa volume states that the primary goal of guidance is the maximum development of each individual consistent with his potential and with the welfare of the social group.[5] The opening sentence of the *Interagency Report* talks of "self-actualization for each individual," and then states that in addition to providing systems of education and training "adequate and appropriate for the development of each individual is the responsibility of providing whatever services may be required to assist him in making the important decisions that will shape his life. This is the major mission of the counselor. . . ."[6]

Much of the same note is struck by the NVGA Anniversary volume. In the first chapter, Carroll Miller, writing on "Vocational Guidance in the Perspective of Cultural Change," reaffirms concern with "the individual in the process of growing up" and concludes, "His needs come out of his total life experience, and he will take help where he can find it."[7]

Donald Super, who contributed the concluding chapter to the above volume, "The Professional Status and Affiliations of Vocational Counselors," underlined the following as the major challenge facing vocational counselors: "Better training in personality and in the handling of personality problems as part of general and vocational development, combined with better use of referred resources for help in personality reorganization."[8]

In the 1960s many of the leaders, including Super and Wrenn, recommended that the vocational aspects of guidance, which had dropped low among the objectives of school counseling, be given a higher priority. This, together with a new concern with helping minority groups, led many of the leaders to recognize that while guidance by its very nature must remain centered on the individual, the profession should be concerned about and make a contribution to changing the institutions which determine the options available to various groups.

We quote Miller again: "Bare-bones vocational guidance of the classical sort, its faith pinned on disseminating information, will prove inadequate in offering any real help to the culturally deprived and otherwise disadvantaged, to the out-of-school unemployed youth, to potential dropouts, and to delinquents from whatever background. . . . Such tasks involve both the providing of new opportunities and assistance in reshaping a way of life."[9]

An even stronger expression of this viewpoint is set forth by Kenneth B. Hoyt in the Van Hoose compendium when he states, "I see environmental manipulation as a means of creating the kinds of positive conditions which will allow students to do things for themselves—and thereby be more free to lead their own lives. . . . I contend that one doesn't have to be very intelligent . . . to realize that for many students certain conditions in their environment are handicapping to them and consequently keeping them from being all they are capable of and wish to become. I further contend that if counselors wish to view themselves as agents of change, they shouldn't hesitate to take an active role in making change take place."[10]

This broadened view is also revealed in the *Interagency Report:* "The primary work objectives of the counselor are to help the individuals he serves understand themselves and their opportunities better in order that they can formulate plans, decisions, and concepts of self which hold potential for more satisfying and productive lives, and to help them implement their decisions and plans. As a secondary and related objective, the counselor seeks to effect changes in the environment which are conducive to increasing individual opportunity for self-development."[11]

At our conference in 1969, Stefflre warned that "it is not realistic to think of counselors as 'change agents' at least in respect to influencing curriculum. The reason is clear: Teachers are not looking for another influence. Counselors need more power than they now have." And Bordin remained skeptical of the interventionist approach, arguing that "the counselor's job is helping people to come to grips with the issue of self. . . . They should not be so terribly involved with external options. More important is what is going on within the individual."

But Schwebel, offering proof that leaders often differ on specifics, was diametrically opposed and argued that "guidance is the handmaiden of the 'status quo.' What is needed now are pressures upon the system to force change."

The weight of opinion seems to be that guidance must remain centered on helping the individual make better decisions about the options he has, but the profession has a role to play in seeking to effect changes in the environment so that more individuals can enjoy a wider range of options.

Although the leadership has been aware of and concerned about the gap between the limited supply of competent guidance personnel and the increasing demand for their services, it has moved only slowly toward group guidance. Of the twenty-four chapters in the NVGA Anniversary volume, only one is directed to this subject—"Strategies of Vocational Guidance in Groups" by Margaret E. Bennett.[12] She tells us that while there has been some experimentation with group strategies, many problems remain to be solved before the strategy can gain widespread acceptance. Hoppock's most recent assessment is: "We have only a few experimental studies in which investigations have compared the results of individual and group counseling but the few that I have seen have shown group counseling to produce equal or better results."[13] And Wrenn adds, "The most urgent need for continuing professional development is in the area of group counseling."[14]

While testing and information dissemination is often carried out in groups, the profession has been hesitant to make broad use of group counseling, although recent experience with the guidance of the hard-to-employ suggests that it is often the method of preference. While the *Interagency Report* included "group counseling" as a basic component of the core curriculum for counselor training, it is not currently offered in many graduate programs and, where it is, it is typically downgraded. In the Conservation conferences little stress was put on group approaches. In fact, Rothney argued that this was not a preferred approach. "The individualization of the process has been overlooked. There are too many groups. There is not enough opportunity to talk about oneself alone with a counselor." However, as Bennett pointed out, group strategies should not be thought of as alternatives to individual counseling but as supplements; the challenge is to combine the two for optimal use of resources and achievement of results.[15]

Since the profession is cautious about changing the emphasis of guidance and about moving far or fast away from a one-to-one counseling relationship, it is not surprising to find that the central recommendation of the Interagency Task Force was directed toward the rapid and substantial increase in the number of guidance counselors. Specifically the Task Force calculated the additional needs over the quinquennium (1966–1971) on the following ratios of counselors to students: in elementary schools, 1:600; secondary schools, 1:300; junior colleges, 1:300. This implies an increase from 35,000 to 116,000 or a net increase of 81,000 or more than 250 per cent in five years!

The estimates of need for the other major federally supported programs, primarily vocational rehabilitation and employment services, were smaller, but still substantial: from a base of 10,000 to 25,000, or a net increase of 15,000, amounting to 150 per cent over five years. The Task Force summarizes its findings and recommendations by stating that "the data lead to the conclusion that the supply of counselors must be increased substantially to meet adequately present and anticipated needs for services. . . . The greatest demand is and will continue to be for counselors to work in educational settings."[16]

There were three major components of the estimated need for a large increase in school counselors: the Task Force stipulated an improvement in the ratio of counselors to students in secondary schools from about 1:500 to 1:300; it looked forward to the staffing of junior colleges' counseling services with trained counselors; and it postulated the rapid penetration of counselors into elementary education. The 1:300 counselor-student ratio for secondary education has long been accepted as a desirable ratio. And few would argue against the desirability of adding substantial numbers of trained counselors to the staffs of the rapidly expanding junior colleges and other post-secondary institutions.

However, with regard to counselors in elementary schools, the Task Force includes a large increment without reference to the small number currently employed or to the major reservations of many leaders about the desirability of moving to expand in this direction. The Task Force had the backing of the Congress which, with the profession's prompting, had amended the National Defense Education Act in 1961 to permit funds to be spent on training of counselors for elementary schools. In its description of the functions of school counselors, the Task Force did not differentiate the tasks that they might perform in elementary school from those that should command their attention in junior and senior high school.

Funds for guidance in elementary schools were among the priority requests of those who testified before the Senate Committee in 1969. For example, the director of guidance for the Chicago schools asked for increased federal support "to make an inroad in the school system at the elementary school level comparable to the inroad previous Title V-A funds made at the high school level."[17] Another witness claimed that funding for remedial work could be eliminated by more elementary guidance. "The sound elementary school guidance program attempts to prevent educational, psychological and physical deterrents to motivation and learning from developing. Guidance should really start in kindergarten or preschool levels."[18] And the President-elect of the NVGA noted that almost one quarter of Title V-A money received by the state of Ohio each year has been used to "encourage the introduction of elementary guidance programs. . . . Even with this small incentive we receive requests from 5 schools for every one whose program we can help to finance."[19]

In the NVGA Anniversary volume, Albert Thompson of Teachers College devotes one paragraph in his chapter on "School Settings for Vocational Guidance" to vocational guidance in elementary schools. He quotes with approval a statement that "guidance in elementary school assists *all* children"; he then points out that the emphasis cannot be on vocational choice because "the vocational maturity level of the elementary school pupils is still too low"; and he concludes by stating that an elementary school counselor "can work constructively with pupils in such a way as to nurture the talents of all children and assist them in overcoming obstacles to success in work and play."[20] Most of the other contributors to the volume do not consider the issue.

Six years later, G. E. Hill of Ohio State directed his chapter in the leaders' compendium to "Guidance in Elementary Schools." He argues that guidance services can help personalize and humanize the child's educational experiences and can be of assistance as he matures. Hill set out nine major ways in which elementary education should be strengthened and claims guidance can contribute significantly to the realization of each of these objectives (but does not specify how). As Hill sees the challenge, "The efforts of counselors in elementary schools are therefore directed toward bringing the resources of the school, the home, and the community so to bear upon the individual child that he will grow up with the best possible chances for becoming a happy, productive child."[21]

The following quotes are from the discussion of guidance in elementary schools by participants at the Conservation conferences:

> Elementary school guidance is largely a curriculum service which involves the counselor with curriculum people. This is a guidance function, not a counseling function.

> It is unrealistic to expect young children to make much sense out of occupational information at the lower grades.

> The elementary school counselor is really a watered-down pupil personnel specialist. She is hired because she is cheaper than other specialists.

> Elementary guidance will be the fastest moving and growing area of guidance. It is in the process of becoming. It is the result of a demand by educators.

> Elementary guidance is conspicuous consumption. No one knows what it is supposed to do.

> The rationale for elementary school guidance seems to be similar to that for early public health measures.... There would be less need for medical care if there were early preventive measures.

> Elementary school counselors should be interested in skill development and in developing attitudes toward knowledge.... It is critically important that somebody help in these areas. The elementary counselor is there to ensure adjustments to sound solutions.

> Elementary counselors are flunkies for principals.

The requirement of 40,000 elementary school guidance counselors adopted by the Interagency Task Force, a figure in excess of the total number of school counselors at all levels in 1966, had the support of the Task Force members. But some of the opinions expressed at the Conservation conferences by other leaders of guidance and related fields indicate serious doubts about the desirability of a rapid expansion of elementary school guidance.

The Task Force knew what would be necessary to meet even part of its additional requirement of over 80,000 counselors for 1971. It stated: "Funding for the recruitment and training of more professional counselors ... will depend largely on the financial assistance of the Federal Government, at least for the next few years."[22] It recommended that "very substantially increased support must be provided both *for preparing and for employing* counselors."[23]

The members of the Task Force did not indicate that they shared the concern David Tiedeman had expressed at the invitational conference on counselor preparation and employment of 1965, the progenitor of the Task Force. Tiedeman was alarmed about the overwhelming government control over counselor recruitment, training, employment, and other facets. He said, "The lines in the profession of counseling are therefore largely etched (1) by the understanding of counseling as held in state departments of education and by state legislators; and (2) by the relation of federal to state government which permits federal intervention largely on an *ad hoc* and generally seriously circumscribed basis."[24] Tiedeman was particularly concerned about the way in which governmental actions tend to fractionate instruction in the university, to favor institutions emphasizing technique over theory, to foster guidance as a technology, and to make counselors remote from participation in determining goals. Although the Task Force mirrored some of Tiedeman's concern about government control, it opted for what it considered the lesser of two evils and recommended the development of more counselors through using government money. After all, the great spurt of guidance and counseling in the 1950s and particularly in the 1960s was the direct outcome of federal financial assistance for professional preparation and employment and there was no alternative source of funding for helping the profession realize its expanded goals.

Specifically the Task Force recommended that new legislation be passed to "provide support for the preparation of counselors for the first full year of graduate education, such support to include traineeships for students and assistance to institutions. . . ."[25] The latter was essential since a large-scale expansion of the numbers in training would be possible only if the educational institutions were aided to expand facilities and staff. Among the interesting aspects of its proposal was the recommendation that this first subsidized year be built around a core curriculum "that would be usable regardless of setting." School, employment, rehabilitation, and other types of counselors "would be educated together in the same basic curriculum during their first graduate year."[26] The plan contemplated that the counselor would learn about his particular setting when he went to work. He would be educated in school and trained on the job.

As the Task Force saw it, "Those who successfully complete the program [would be able] to function at entry levels of employment in their profession, under appropriate supervision."[27] In addition some would "go on to a second, third or fourth year of graduate training."[28] While the Task Force was willing to innovate with respect to the first year's training, it did not want to precipitate a head-on conflict with the key professional groups which had long advocated a basic two-year master's degree program. It therefore distinguished between *minimum* functional competence— one year of training consonant with the prevailing pattern—and *desirable* functional competence—which would require two or more years of formal academic training. The Task Force took explicit note of the fact that most of the approved graduate training programs for rehabilitation counseling which receive federal support require two full academic years; that the Consultants on Counseling and Testing of the Federal Advisory Council on Employment Security had recently made a similar proposal for professional preparation of counselors in the public employment service. The APGA policy statement, *The Counselor: Professional Preparation and Role* (1964), had laid out a program which would require a minimum of two years of graduate study. The Task Force also noted that doctorates were preferred for counseling psychologists. The push toward a basic two-year program had been a part of the scene at least since the early 1960s, when Wrenn wrote *The Counselor in a Changing World.*[29]

It is worth noting briefly what the Task Force hoped would be squeezed into the one-year core curriculum:

Basic psychological principles

Theory and techniques of individual and group counseling

Psychological appraisal, including individual and group testing

Knowledge of the cultural environment, economics, and the labor market

Educational and occupational information

Professional ethics

Statistics and research methodology

and "to the extent practicable, supervised practicum experience."[30]

The Task Force did not translate these competences into learning time or show how they could be acquired within one academic year.

In addition to the particular hurdle of inadequate financing for counselor education to which it was specifically responsive, the Task Force stated that there were other factors acting as a deterrent to recruitment: Among these are "lack of attractiveness of counseling as a career," and "the frequent requirement that school counselors have a teaching certificate." With regard to this last, the report stated that "Task Force members differed in their opinion as to the desirability of removing this requirement."[31]

The Task Force lent its prestige to enhance the power and influence of the professional guidance establishment. Of its ten recommendations, four were specifically directed to the appointment of consultant, advisory, and coordinating bodies to government agencies in which the leadership of the profession would play a critical role.

The Task Force went out of its way to strengthen the trend toward professionalism. While it noted that persons other than counselors sometimes counsel, it stressed that "a unique combination of job functions, competencies, and premises ... distinguishes counselors as an occupational group." It also remarked that the counselor "in any setting should be prepared and should be professionally competent to accept responsibility for and engage in [counseling] activities."[32]

In recommending a major federally subsidized training program for "professional" counselors, the Task Force demonstrated that it sought a solution to the urgent manpower problem by ways other than that pursued by the federal government via the Projects CAUSE, which trained counselors in special short-term courses. However, it stated, "Nonprofessionals are being used as support personnel to professionals in a number of occupations ... [and] it is the view of the Task Force that this approach should now be systematically and judiciously developed in federally-supported counseling and guidance programs." It added that "the basic reasons for the use of counselor support personnel are to facilitate service, and to increase the effectiveness and productivity of professional counselors." To reassure the profession, the Task Force pointed out that if more support personnel were employed, "the expressed demand for counseling may increase. Furthermore, counselors will have to undertake new training responsibilities and new supervisory responsibilities." Then the critical reassurance: "The employment of counselor support personnel should, therefore, not be seen as a method to reduce the demand for professional counselors, from a long-range point of view. Although this may occur as a short-term result, the long-range result cannot legitimately be foreseen as one of reducing demand or need for professional counselors."

The "judiciousness" of an effort to employ support personnel was spelled out further. Support personnel would work only in locations where their activities are under the direction and supervision of professional counselors. The concept of levels of preparation would distinguish support personnel from professional counselors, and the occupational rationale for using support personnel is that in their absence their activities "might properly be assumed by professional counselors." Support personnel would be engaged in "prescribed and limited procedures . . . not requiring analytical judgment or interpretation." Professional counselors on the other hand would require "extensive knowledge . . . of program objectives and operations, extensive use of technical knowledge and skills . . . and considerable use of judgment" based on their academic and on-the-job achievements.[33]

The caution with which the Task Force dealt with this problem is underscored further by its explicit references to "the policy of relevant professional organizations." The Task Force called attention specifically to the statement adopted by the Executive Council of APGA in 1966 on *Support Personnel for the Counselor: Their Technical and Non-Technical Roles and Preparation* and reproduced the eight-page report in its entirety. The APGA policy statement made these critical discriminations between the professional counselor and support personnel:

1. The counselor performs the counseling function . . . while support personnel contribute to the overall service.
2. The work of the counselor involves synthesis and integration . . . the work of support personnel tends toward the particular.
3. The counselor bases his performance on use of relevant theory.

Functions of support personnel are characterized by more limited theoretical background.[34]

Having abundantly indicated its sensitivity to the competition, confusion, and conflict that might arise if the matter of support personnel were not handled with discretion, the Task Force finally made the following recommendation:

that Legislation be prepared to support a program of experimental and demonstration projects for planning the preparation of, preparing, and appropriately using the services of counselor support personnel.

It joined this modest proposal to a recommendation that an advisory panel or panels be appointed "of appropriately qualified experts or consultants . . . to review and make recommendations."[35]

There is no reference in the NVGA Anniversary volume to support personnel. Super concludes his contribution by calling attention to two levels of counselor training and certification if individual and social needs are to be met. He looks forward to two years of professional preparation for most counselors of whom a minority will acquire their doctorates.[36]

To the slow but steady effort of the guidance and counseling leadership to establish the two-year program as the norm—there were some dissenters like Hoyt who considered it impractical[37]— the apparent success of a countermove under governmental aegis to train counselors in an eight-week program proved threatening. Although the Task Force was charged with the assignment of developing a program that could help meet urgent manpower requirements by increasing the supply and improving utilization of counselors, they were not willing to take more than one small step with respect to support personnel and they recommended that even that remain under the control of the professional establishment.

The following statements which concerned the matter of support personnel were made at the Conservation conferences:

The new approach would take guidance apart and let licensed personnel handle certain things and let others handle interpersonal relationships at which they are particularly adept.

The non-professional should be kept in mind when we talk about improving the graduate curriculum. Tracks should be split—between the well-trained and the less skilled. Guidance personnel would not be giving up much if some of their present functions were allocated to aides.

We have to learn how to use paraprofessionals.

The counselor-client ratio could stay where it is if the counselor performed only certain jobs.

We must remember that there are two million paraprofessionals—the teachers. We must learn to utilize them in guidance.

In contradistinction to earlier quotations from the Conservation conferences we should note that most of the statements about paraprofessionals reported above were the opinions of persons not from guidance but from allied disciplines. The guidance representatives did not accept the need for paraprofessionals any more than did the members of the Interagency Task Force or the contributors to the NVGA Anniversary volume.

The issue of restricting certification of school counselors to individuals with a teaching license who have served in the classroom has disturbed the field for some time. The leadership split. In his 1964 article for the NVGA Anniversary volume on "Professional Status and Affiliations," Super argued that to advocate that school counselors understand schools was a reasonable requirement but to insist that they first become teachers "is the most expensive, the most time-consuming, and the most deterring to non-teachers."[38] On the other hand, Kenneth Hoyt continues to assert, "I want to see school counselors with teaching certificates and demonstrated successful teaching experience."[39] As we have noted, the Task Force, after calling attention to the detrimental effect of this requirement on recruitment, stated that it was divided between recommending its retention or abolition. At the Conservation conferences the following statements were made:

There is too narrow a reservoir from which counselors are drawn. They should be drawn from the whole spectrum of disciplines.

Certification standards have hamstrung the profession. In New York State, an ad hoc committee, studying certification of pupil personnel specialists, recommended two full years of graduate training and further recommended that completion could be used as an alternative to teaching. The New York City principals were the only group opposed to this recommendation. They advocate five years of teaching experience.

Counselors should have the BA plus graduate work. If they make counseling their vocational choice in their junior year at college and major in related courses, this would mean four years of training—junior and senior years in college and two years of graduate school.

We must think of the present framework of guidance. Guidance for whom? We give the same kind of training to counselors and teachers regardless of the functions they will perform or of the student body. There should be greater differentiation. They (guidance personnel) do not need a year of graduate training.

Part-time training is not sufficient for people who are working full-time in the school setting. If counseling is not a lifetime job (for many men who will move up the administrative hierarchy), why not shorten the length of training?

The way to do it is to do away with the teaching requirement.

Throughout these far-ranging comments there was no consensus in favor of the present teaching requirement. Instead, there is intragroup conflict; school counselors, supported by school administrators, tend to believe that it is to their advantage to retain the requirement so as to maintain job control and affiliation with the field of education, while many of the leadership, who hope to speed the professionalization of the field of guidance and counseling, see it as an impediment. Although the latter have gained allies among those who believe that the requirement is a deterrent to recruitment, the center of gravity remains with the traditionalists. If the American Association of School Counselors were to withdraw from the APGA as has been proposed, and were to join the NEA, the prospect of reform would all but be eliminated. Nevertheless some states are considering action to remove the teaching requirement.

With regard to the specific matter of guidance manpower, the position of the Task Force was as follows:

—Dissatisfaction with the one-year, part-time training program for most school counselors.

—A clear preference for a two-year full-time graduate training program.

—A split on the requirement of teaching experience for the certification of school counselors.

—A cautionary view toward support personnel.

The Task Force was responsive only to the first issue. However, it did not explain how one could acquire the basic competences it had delineated within a one-year full-time training program.

The several recommendations of the Interagency Task Force were submitted to the Manpower Administration, U.S. Department of Labor, in the fall of 1967. Despite the fact that the membership of the Task Force was broadly representative and that all fifty members were in general agreement about the steps that were urgently required to expand counselor manpower, the key administration officials failed to act. Neither the Department of Labor nor the Department of Health, Education and Welfare—the two agencies most directly involved—took action to draft the recommended legislation. Consequently the support of the Bureau of the Budget and of Congress remained untested. The gap between government administrators and the professional guidance leadership in basic posture toward guidance and counseling was widened by this failure of government officials to act on an interagency report for which their own staffs were heavily responsible. Thus, when the budget squeeze took effect at the end of the 1960s, the attitude of both the Administration and the Congress reflected kind words but little cash. (The most recent appropriation [Fiscal 1970] for guidance under NDEA, Title V-A, was $17,000,000. The administration had asked for no specific funds for guidance, while the APGA had asked for $30 million as a "bare minimum" for 1970 and $54 million for 1971.) The Interagency Task Force's proposals never were given their day in court.

The one conclusion we can draw is that counseling's manpower problem is unresolved and, in light of government's present disinclination to underwrite the costs of training, it is unresolvable. There is simply no way to bridge the gap between the personnel standards and goals which the leadership has espoused and the realities of the labor market. We will return to this dilemma in Part Four.

Other related issues have not been appraised and for them no
soultions, not even partial solutions, have yet been proposed.

If it is true, as most of the leadership believes, that counseling
skills are the hallmark of a competent counselor, how can we
expect significant progress in the field when even the totally subsidized one-year graduate training program that the Task Force
recommended includes a practicum "where practicable"? It is
essential, as Super emphasized at the Conservation conference, that
counselors have field experience and that such experience be supervised by competent staff.

Another difficult problem is presented by the belief that the key
to effective counseling is empathy rather than technical skill and
that empathy is more a matter of personality than training. If this
premise is granted, or granted in part, it carries many implications
for the recruitment, preparation, and use of counseling personnel
that the profession must still confront.

One gain from manpower stringencies can be the review of
conflicting demands in order to reallocate, whenever possible, the
limited resources to priority needs. The bland way in which the
Task Force sought to legitimize a demand for more than 40,000
guidance personnel for elementary schools in the face of manpower
stringency and with critical questions about the function of guidance
in that setting unanswered is one more illustration of a policy
stance without concern for the balancing of resources and requirements, present or prospective.

Another conventional response to manpower stringencies is to
explore how changes in utilization of personnel might reduce the
need for additional staff. One might assume that attention would
be directed to exploring the potentialities of making greater use
of group techniques. However, support for this approach does not
appear to be growing or is growing only slowly. We should note
that, although the Task Force attempted to find answers to the
tight manpower situation, it did not devote one paragraph of its
report to group approaches.

At present guidance is closely linked to the school. Even the
Task Force, which was established because the federal government
wanted to provide services for out-of-school youth, paid relatively
little attention to the non-school population, particularly adults.

This has been characteristic of the leadership as a whole. With the exception of schoolchildren, the only significant clientele in which it has evinced interest until recently has been physically handicapped adults.

The Task Force stipulated that henceforth all guidance counselors should have the same academic training and that they should learn about the specific needs of the population they will serve through supervised on-the-job employment and further training. Until a broad-scale effort is initiated, the validity of the philosophy of this bifurcated training—general knowledge acquired in the classroom and specific know-how on the job—will remain untested.

While there are many differences among the guidance leadership as to the priorities for strengthening the profession there is one broad area of agreement: more and better-trained personnel is the preferred cure.

PART IV

POLICY

16

ADVICE TO

ADVICE-GIVERS

GUIDANCE IS beset by claims and counterclaims. Its enthusiastic protagonists believe that the field is making a major contribution to the welfare of individuals and to the progress of society. They argue that if more funds were invested to train guidance counselors, to establish new guidance programs, and to improve existing ones, the contribution would be even greater. When the leadership is challenged about a deficit in accomplishment, the answer is a simple one: counselors have an excessive caseload.

But during the last decade there has been a substantial increase in available resources and caseloads have dropped to the desired level in some environments such as Suburbantown. Yet the promised results are still not forthcoming. Observations, impressions, and systematic investigations of guidance programs generally do not confirm claims that guidance plays a decisive role in the career plans and outcomes of its clients.

School counselors appear to spend the bulk of their time in approving courses of study, in assisting with college applications, in dealing with rule infractions, and in test administration. Few spend a significant amount of time in activities specifically designed to lead to improved decision-making and long-range planning, the expressed goals of guidance. Furthermore, while most of the leader-ship and practitioners proclaim that guidance has the responsibility of serving the entire adolescent group, there is considerable evidence that middle-class students preparing for college predominate among its clients and that far less attention is paid to the educational and vocational problems of the large numbers who are not college-bound.

Employment counselors tend to provide routinized services to their clientele and have demonstrated inadequacies in dealing with the problems of the hard-to-employ. Despite the developmental approach espoused by the profession, the adult population receives relatively little attention.

Rehabilitation counseling, by its selective focus, has been able to achieve more success than other forms of guidance. But the specialized character of its clientele and the wide range of the services on which it can draw prevent its becoming a model for guidance services for the general population.

The gap between unlimited aspirations and mundane achieve-ments has many causes. But predominant among them is the lack of congruence between ends and means. Counselors say that they help their clients realize their full potentialities. But it is difficult to trace the consequences of their actions. It is hard to think of other services in which intervention alone is equated with results.

In light of these ambiguities and confusions, what can be said about the present and potential value of guidance? Some analysts believe that its potentialities are so modest that it is not worthwhile to invest additional resources in an effort to change and strengthen the field. These skeptics do not believe that guidance can signifi-cantly affect people's lives in the face of the powerful institutions that shape career outcomes—the family, the school, the labor market.

To buttress their skeptical attitude toward the potentialities of guidance and counseling, these observers call attention to the following "facts of life" which they believe justify a withholding attitude:

—Since many young people see guidance personnel as authori-tarian adults who try to control and regulate their lives, few are likely to benefit from their services.

—Differential aptitudes and interests are developed early in life and are subject to change only with great difficulty.

—Guidance cannot affect the type of jobs that employers have to offer nor add to a worker's skills.

—Guidance for education and work makes little more sense than guidance for marriage. People may act irrationally but they often are able to change if they are dissatisfied with the choices they have made.

—Without the help of guidance young people come to recognize that adults fare better or worse in the labor market as a result of their preparation and skill and the position of their family.

—Those who are intent upon careers seldom need prodding or support.

These strictures, reservations, doubts cannot be blithely ignored. Each makes a relevant point. Together they are a challenge to the advocates of more and better guidance services. Yet each argument can be countered.

—The response of most youths to adult aid can be affirmative if the adults are sensitive and perceptive and if they encourage free interaction among peers without authoritarian intervention.

—Differences among individuals have little to do with the validity of guidance. Every person has some options, regardless of his aptitude or interests, and it is desirable to encourage and assist him to make an informed choice.

—Guidance does not claim to be able to influence the demand for labor. But it can convey labor-market information to the job seeker so that he can make a knowledgeable occupational decision. Moreover, while guidance cannot provide a worker with additional skills, it can encourage him to enroll for and complete skill training.

—Guidance cannot guarantee successful career choices, but decisions will be more satisfactory if they are made with deliberation and if the critical factors are weighed.

—To be informed about job requirements is not the same as to meet them. To fulfill vocational aspirations, one must know how to proceed to meet specific requirements.

—Differences among the career aspirations of people are not necessarily related to their need for guidance. Whether a person aims for a career in the traditional sense or for a secure job, a gap exists between his aspiration and its realization. Guidance along the path can often assist the individual to reach his desired goal.

We believe that there is a rationale for guidance services which derives from more modest aspirations than the practitioners in the field have enunciated. Guidance, like education, has been caught up in its own rhetoric for so long that it balks at anything less than remaking man and society. We prefer to present a limited set of challenges to guidance which, if effectively met, would justify not only the present level of social investment but a larger one. These are our premises:

—Everybody is confronted repeatedly with the need to make decisions with respect to education and work. These decisions can be facilitated if people have relevant information about the shorter and longer consequences of alternative choices.

—Better decision-making with respect to career development also requires the clarification of goals, the development of plans, and their implementation.

—People need help in learning to negotiate complex and changing institutions—the educational system, the Armed Forces, the labor market.

—While informal advisers such as one's peers and especially one's family help young people to define their goals and initiate them in the ways of the institutions of our society, they frequently do not have important information or objectivity.

The case for career guidance is embedded in the foregoing propositions. It does not follow that without career guidance, many young people and adults would make faulty educational and occupational decisions. Many would not or, if they did, they could correct their mistakes without serious loss. But many others would make better decisions if they had clearer goals, improved information about alternatives, and assistance in implementing their choices.

The rest of this chapter is devoted to the actions which the guidance and counseling profession might take to realize its potentialities more effectively. In formulating our recommendations we have been acutely aware of the margins that restrict the profession. To assume that it can reverse course, deny its history, or operate without reference to manpower, money, and other constraints would be as foolish as to assume that the *status quo* cannot be altered.

In seeking a framework within which to place our advice to the advice-givers, we have identified *within* the guidance movement the following centers of power, authority, leadership:

The counselor educators

The counselor supervisors

The guidance researchers

The guidance counselors

The professional organizations

We have pre-tested each of our recommendations to be sure that one or more of the foregoing groups is in a position to act on them, although individually and even collectively they may not be able to implement them. The guidance field may require support and action from outside forces, and to these we direct our attention in the following chapter.

We stated at the outset of this study that our concern is with educational and vocational guidance. We find, however, that those who engage in providing guidance services often perform a wide variety of additional functions, ranging from counseling for personal adjustment to handling disciplinary problems. Guidance has an expressed goal—"the full use of human potential." We are pleading for a refinement and specification of this overambitious goal.

Since public funds are tight, guidance must present a strong case to obtain the resources it needs. Our *first* and overriding recommendation is that educational and occupational guidance be made the primary commitment of the profession. This recommendation seeks to bring guidance back to its origins. It postulates that education and work are critical dimensions of human life and experience and that improved decision-making through guidance intervention can make a difference for a considerable proportion of the total population.

The priority claim for career guidance implies a shift in focus and resources away from certain objectives that have won adherents in years past. In the first instance, it means that school counselors can be concerned but cannot alone deal with all the developmental problems that young people are likely to encounter, from conflicts with parents to experimentation with drugs. This is not to deny that such problems are pervasive, that they frequently swamp more mundane matters of educational and occupational decision-making, nor does it argue that they should go unattended. But if guidance counselors are to develop competence they cannot at one and the same time be informed sources of career information and assistance and continue to serve as psychotherapists or administrators. They must rely more on referrals to psychologists and social workers. The burden of this recommendation is that guidance counselors should no longer devote most of their time to such tangential activities.

However, our recommendation does not imply that guidance counselors, or for that matter any group of advice-givers, can afford to operate except on a basis of an understanding of the stages and varieties of human development. The greater their understanding the better. But regardless of their psychological sophistication, this knowledge alone does not suffice. Guidance personnel must become more informed about work and careers and about the pathways into them. This is, or should be, their unique role. In the other areas where they are active, there are other professionals, usually with more training and expertise.

Our *second* recommendation is that the guidance leadership seek to inform employers of counselors and instruct future counselors that their role is that of specialists who help clients with respect to their career development; their role is not to serve in a line capacity to accomplish organizational goals. This is particularly apposite with respect to guidance personnel in school settings where so many young people correctly see the guidance specialist as part of the administration whose advice is often more responsive to the aims of the school than to student needs.

Clearly no staff person can be indifferent to the ends of the organization which hires and pays him. Yet there are important differences between the ways in which professional groups see themselves, their work, and their responsibilities and how non-professionals view themselves. Every professional has the obligation to do his work in consonance with his understanding of best practice; he is required to be sensitive and responsive to the needs of his clients; and the true judges of his behavior and performance are not his employer but his professional peers. If guidance counselors are to move more rapidly toward professional status they will need to be helped by counselor educators to consider themselves as professionals and they must have the help of their professional societies to establish and maintain substantial independence from the dictates of the administrators who hire and employ them. But above all the counselor must have and be able to make effective use of skills and competences that people want and will pay for through taxes or fees because they believe they can benefit from the service.

One of the reasons that school counselors identify with the administration is that for many the only career advancement is to move from guidance into administration. Many people change their roles as they move up the hierarchy: the professor who becomes a dean; the researcher who becomes a laboratory director; the priest who becomes a bishop. That is the nature of the occupational world. However, one of the disabilities that guidance faces in almost every setting is its foreshortened promotion ladder. There is little room for guidance personnel to advance except by moving over or out. If guidance gains more public support; if its employment base is both broadened and deepened; if it makes more use of support personnel, it should be possible to moderate, though it will probably not be possible to eliminate, the outflow of the many who want to improve their career opportunities.

The inevitability of the movement of many school counselors, as well as employment and rehabilitation counselors, into administrative or training positions if they are to keep their career options open is not necessarily all loss. As administrators, former counselors should have more understanding and support of their guidance staffs and what they are seeking to accomplish. As educators they should be able to sensitize their students to the impact of work realities.

Our *third* recommendation relates to the need for linking guidance to other services. Sophisticated observers of the current scene know that in guiding and counseling the underprivileged, the critical factor is whether the counselor can intervene in some direct way to better the life conditions and circumstances of his client. If he can get him into a training program or if he can get him a job, he may be able to counsel him later and to help clarify his position and future prospects. But unless the guidance counselor can deliver concrete help, he might as well forgo the counseling effort. Clients who are outside the mainstream need a sign that counseling is not one more attempt at whitewash. Sometimes the counselor must use bait to entice clients to seek them out. In Project SEEK, an effort to provide remedial aid in colleges to disadvantaged students with inferior educational preparation, one of the principal pieces in the counselor's armamentarium is financial support provided students. The checks are presented by counselors and provide them with the leverage needed to establish contact with these students and to encourage them to return for counseling and related services.

Our *fourth* recommendation flows directly from the preceding ones. If career guidance is to be the critical intervention and if guidance counselors are to become staff specialists, then it follows that the education of counselors must be responsive to these facts. The major reforms of the educational and training program must be along the following lines:

—More emphasis on the world of work and on the pathways into it.

—Greater stress on training the guidance counselor to mobilize and utilize informational and other resources existing within his setting and on the outside.

—Supervised field work in a relevant setting to improve the trainee's ability to listen to and interact with his clients and to observe how people change their attitudes and behavior.

Unless there is a large-scale public underwriting of graduate counselor education, which we will discuss in the next chapter, there is little prospect of satisfactorily accomplishing these objectives within the prevailing pattern of one year's graduate study on a part-time basis. Even the Interagency Task Force did not recommend that a practicum must be made part of a full-time curriculum limited to one year. One way out of this dilemma is to encourage college students to see the study of guidance and counseling as a field in its own right, not as a substitute for professional training in psychology or psychiatry or eventually as an escape route from teaching. If they were to enter graduate school with a foundation in economics, sociology, and psychology, a year's intensive full-time study plus an apprenticeship might be, if not ideal, at least a sound advance. In the absence of radical changes in the financing of counselor education and in salary levels, neither of which appears imminent, this looms as a feasible short-run reform.

If young people are to be encouraged seriously to consider guidance and counseling as a career rather than as a derivative or residual choice, and if they are to use their time in college to move in this direction, the almost universal state regulation that only teachers can become certified school counselors should be rescinded. This is our *fifth* recommendation. The leadership should speak out clearly on this issue. If it does, it is likely that one state after another may favorably consider a change in the licensing requirements.

In any case, a major effort must be launched soon since guidance cannot move toward professional status if it continues to insist that a teaching license and classroom experience are essential for the proper discharge of the functions of career guidance specialists in a school setting. This is a false hypothesis. The fears of the rank-and-file guidance counselor that he will lose prestige and bargaining power if the requirement is eliminated should be thoroughly aired and assessed. If these fears are groundless, the leadership should reassure the membership. If these fears have validity, it is the task of the leadership to find alternative ways of protecting the rights of school counselors while gaining support for the removal of this anachronism.

Guidance counselors should no more be compelled to have teaching experience than school social workers or school psychologists. If school counselors were to feed back to the teachers and administrators what they learn about the weaknesses of the curriculum and if they played an active role in curriculum reform, one might argue with more justification that they need teaching experience. But counselors do not need to be curriculum experts; in fact, they are not and are not accepted as such. When it comes to simple feedback, the reports of a guidance specialist who is recognized as competent in his own field should have sufficient authority. The school nurse and social worker have just that. And that is all that is required.

As the Interagency Task Force and similar groups have made clear, the retention of teaching experience as a licensing requirement for school counselors can result only in intensifying the manpower problems of the guidance field. It establishes a narrow funnel through which recruits must pass. While ignoring subtle arguments about the dominant characteristics of teachers and counselors and the overlap between them, we cannot ignore that the key to success in the classroom may be linked to a more authoritarian approach than should characterize guidance. To exaggerate to make a point, we could argue that the last group from which counselors should be recruited are successful pedagogues. And a rationale has not yet been developed for centering the selection on the teacher who is fleeing the classroom, although many unsuccessful teachers make their way into guidance.

There is another drawback to the certification requirement, which involves salary levels and retention. It inflates the guidance budget by the automatic increments that teachers earn. The preferred approach would be one that recognizes the guidance specialist as a professional with an independent salary scale. But this would require greater professionalization all along the route, from education to supervision.

We are not stating that the retention of the teaching requirement is totally without merit. But the weight of the evidence appears to be overwhelmingly against it.

A further recommendation deals with the priority areas where career guidance should expand. We might raise the antecedent question of whether current guidance personnel should be reallocated. We have decided to by-pass this question because we believe that no clear case could be made for withdrawing a significant proportion of available resources from the principal areas where they are now concentrated—in secondary schools, rehabilitation programs, and the Employment Service. We prefer to rest with the recommendations already advanced for a shift in focus among these settings.

Our *sixth* recommendation is to expand guidance resources for youth, in and out of school, as well as for adults, and to retard the slow but steady trend toward bringing guidance services into the elementary school. Many secondary schools still have a high ratio of students per counselor and various subgroups of high school students receive little or no guidance services. We will address both of these issues after clarifying our broad position.

Our recommendation that services for young and mature adults be expanded is predicated on the following: the limited amount of such services currently available, except for particular groups such as veterans and those in rehabilitation programs; the inevitable tendency for young people to delay their occupational decisions as a concomitant of the elongation of their education and training; the tendency of young adults to reopen their tentative decisions as a result of early experiences in the military or in the civilian labor market; the increasing number of mature women who wish to enter or return to the world of work; and the large number of middle-aged adults who seek to make job and career shifts. All of these groups need guidance; few of them have access to it.

The only significant financing of guidance to date has been derivative—that is, in connection with major programs focused on education, vocational rehabilitation, or employment. Consequently, the recent strategy of the guidance profession has sought to profit from the mounting public concern over education of the young by appealing for the incorporation of guidance services into programs to strengthen early education.

But what specialized skills does the typical guidance counselor have that can contribute to the priority task of improving the performance of elementary school pupils? We noted earlier that teachers are disinclined to listen to their guidance colleagues about curriculum. Moreover, it was pointed out in our Conservation Project's conference that there is little or no opportunity in elementary schools for the guidance specialist to utilize his counseling skills. If a counselor has training and expertise in community relations he might serve to link parents more closely to the school. But he rarely has such skills and in any event that would appear to be the appropriate role for the principal. Most counselors have had a course or two in psychometrics and one might point to this as qualifying them to contribute to pupil assessment. But they are not as skilled in this area as are school psychologists who are increasingly available. Moreover, as we have noted, there is a growing belief among many critics of the performance of elementary schools that the last thing they need is more testing.

To suggest that neither more guidance nor more testing is the answer to the malperformance of the elementary school is not an endorsement of the status quo. Clearly, when a child fails to acquire basic skills in his first years in school—as so many do—the rest of his years in school are likely to be of marginal value. Many reforms are required which involve staff, curriculum, community relations.

We do not argue that if elementary schools hire guidance personnel there will be no work for them. We are merely stipulating that properly trained guidance counselors primarily concerned with career development have little to contribute to the elementary school. They can be used to expand the principal's staff but, as we have indicated, we think that would be an error. They can substitute for a school psychologist but, as with most substitutes, they will usually operate at a lower level of competence. They can be mediators for children with learning and adjustment difficulties, but they are likely to have little leverage either with the teaching staff or the administration to bring about meaningful changes. They might be able to stimulate some interest in building an occupational unit into the curriculum, but most are not particularly competent in this area. For these reasons we strongly urge the guidance leadership to reconsider the steady drift toward elementary school guidance and to take a public stand against such expansion.

In contrast, we do urge the leadership to recognize the need and press for the expansion of guidance services for young adults and for the mature population. We urge them to shift available guidance resources in high schools from the privileged to those groups who need express help in career planning, such as those requiring special assistance in order to attend college; to the non-college-bound who need help in making a transition into training, work, or the Armed Forces; and to girls and members of minority groups for whom many options are opening up for the first time.

We realize that all who are bound for college need help in filling out the necessary applications, but we question whether this requires most of the time of a skilled guidance staff. We believe that the guidance staff might limit its efforts to broad group indoctrination sessions about college admissions for middle-class students and their parents. There is considerable evidence that indicates the preference of educated parents to be operative with respect to their children's choice of a college. School counselors should be available to those who seek them out but they should not preempt this area.

In any case, they must do more for the non-college-bound. Otherwise they discriminate, which is no less reprehensible because they may do so unwittingly and without deliberate design.

Our recommendation that special attention should be devoted to females and members of minority groups flows directly from the theory and practice of career guidance. These are the two groups that are most likely to be misinformed about their options; they lack adequate models; their informal informational systems are likely to be deficient. These shortcomings reflect a sudden and substantial change in the paths that have opened up and the opportunities that lie at the end. An important social role for guidance and counseling is to cut the time lag between the new reality and the awareness and response to it, particularly among the young generation which is making its plans for the future.

We know that many young people who drop out of high school or who even acquire a diploma flounder in the labor market for several years while they consider or reconsider their job and career objectives; a significant minority become interested in returning to school or in entering formal training programs in order to add to their competences and thus broaden their opportunities. While they pick up a lot of information from employers, co-workers, and friends, much of it is misinformation and they often could profit from an opportunity to explore in more depth the range of opportunities open to them. This would require that they have access to a competent guidance service which has a broad overview of the whole gamut of educational, training, and employment paths and institutions.

James Conant and John Gardner separately advanced the recommendation in the early 1960s that each high school should assume responsibility for providing career advice and assistance to all alumni, dropouts and graduates, until they are twenty-one.[1] We commend the intention but we believe that their recommendation is faulty: high school guidance staffs would find it difficult to develop broad competence over the whole job domain; it would be difficult to achieve economies of scale; young people most in need of help are antagonistic toward an institution which many of them found to be oppressive and unrewarding; and many youths move away from home.

The Employment Service has an unfortunate record in terms of attracting young and mature adults with career problems and helping them. Even with respect to its primary function of placement, its record leaves a great deal to be desired. Nevertheless, we believe that it is more sensible to build on the only major labor-market institution which has offices throughout the country and to try to strengthen it so that it will become more responsive to the needs of youth than to try to duplicate it, with almost certain failure, by expanding the functions of the high school counseling staff.

In view of the nature of the labor market, the counseling and guidance services of the Employment Service should be expanded and strengthened not only for youth but also for adult men and women who want to explore a job or career change or who are returning to work and need assistance. The large and growing numbers of "loosely attached" workers underscore the desirability of expansion and improvement of guidance services. Once again we stress that an effective service would have to offer advice with respect to the gamut of education, training, employment, and even retirement.

In addition to the Employment Service, we believe that expansion of services should also be centered in post-high school training and educational institutions and in non-profit and even profit-seeking guidance agencies.

The supporting arguments are ready at hand. The elongation of the educational-training cycle implies that more and more young people will delay considering their occupational choice until they are out of high school. The large and growing proportion of young people who are going to community colleges need advice about occupational programs and about transfer possibilities. Too many of them drop out or complete their studies without clear ideas of the next steps to take and they could profit from career guidance. This is one locus for priority expansion.

With regard to four-year colleges and universities, we believe that while there has been considerable improvement in the provision of psychological counseling, especially in large institutions, too little attention has been directed to career guidance. Although many students need help with respect to their developmental problems, this should not obscure the fact that larger numbers could profit from being encouraged and helped to relate their educational decisions to a career strategy. Once again, women and minority group members should receive special attention since they are most likely to need help with respect to their career development.

This then is a summary of our *sixth* recommendation, which is concerned with priorities among clientele groups:

—A moratorium on the expansion of guidance into the elementary school until its functions have been more clearly delineated and alternative solutions explored.

—A redirecting of guidance services in high school toward non-college-bound males, toward girls, and toward minority group members.

—A high priority for the expansion and improvement of guidance services in the Employment Service for youth and adults.

—A high priority for the expansion of guidance services in community colleges.

—An expansion of career services in senior colleges.

Our *seventh* recommendation relates to the several actions which would improve the effectiveness of the guidance profession through new patterns of work and manpower utilization. The first and simplest action is to shift wherever possible away from the one-to-one relationship between counselee and guidance specialist that has been the dominant pattern since the inception of the movement. In the absence of unequivocal evidence that this is the only relationship that is appropriate, the guidance leadership should explore systematically what functions can be equally well and perhaps even better performed on a group basis.

Many aspects of course selection and college admissions—the two functions on which high school counselors spend so much time —can be handled on a group basis. Moreover, as we have noted, group counseling appears to be the preferred technique in dealing with young people who are "loosely attached" to the labor force. They trust each other and are able to learn from listening to each other and they apparently are reassured when they learn of common problems. If, as we suggest, more emphasis be placed on group techniques, counselor educators should include them in the required curriculum and practicum.

A second action involves intensified efforts by guidance counselors to obtain assistance from their colleagues. We are reminded in this connection of Felix Robb's statement at the Conservation Project's conference that, from the viewpoint of guidance, teachers represent a force of two million paraprofessionals. While teachers may resent counselors' coming into their domain with ideas about restructuring the curriculum and about other adaptations in school procedures and practices, they are likely to agree if they are asked to assist in the guidance task. With justification, teachers believe that they are often in a preferred position to make recommendations to students about course selection. Similarly they might be willing, especially in connection with instruction in English and social studies, to give more attention in the classroom to the world of work and the paths leading into it. In addition, they are often better able than the counselor to identify the underachiever or the student with unusual strengths. Indeed, unless school counselors can work with and through the teaching staff, they have little prospect of making more than a marginal contribution to the student body.

Similarly, the employment counselor should develop closer working relations with other members of the Employment Office staff, in particular the job developer and the placement officer. The rehabilitation counselor faces the challenge of improved coordination with his colleagues.

A third action is to create more effective liaison between the institutions that contribute to career decision-making and the encouragement of guidance personnel both in their basic training and subsequently to use lateral coordination involving contacts outside their own setting. Closer liaison is important between school counselors and employment counselors; between guidance counselors in every setting and professionals who are qualified to handle clients who need specialized help; between employment counselors and the staffs of health and welfare agencies in order to resolve problems that interfere with the realization of career objectives; between guidance specialists at different levels of the education-training-employment structure as well as between them and admissions, training, and employment staffs who make critical decisions.

Another desirable action is to encourage guidance personnel, particularly those in secondary school, junior college, and college, to learn to make greater use of the specialized resources available in the community in order to help them explicate and concretize many of the realities of the world of higher education, of work, and of the Armed Forces, and to let informed outsiders answer many of the questions which concern their clients. As Ralph Tyler has stated repeatedly, it is a pervasive error for schoolmen to try to do too much on their own while neglecting valuable allies. Guidance specialists are prone to make the same error.

We now present a challenge to the traditional ways in which guidance counselors have carried on their work in the past, one which contains the greatest promise of improvement in the future at a cost that the community may be willing to bear. The guidance literature is replete with complaints from practitioners that they are forced to spend a disproportionate amount of their time on clerical and administrative details that detract from their ability to help their clients with their career problems. In addition, the profession has insisted that it does not have and is not likely to have in the near future the trained manpower it needs to meet the priority claims for service even for those population groups which society has singled out as entitled to service.

The logical response of the profession would be to seek to attract a large number of less trained persons at lower salary levels and to restructure the way in which the total workload is performed and thus increase the total output of services. But, as we saw in the last chapter, the guidance profession is unwilling to endorse a rapid increase in the number of support personnel.

We believe that this is an error and that if career guidance is ever to make a serious attempt to meet the potential need and demand for its services, it has no alternative but to experiment with making greater use of support personnel. We have suggested many alternative ways in which career guidance might be strengthened through new work patterns, so that we do not need to spell out again the ways in which support personnel can be most effectively absorbed and used. But the principles are clear. The first is to designate those functions which require less training time and assign them to the support group.

As we have seen, the leadership is convinced that a reallocation of some of its functions might jeopardize the improvements in professional education and training for which they have striven for so long. But at present there is little if any momentum in the direction of the two-year training program. Graduates of the present one-year part-time training program are concerned that the distinctions between them and the baccalaureate holders who undergo short training on or off the job will be obliterated with corresponding loss of prestige and income for those with master's degrees. This is not an irrational fear, but there are factors that should be added to the equation in order to allay it.

It is not necessary that support personnel be recruited from among college graduates; in fact, there are reasons that they should not. They would be overeducated for the functions allocated to them and their salary levels would tend to be higher than others with less education who could cope with the work. It would be better to recruit personnel from among high school and junior college graduates. In this case, the distance between the present certified or otherwise recognized "professional" counselor and the support personnel would be widened. However, it would be necessary to provide for career progression for support personnel in which both experience and additional education would play a part.

Second, the prospect that the professional counselors' work would become more interesting if it were expanded to include the training and supervision of support personnel should be evident. In addition, it would be easier to develop more supervisory positions when the base is broadened. And, as everybody in guidance so well knows and has lamented frequently, the field at present lacks a broad promotion ladder.

Third, as experience with the loosely attached in the labor market has demonstrated, there are critical functions, such as outreach, which can be performed best by support personnel. A white female counselor may guide a youth from the ghetto just as well as a black male counselor, but she is unlikely to be able or willing to go into the ghetto and find him and coax him into the office for service.

We believe that all elements of the guidance profession should recognize the need for and desirability of attracting more support personnel as part of the larger objective of redesigning the way in which they carry out their work so as to broaden services at a cost that the American people can and will support. The major challenges we see in this connection are for more controlled experimentation in the use of support personnel, the adjustment of the education and training structure of professional counselors to reflect such a trend, and improved supervision.

We have referred earlier to the fact that the counselor educators are fully aware that the most serious weakness in the present education and training is inadequate field training. Even when there is field training, the quality of the supervision is often inadequate; it tells counselors what they should do but does not alert them to what they can do within a particular setting and it fails to monitor their counseling. A second weakness is that often newly trained counselors are thrown into work with no instruction, guidance, or support. With rare exceptions, such as the Veterans Administration and well-run community agencies, there is conspicuously little supervision of the day-to-day work of the counseling staff. Each counselor is permitted to act as if he were a private practitioner who must meet the vagaries of competition and attract and hold his clients on the basis of demonstrated competence. But most clients are assigned; they seldom have any recourse if they do not like their counselor; and there is little or no check on outcomes. There is much to be said for introducing more "choice" in the selection of a counselor by a client as well as more follow-up of his response, subjective and objective, to the services which he received.

Counselors should be informed while in training that as part of their professional development they will be subject to continuing supervision by senior guidance staff, not only to help them to acquire greater competence but also to protect the client. No profession can progress if each practitioner makes his own rules and works alone, without active supervision or structured exchange of information with his colleagues.

An expanded and improved system of supervision of and by guidance personnel is a *sine qua non* for any additional investment of the American people in a service which, while having the potential for improving the career development of many individuals, can be harmful in inexpert hands. Improved supervision is urgent if, as has been strongly recommended, the field plans to attract and use large numbers of support personnel. Without supervision there can be no responsibility, and without responsibility there is no accountability. Without supervision, there can be no professional growth.

Our *seventh* recommendation, therefore, involves the reorganization of the work patterns of career guidance. In summary, it includes the following:

—Greater use of group techniques.

—More interaction between counselors in their own and other settings, and with specialized community resources.

—The attraction and effective use of large numbers of support personnel to enable counselors to broaden their services and yet keep within manpower and money constraints.

—Stronger supervision to insure quality control and systematic progress of counselors. Improved supervision will be more urgent if changing work patterns accompany the employment of large numbers of support personnel.

Our *eighth* and last recommendation to the profession is that the leadership encourage accountability and innovation. As we have seen in Chapter 13, it is not possible at present and it may never be possible to develop a scientific approach for appraising the effectiveness of guidance and counseling, but it does not follow that the leadership and the profession as a whole do not have to strive continually to improve effectiveness.

There is today little meaningful data about counselor interventions and client outcomes. A first responsibility of every guidance supervisor is to insist upon the collection of operational data, especially follow-up information, and to provide for its analysis. Such data might not provide unequivocal evidence about the utility of guidance in effecting critical behavioral outcomes, but systematic information could be highly illuminating in assessing actions taken after guidance intervention. Perhaps the most important gain from the collection and assessment of operational data would be the opportunity that it would offer supervisors and administrators to use the results for planning, programming, and on-the-job training. Practitioners would have to look at their performance. The discipline of self-criticism is essential if a professional ethos is to prevail.

The several recommendations advanced for the increased use of support personnel and alterations in work patterns to include broader use of group techniques will lend themselves to experimental designs. It is important that the leadership carry through an experiment on a sufficiently large scale that greater reliability will attach to it than to a single effort where idiosyncratic factors might prevail. While cooperative research is never easy to plan and carry out in applied fields, including guidance, it is essential if progress is to be made. The group of regional educational laboratories financed by HEW and the multiple units in which guidance services are provided in the Employment Service and in vocational rehabilitation agencies provide a favorable background for cooperative research. The missing link is a research orientation with strong leadership both within and outside of the individual guidance systems. Research is the cutting edge of every profession; unless interest can be awakened and resources commanded for research, the discipline cannot grow into professional status.

The guidance movement is only sixty years old and much of its growth, at least in numbers of practitioners, has occurred recently. It has spent much of its organizing and structuring efforts on seeking to define a unique role for itself, particularly in relation to closely allied fields such as teaching and psychology. This has made its outlook and orientation parochial. The leadership and the rank and file appear to be preoccupied with intraorganizational and professional nuances.

The hallmark of a profession is that it assumes a leadership role in seeking to improve the quality, broaden the range, and otherwise enlarge its contribution to the public weal. Guidance has not yet risen to this challenge. It has continued to neglect the needs of large groups. Moreover, until recently it had not joined with other professional and political groups to point out the necessary reforms in basic institutions, particularly the schools and the labor market, or the need for new transitional mechanisms from one to the other if the promise of career options for every American is to be a reality. The guidance profession has been in a preferred position to learn about the shortcomings of education, particularly in high schools. But its leaders have not been in the forefront of those recommending reforms so that high schools can better serve the many students who today are being more abused than educated. As it seeks to grow into full professional status, guidance must be more concerned with matters of public policy; it must use its special insights and strengths to contribute to the formulation of better policies.

It is not enough for a group to want to become a profession or to keep repeating that it is one. A group becomes a profession by earning the public's confidence. It must be sensitive to the needs of the public for its services, take the leadership in seeking to meet them, be willing to account to itself and to the public about the quality of its services, seek to improve them through research and demonstration, and join with other concerned groups to help bring about changes in the underlying institutional structures which are desirable in their own right and essential if the profession is to fulfill its social obligations.

There is only one way to read the record to date. Guidance has been ingrown and introspective. Its best chance to gain full professional status is to act like other professional groups.

We have now completed our major recommendations to the guidance field. They are recapitulated below:

—Educational and career guidance should be the primary commitment of the profession.

—The primary responsibility of the guidance counselor should be to his client rather than to organizational goals as defined by the administrator.

—Guidance can be effective in helping disadvantaged groups only if it couples its services with other inputs that can help change the clients' reality situation.

—The education of guidance personnel must include more training in the dynamics of the labor market. Moreover, supervised field work in appropriate settings should be an integral part of all professional training.

—More services should be provided in high schools for non-college-bound youth, girls, and minority-group members; more attention should be devoted to the needs of college students for career guidance; services for mature men and women should be broadened; guidance in elementary schools should not be expanded.

—The requirement of teaching experience for the certification of school counselors should be rescinded.

—Improved counselor performance should be sought through more emphasis on group techniques; more reliance on non-guidance colleagues and other specialized manpower resources; greater use of support personnel; and improved supervision.

—More rapid progress toward professionalization can be made through actions aimed at improving accountability, taking more steps to innovate, expanding research, and playing a more active role in formulating policies and programs aimed at meeting the needs of the public for improved services.

17

ADVICE

TO THE PUBLIC

NO OCCUPATIONAL group is in charge of its own destiny. Its activities are circumscribed by law and by public attitudes and actions. For example, governmental action is required to implement three of the major recommendations made to the guidance profession in the last chapter: the elimination of the requirement of teaching experience for school counselors; interdiction of the expansion of guidance into the public elementary school; and expansion of guidance services to young and mature adults.

Other recommendations which we advanced require help from the public if they are to be effectively implemented: making career guidance the critical concern of the profession; enabling guidance personnel to be primarily concerned with client needs rather than with organizational objectives; redirecting the use of many existing guidance resources toward women and minority groups; and tapping into new manpower sources to expand the effectiveness and efficiency with which guidance services are rendered. For each end public understanding and support are crucial.

It may be helpful to stipulate at this point the major groups to which the recommendations in this chapter are addressed. Present and potential clients are important, as are families, because much of guidance is directed toward children and young people. A practitioner's success often depends on his client's understanding of the scope and limits of his own capacities and on his client's ability and willingness to cooperate in achieving a particular objective. A patient cannot expect his physician to cure him and keep him healthy if he does not follow the regimen laid out for him. In every service, the outcome depends on the cooperation of the client in a mutual relationship, and order of his family as well.

The educational establishment in which the majority of guidance personnel work and will continue to work is the second important group. Many in the educational hierarchy consider guidance personnel part of a large and growing group of ancillary manpower that is available to the superintendent and the principals to keep their schools functioning more smoothly. As Ralph Tyler has stated in his insightful piece in *Agenda for the Nation,* the scale and complexity of the educational enterprise are so overwhelming that educators have forgotten that the schools are not an end in themselves but exist to serve students.[1] The future of guidance will depend in large measure on the understanding, sympathy, and support that it is able to elicit from the educational leadership. School counselors will have a unique function only if, and to the extent that, the educational hierarchy accepts and furthers their role as facilitators of student progress through the institution and beyond.

Federal, state, and local government, mainly because of their control over budget, will determine both the directions and the scale of guidance. But the reach of government is more extensive. For instance, governmental units are the direct employers of the overwhelming majority of guidance counselors, from those employed in the Veterans Administration to those hired by a local school board. State governments control licensing and credentialing. As the principal sponsors of higher education, they likewise exercise a major influence on the education and training of guidance counselors. The federal government underwrites the Federal-State Employment Service, which is the major institution for counseling adults. The U.S. Department of Labor (with help from state and local government) collects most of the information which the field uses, and the U.S. Office of Education in the Department of Health, Education and Welfare has various responsibilities for guidance services in rehabilitation and vocational education, for financing the principal subsidized programs of counselor education, and for supporting experimental computerized systems. In addition, this agency serves as the conduit of funding to the states and localities for programs in elementary and secondary education, some of which are directed to guidance.

In meeting its large-scale needs for military manpower, the federal government is involved in four types of guidance efforts related to the recruitment, educational improvement, retention, and separation of servicemen. The Veterans Administration is responsible for guiding ex-servicemen.

Profit-making enterprises have some limited leverage. They produce much of the occupational information available. Recently, usually with the stimulus of federal financing, they have been involved in experiments devoted to the development of computerized guidance systems. There are a limited number of profit-making organizations which provide guidance services to the public for a fee, particularly in relation to college admission and job placement. Also, large corporate enterprises have just begun to explore the potentialities of guidance for their own personnel to facilitate the adjustment of the hard-to-employ and to assist those who are approaching retirement. Although these efforts are relatively small at present, there may well be substantial growth in the future.

The last critical centers of influence are the non-profit organizations. They were responsible for launching vocational guidance and they have always made significant contributions. A limited number of community agencies and universities provide guidance services to the public, usually on a sliding fee basis; private universities play an important role in counselor education; foundations have supported experimental and research efforts; and governmental agencies have contracted with this sector to undertake research, demonstration, and service programs.

To recapitulate, these are the principal leverage points outside of guidance itself that can have a major influence on restructuring the field:

Clients and their families
The educational establishment

Federal, state, and local governments
Private enterprise
Non-profit organizations

The recommendations that we will now present and discuss are directed to one or more of the foregoing groups, since they are in a position to implement them or to help to implement them. Most of our recommendations will require cooperation among these groups, together with the support of the guidance profession itself.

We will begin with a discussion of the public's expectations of guidance. We have argued that there are significant margins where effective guidance services can make a difference in the work and lives of young people and adults. But we have stressed that guidance should not be looked upon as a cure-all for the malfunctioning of the family, the school, or the labor market, because only disappointment and frustration will ensue from an overevaluation of its potential.

On occasion, Congress has acted as if guidance, instead of being a facilitating service, could be relied upon alone to alter career outcomes. If legislators are short of money or do not want to increase their appropriations, that is their right and privilege. But they should not delude themselves or attempt to delude the public that modest additional expenditures for guidance can fill a major breach in the performance capabilities of the school to teach effectively or the job market to provide adequate employment.

Parents and young people often have false expectations of guidance which derive from the guidance leadership itself. The school counselor can encourage and help some young people who are seeking to clarify their educational and career goals. But most of those who can be helped are youngsters with expressed interests who are ready to search. Exceptionally skillful counselors may acquire allies (teachers, administrators, parents) in their attempt to change the atmosphere of the school in the direction of a heightened concern with educational achievement and career development, and they may thus be able to encourage more young people to make better educational and vocational decisions. Parents who are concerned about the career development of their children should encourage schools to make this the center of their guidance programs and lend their aid and support to move in this direction.

If parents are to play a more active and constructive role several preconditions must exist. First, they must be organized into effective parent associations or into some similar arrangement which will insure that their voices will be heard and listened to by those with the authority to act. Next they must have access to information about how the guidance staff spends its time and some indication of the outcomes. The parent group must also have a nucleus of informed persons within its own ranks or advising it so that it can understand what a career-oriented guidance program might be expected to accomplish and the alternative ways in which it might realize its goals. Parents must be better informed about the potentialities and limitations of various testing programs for guidance.

Some persons who face serious career problems may expect too little from guidance. We know from the manpower efforts directed at the hard-to-employ during the last decade that many people who need help most do not apply to agencies where help is available because they do not want to risk still another defeat. Improved outreach can often help. While guidance alone is seldom able to provide all the answers these people need, it is often an important supplemental tool in connection with training and placement services. Greater understanding is needed about what can be reasonably expected of guidance by the public.

With respect to expectations, therefore, more effort is needed to assure that the concerned segments of the public—providers and users alike—recognize that guidance can make a contribution to improved career decision-making and work adjustment of many persons, but it cannot compensate for the ineffective performance of major preparatory and employing institutions.

If guidance were accorded its correct role, that of a facilitating mechanism which can contribute to improved career decision-making and adjustment, and were not considered a cure-all for complex personal and social inadequacies, it might receive more support for its actual potential and generate less frustration because of its inability to accomplish the impossible.

An arena where the governmental and private sectors play an important role in the provision of guidance services is the broad field of information for counselors and clients. While, as we have noted, every individual constantly is collecting information about the world about him, we are referring here to formal sources of information about education, jobs, and careers.

We are concerned with two aspects of educational and occupational information primarily—availability and use. The lack of availability of information is largely the fault of the compilers and purveyors of information, particularly the federal government. The inadequate use of information can be ascribed in large measure to the guidance field, which has neglected this function in its training and practice; however, often the producers have also been at fault in this regard because of unimaginative presentation of materials.

The chief producer of occupational information is the U.S. Department of Labor. While most government material is superior to privately published information in terms of cost and validity, the content and presentation of the Department's data have deficiencies which have been discussed in Chapter 12. Furthermore, there is a demonstrable lack of coordination in output among the various governmental agencies engaged in production and dissemination of data. We believe that the production of occupational information is the responsibility of the federal government, supplemented by state and local efforts, because the government accumulates most of the requisite data and because it is to the government's interest that its citizens be well-informed about work opportunities. Therefore, we recommend that more attention be paid to the ways in which various branches of government can best contribute to a coordinated and efficient information apparatus.

The *Occupational Outlook Handbook*, published by the U.S. Department of Labor, is the principal source of occupational information for guidance. Its limitations as a guidance resource include the following: it does not provide counselor or client with local or regional information about present and prospective job opportunities; it is written in a style that does not attract many terminal high school students; it is not an instrument designed to make either counselor or client aware of alternative portals of entry into work and their implications. Except for minor improvements, the format of the *Handbook* has not been changed during the twenty years that it has been published.

We recommend therefore that a broadly based committee be established by the Secretary of Labor consisting of representatives

of his own Department, members from major federal agencies such
as the Departments of Defense, HEW, Veterans Administration,
National Science Foundation, and representatives of state governments, the guidance profession, foundations and community agencies, private communications enterprises, trade unions, and representatives of the consuming public, in order to review the need for
objective job and career information and the extent to which this
need is being met; to delineate what additional information should
be collected and by whom; and to consider the ways and means of
adapting these materials for local and regional purposes. Since
information-gathering, particularly on a continuing basis, is costly,
the committee should formulate two program recommendations:
minimum and desirable. It should distinguish between counselor
and client users of information and among clients of different ages
and education and it should use these distinctions as guidelines
for their deliberations.

There have been studies and recommendations related to various
facets of information-gathering and dissemination, such as the
Report by the Advisory Committee on Research to the U.S. Employment Service in 1968.[2] But there has been no broad-scale
consideration of the informational needs of all types of clients. In the
meantime, information activities have been fragmented within and
without the government and this has led to overlapping, inadequate
coverage, and hit-or-miss utilization.

The best data in the world are wasted if they are unused. Therefore, hand in hand with a delineation of the necessary information
must be a consideration of how to insure that potential users will
in fact use it. With regard to the current experimental programs
involving the computerization of information, we doubt whether
at the present time the computer can make the fundamental contribution to information dissemination visualized by its protagonists.
Even if we disregard the critical problem of updating data inputs,
the cost of computer installations can be justified only if they are
in constant use. Yet large numbers of high school students, for
whom most of these efforts are designed, are notoriously uncon-
cerned about serious career exploration and, while they may try
a computer as a new gadget, it is questionable whether many would
make effective use of it. While young people who are college-bound

and mature adults might be more willing to use a computer capability for career information and decision-making, we must recognize that at present and probably for a considerable time to come, the "software" is likely to be so deficient that computerization will remain a promise rather than a reality even if the financial barrier could be pierced.

On the other hand, printed and audio-visual media are worth improving; they cost much less to produce and they are worth having available even if they are not utilized by all students. Audio-visual presentations, in particular, appear especially useful for those persons who have reading difficulties and for the many more who, because of the pervasiveness of television in their lives, are more attuned to such presentations than to the written word. The government has produced some materials of this sort, but the committee we have recommended forming should also consider the variety of ways that this effort can be improved and supplemented by private and public undertakings.

In the meantime, we recommend that the government defer further investment in computer systems. If private concerns wish to experiment in this area, this is their prerogative and they may well arrive at economical and imaginative solutions. Local school systems might facilitate such experimentation by entering into cooperative purchasing arrangements which would provide a larger market for private enterprise.

We see a priority need for the federal government to work in close association with the states for the systematic collection and distribution of information directed primarily to counselors with selective adaptations for clients about all post-secondary educational and training institutions in each major labor market, and in more sparsely populated areas on a regional basis. At present, to quote the National Industrial Conference Board, there is a "program jungle" of governmental and non-governmental efforts whose numbers and character are constantly changing.[3] These include private business, technical, and trade schools; apprenticeship programs; institutional training programs in the public, non-profit, and corporate sectors; corporate in-service training; and governmental training programs directed at particular population groups. Information about these programs is not easy to collect and even more difficult to evaluate, yet counselors and clients have urgent need to know about such opportunities in order to assure their optimum use.

A related body of information that needs to be kept current pertains to financial aid that is available for study and the conditions governing its allocation. Here local and even regional information may not suffice. The National Negro Scholarship Fund has for many years informed Negro graduates of Southern segregated high schools about college scholarships in predominantly white institutions, but this has been a specially tailored effort. Many youngsters from low-income and minority families with a diversity of talents and interests—academic, artistic, athletic—graduate from high school every year without knowing about opportunities that could have life-long consequences.

We recommend therefore that one of the foundations explore the most effective ways of improving the dissemination and utilization of current information about financial aid so that it will come to the attention of young people outside the main academic stream.

Many guidance counselors and their clients have an imperfect understanding of the ways in which the educational, training, and labor-market structures actually operate. In recent years Congress has made small appropriations to the Department of Labor and larger but still modest appropriations to the Department of Health, Education and Welfare to stimulate research into the critical areas of how people prepare for work, enter, and adjust to it. But we know too little about these processes, and what we do know often filters down slowly if at all to the guidance profession. The National Manpower Advisory Committee recommended some time ago that Congress allocate about 2 per cent of the annual appropriation for each of its major training programs for research, since this is the only hope for our moving from rehabilitation to prevention.[4] We strongly question the suggestion of Congresswoman Edith Green during the 1970 Congressional hearings on appropriations for education and guidance that in light of the stringency of program funds, all appropriations for research be stricken until the budget eases.[5]

The matter involves more than federal funding for research. The major educational and training systems have an obligation to learn much more about the people who go through their hands. Many do not have reliable data about their dropouts; others know little about their graduates. Responsible administrators of preparatory institutions should take steps early to remedy at least those information deficiencies that cost little to rectify. Employers should also be willing to contribute more information about the world of work, including whom they hire, train, promote, or separate.

Improved information is basic to improved guidance and much remains to be done. To recapitulate:

—The U.S. Department of Labor should establish a broadly based committee to review the unmet needs of counselors and clients for objective job and career information and to recommend the best ways to present it.

—At the present time the federal government should make no more funds available for experimentation with computerized guidance systems and should leave further development to the private sector.

—An intensified federal-state effort should be made to collect and distribute systematic information about all post-high school educational and training institutions primarily on a labor-market basis.

—Foundations should explore how current information about financial aid, at the national, regional, and local levels, for study in both academic and non-academic fields, can be made more readily available to counselors and prospective students.

—Federal and state governments and foundations should expand research funds for the study of the world of work, particularly of the operations of the labor market and for longitudinal studies of career development.

—More effort should be devoted to translating relevant research findings into materials that practitioners can use.

—Responsible officials of the principal educational, training, and employment structures should collect, analyze, and make available on a recurrent basis information about the people they train and employ.

Among the challenges people encounter during both their training periods and their working lives is to understand the alternate paths from one institution to another. Guidance must constantly attempt to facilitate transitions from one level of school to the next, from school to job training, from civilian life to the Armed Forces, from school to work, from training to work, from home to work, from job to job, and from work to retirement. These are the principal transfers, and the effectiveness of a guidance system can be enhanced if the public helps to clarify these linkages.

To illustrate briefly: it is an error for parents to leave the career guidance of their children completely to the school counselor. Even if there were more counselors and they were better trained, youngsters would still need parental and other inputs. The importance of parental and community involvement in the school in general and in the guidance effort in particular is heightened when the larger environment contains broadening opportunities. Thus, blacks today are taking increased interest in their children's schooling because of the new options that have become available to them.

The operation of schools remains largely the responsibility of local government. But local control does not mean that guidance personnel should be left to their own devices. Every community expects the schools to prepare its children to function successfully in the larger world. The board of education as the representative of the local taxpayers has the obligation to insure that career guidance proffered in the schools is current, reliable, and relevant. If it is unable or unwilling to do so, parents might want to consider alternative ways of providing guidance services to their young, including taking guidance out of the school and locating it in a community agency.

There is another critical issue. In many school systems, the personal records of students, which include materials that were acquired in confidence, follow each pupil from grade to grade. This breach of confidence raises questions relating to the protection of individual rights and to public morality.

All school personnel—and guidance counselors in particular, as self-defined student advocates—have a responsibility to review their policy with respect to pupil records. Parents should be aware that in many states they have the right to see their children's records and they should press for this right where it does not now exist. We support the recommendation of the Massachusetts Advisory Council on Education that school counselors refrain from making subjective assessments of students for any post-secondary institutional, educational or employment. If counselors seek the full trust of their clients, they must not be judgmental.

We have called attention to one way in which guidance counselors, particularly in the educational system, can increase their resources and improve their performance, which is to use the latent manpower resources of the community, particularly those in the world of work, to help students engaged in career explorations. While the guidance staff should take the initiative in this regard, the fact remains that many do not know how, or are too timid, or simply do not think that the effort would be worthwhile. In vocational education, advisory boards have long had a role to play with respect to curriculum, and while many have not discharged this responsibility effectively, a minority have done so. Recently, large corporations have begun to "adopt" certain ghetto schools and have assisted with the guidance and particularly the training and employment of many young people who leave the educational system. Because of the tendency of schoolmen to keep the community at arm's length and to consider the community as apart from the total educational experience, it is essential for business, labor, and other key institutions in the world of work to determine what they might be able to contribute to the career development of young people and to take the initiative in establishing a relationship with the educational system in order to set up effective advisory committees and to provide opportunities for work exposure and experiences.

We have noted that many local Employment Offices have worked out relationships with schools in their localities which have made it possible for their staffs to provide group testing, group counseling, and a limited amount of individual counseling for members of the senior class. We recommend that, as the guidance resources of the Employment Service are expanded and improved (as recommended below), school authorities facilitate liaison between their guidance staffs and those of the Employment Service.

In many countries, such as Great Britain, Sweden, Germany, where there has been a much more sustained and aggressive effort to facilitate the transition of young people from school to work, an unsolved issue has been the respective responsibilities of school and employment office staffs. As we have indicated, we do not believe that the school counselor, particularly in a metropolitan area, can become an effective employment counselor and we therefore recommend that the primary responsibility in this regard be placed on a strengthened guidance operation in the Employment Service—but with improved liaison with all high schools rather than, as at present, with only some. Moreover, to be effective, such liaison must be initiated before students are in their senior year. Clearly a substantially strengthened youth guidance program centered in the Employment Service will require public support as well as public financing. We also recommend that programs designed to acquaint school counselors with the workings of the Employment Service be expanded both during training and later. Resources should be made available by the Employment Service, and school systems should encourage counselors to spend their summer vacations in an Employment Office.

The Armed Forces also have had entrée over the years to a large number of high schools where they have had an opportunity to work with the guidance staffs and recruit interested seniors. They too have been doing group testing in the schools. The public issues involved are whether this practice is sound and should be continued; the criteria the Armed Forces use to select or neglect schools; and the place of draft counseling.

As long as the Military Training and Service Act remains in force, there is no reason that discussion of the Armed Forces as a career, or as a stage in a career, should not be part of a high school guidance program. Insofar as draft options are concerned, we agree with the member of the New York City Board of Education who stated that the real challenge in this area is to insure that all young men in high school have an opportunity to obtain objective information about the Selective Service law so that they can weigh it in formulating and carrying out their career plans.[6] Clearly this will come about only if the public recognizes the importance of the draft for career planning and insists that it be incorporated into school guidance service. Without strong public pressure, the educators will not do this. Since the draft is a critical factor in career planning, we recommend that draft counseling be incorporated into school guidance programs, except where the student body so distrusts the establishment that an alternative community effort is preferable.

It is also important to assist veterans in their transition back to civilian life. In recent years the Armed Forces have expanded their separation counseling, but they are often unable to provide effective help since most men want to return to their home communities and want to know about opportunities there. Broad generalizations about job and career trends will not help them unless it relates to their entitlements and benefits under the GI Bill or unless, as with Project TRANSITION, they are willing to enter training while still in uniform, with an eye to eventual employment.

The American people have always felt a special obligation toward the veteran, particularly the combat veteran, and the current and prospective release of large numbers of them to civilian life points up the need for improved services. We therefore recommend that the Secretary of Labor, after consultation with the Veterans Administration and other appropriate governmental and non-governmental groups, take early action to strengthen the career guidance services available to veterans.

One important transformation in recent years has taken place in the Employment Service, as it became more heavily engaged in assisting the hard-to-employ. Its employees have been pressed to get out of the office and into the community and to work cooperatively with other agencies. This trend should be encouraged by government administrators and by community representatives. In many instances, meaningful guidance services for the hard-to-employ can be provided only as part of a larger rehabilitation program which might include health, legal, and educational services.

The movement under way to encourage the states and, *pari passu,* the larger cities, to develop a manpower planning and coordinating council under the Manpower Development and Training Act would provide an important new mechanism for improved linkages between the Employment Service and other concerned and involved groups and organizations. Such a council should encourage the implementation of the directive of the 1963 Vocational Education Act which obligated vocational educators to look to the Employment Service for labor-market trends for curriculum building and review and for information needed by their guidance services. Since these are two powerful bureaucracies, it will require strong leadership on the part of governors and strong community pressures to improve these critical services so as to speed effective liaison between the Employment Service and vocational education programs.

In considering any aspect of labor-market behavior in the United States, including the operation of guidance services for adults, one must take into account the antagonism toward the Employment Service characteristic of most large employers and the disinterest of organized labor in its operations. Nevertheless, we recommend that the Employment Service explore how it might cooperate with the Social Security Administration, employers, and trade unions and begin to provide orientation and retirement counseling to the rapidly increasing number of older workers. We recommend that a foundation finance an exploratory investigation of the need for the guidance and counseling of older workers to determine how existing institutions, private and public, might more effectively provide it, whether additional structures are required, and how they can best be put into place.

This account of how public concern, interest, and support could help to bring about more effective linkages between key institutions and thereby contribute to more effective guidance services has been selective, not inclusive. Among our principal findings and recommendations are these:

—Parents, sometimes individually but primarily collectively, must be involved in the direction, scope, and emphasis of school guidance services.

—Interested community leaders, especially in business and labor, should take the initiative in making themselves available to assist in school guidance programs.

—The Employment Service, working in closer liaison with the schools, should provide improved transitional services for terminal high school students.

—The military should have continued access to high school seniors to describe military options; in addition, draft counseling should be added to high school guidance services.

—The present structure of guidance services for veterans should be strengthened.

—Closer liaison at state and local level should be maintained between the Employment Service and other manpower and manpower-related agencies.

—Foundation support should be elicited for the establishment of a model of guidance and counseling services for older workers as they approach retirement.

In the remainder of this chapter, we will attempt to specify as clearly as possible our additional recommendations to the several branches of government which, as noted earlier, have the major leverage to alter the scale, scope, and quality of the guidance services to which the American people have access.

We will start with current practices but we will not, of course, be bound by them. School guidance grew slowly but steadily under the impetus of increased state and local expenditures for education. Many communities, especially the affluent suburbs and the large cities, now consider guidance a desirable, even necessary, service which can help the schools achieve their primary mission of providing educational opportunities for every child. Since 1958, the federal government has provided major financial assistance for the training and upgrading of school counselors and it has provided grants for strengthening existing guidance services and experimenting with new programs. The 1970 Congressional hearings on appropriations for the Departments of Labor and Health, Education and Welfare had to consider the administration's recommendation that no specific funding be made for guidance and that a reduced grant be made for a series of other educational services. During the course of the hearings, the following points were made by witnesses:

—One counselor in every ten is paid out of NDEA Title V funds.

—In its early years NDEA supported guidance counseling and enabled many schools to provide a service that theretofore had been limited to a few localities.

—After the mid-1960s, federal funding of guidance steadily decreased until the burden fell almost entirely on the local education budget, which was already overburdened by other demands.

—In 1967, when the federal contribution for guidance was $24 million (Title V money), the local contribution was over $252 million.

—To withdraw the federal "seed" money at this critical time would have a disastrous psychological effect on the willingness of communities to support guidance and would result in decreased services.

—During the first half of the 1960s, annual federal appropriations

were in the $14.5 million range; in 1965, they were increased
to $20 million and for the three years following, to about $24.3
million. In 1969, they dropped to $17 million or 69 per cent of
the authorized sum; and, as noted above, the administration
recommended no specific funding for 1970 while the Congressional authorization for that year was $40 million!

From this testimony, as well as from other sources, we can see
that federal financing had a considerable impact upon the expansion
of school guidance service in the 1960s. Its primary leverage was to
strengthen the supervisory efforts at state level, to train counselors,
and to support programs at the local level.

So much for the past. What should be the stance of the federal
government toward the future financing of school guidance? With
respect to the financing of guidance services in junior and senior
high school, we believe that in general the federal government
should not be directly involved. It became involved in response to
the public's distress at the Russians' launching of Sputnik, but this
is no justification for its remaining in the picture. Nevertheless, since
many state legislatures meet only biennially, we believe that it
would be destructive for the federal government to make radical
changes without giving the states due warning.

If the federal government continues to provide special funds to
help improve the quality of the educational services available to
targeted populations, we agree with the administration that such
funds should not be specifically mandated by the Congress to guidance or other services but that their distribution should be left to
the states and localities under broad federal guidelines. We understand the fear of the guidance leadership that the educational establishment might exclude guidance. This issue should be decided not
in the halls of Congress but closer to home. If a school district is
short of modern textbooks, it might be better for the authorities to
use the "extra" money to purchase them than to hire one additional
school counselor.

We have strongly urged that no additional public money be put
into elementary school guidance until many other guidance needs
are met. We repeat that recommendation here and note that one
of the reasons the guidance establishment is interested in federal
"seed" money is exactly because it can be used to expand guidance

in elementary schools. Consequently, if the federal government is to leave the financing of routine guidance services to other levels of government, this would have the benefit of shrinking a movement which we believe to be badly conceived and poorly executed.

We view with some concern the fact that so much of the money that guidance has received from the government has been used for mass testing programs. We question whether many of these tests can add to the effectiveness of a guidance program. Their rationale lies more in the educational realm than in the domain of guidance. We believe that additional government funds should be spent for improving the staffing of guidance programs and for their informational resources, rather than for testing.

The role of the federal government in financing the education of school counselors is more complicated. We believe that it was an error for the federal government to reinforce the requirement that all school counselors be teachers by limiting NDEA assistance to persons with teaching licenses. Moreover, more NDEA programs have been directed at upgrading the guidance staff than at adding to the supply of new counselors trained in a professional full-time program.

We do not believe that the federal government should indefinitely finance the upgrading or basic training of school counselors. A program that has more merit and is more consistent with the actions of the federal government in other shortage areas of professional manpower is to use federal funds to increase the training of a professional leadership cadre for teaching, research, and administration. The government has underwritten various fellowship programs. We recommend that it shift more funds away from practitioner to faculty training. We recommend, moreover, that it eliminate the requirement of teaching experience for eligibility. Support for this recommendation is the shared concern of all people informed about the shortcomings currently prevaling in many counselor-training institutions.

The federal government is involved in other guidance and counseling training programs which are conducted under separate appropriations for the Veterans Administration, the National Institute of Mental Health, and the Vocational Rehabilitation Administration. These are long-established programs geared to two-year full-time training programs plus supervised field study or to the doctorate. These programs pass muster, especially since a fair proportion of the graduates are employees in mandated federal guidance programs.

We do not agree with the recommendation of the 1967 Interagency Task Force that the federal government, in addition to continuing to underwrite these training programs, undertake a new one in which it would pay for the one-year full-time graduate education of all guidance and counseling personnel. We can find no basis for singling out guidance personnel to receive such training support in the face of established federal policy which has been, and in our opinion should continue to be, more selective by centering on stipends for advanced graduate training.

Moreover, we do not agree with the Task Force that the federal government should make experimental and demonstration grants for the purpose of training support personnel. We believe that the large number of state-controlled community colleges offer ample opportunity to experiment in developing special curricula. However, our preference is for emphasis upon on-the-job training. Moreover, we believe that the nub of this issue is not training, but the willingness of agencies to hire and use support personnel and that federal grants for training would only muddy further the already murky waters.

There is one problem that might be eased if the federal government were to increase substantially its appropriations for across-the-board training of guidance counselors. We refer to the difficulties that the states face in attracting, upgrading, and retaining adequate numbers of guidance specialists. This deficiency is serious because we expect, as indicated earlier, that the Employment Service will play a large and strategic role in the priority area of expanded services for youths and adults. To help the states meet this manpower problem, we recommend increased Congressional appropriations to enable the Employment Service to:

Undertake more in-service training

Cover the tuition costs for extramural training

Grant leaves of absence for one year for full-time study for guidance counselors who have demonstrated superior performance.

The strengthening of the Employment Service's capability to provide more and better guidance and counseling services cannot possibly be accomplished solely, or even primarily, by subsidizing the training of its existing staff. The Employment Service must be able to offer better salaries; it must be able to provide more opportunity for guidance counseling; and there must be more of a career ladder before it can expect to attract and retain a stronger staff of guidance personnel.

For the Employment Service to move rapidly in this direction requires, *inter alia:*

—An expressed commitment by the Congress, with supporting financing, that improved guidance services for youth and adults is a priority task for the Employment Service.

—Additional staff personnel for the U.S. Department of Labor to enable it to provide leadership in the guidance field.

—Authority for the U.S. Department of Labor to establish minimum standards throughout the Employment Service with regard to hiring and promotion of guidance personnel and to the quality of services to be provided.

With respect to the range of problems dealt with in this and the preceding chapter, state governments have considerable leverage to affect outcomes. Many have failed to take any leadership with respect to the improvement of guidance services; some have done a little; no state has moved on all the fronts where it could take constructive action. Yet most states are in a position to exercise major influence on local school systems. We will outline below the principal affirmative state actions which can improve the level of guidance services:

—Mandate that guidance be provided by all public junior and senior high schools and junior and senior colleges and provide financial assistance where necessary.

—Establish a supervisory unit to oversee all school guidance and to stress accountability.

—Help to make career guidance the major commitment of school counselors.

—Take no action to encourage the introduction of guidance services into elementary schools.

—Eliminate the teaching requirement for certification of school counselors.

—Act to strengthen the institutions responsible for the training of guidance personnel, particularly school and employment counselors.

—Strengthen the guidance operations of the State Employment Services by offering more professional opportunities and higher salary levels, and encourage improved linkages between the Employment Service, the schools, community agencies, and employers.

—Cooperate with federal and local governmental agencies to improve the quality of career information available for the use of counselors and clients.

While this chapter has been largely concerned with the ways in which the federal and state governmental machinery can and must be used to improve the quantity and quality of guidance services available to the American people, we do not consider that government is the sole instrumentality for channeling public opinion, pressure, and support directed to this objective. We have called attention in passing to the contribution that foundations have made and can continue to make to explore new functions. We have noted that parents should organize themselves so that they may be able to lean more successfully against a rigid bureaucratic educational structure. We have called attention to the desirability that employers, trade unions, and other community groups take the initiative vis-à-vis the schools to play a larger role in the guidance and counseling of young people.

We offer this brief recapitulation to underscore our belief that critical as is the role of government in the reform of guidance, there is a place—an important place—for non-governmental organizations in this effort. We say that if the improvement of guidance is seen solely, or even primarily, as a function of governmental appropriations of larger sums and of government officials' use of them as they have in the past, progress will indeed be slow.

The burden of this book is to stress the need for redirection of guidance through the establishment of priorities for expansion and for improved supervision and accountability. None of these objectives can be accomplished without the active and continuing participation of the public. Certainly, a higher level of governmental financing is needed if guidance services are to be improved. But we believe that additional financing must be part of a larger program of structural and operational reform. And these reforms will be made only if the public makes them a condition for additional support.

The several recommendations advanced in this chapter can be summarized as follows:

—The public must realize that while guidance can make a contribution to improved career development, it can never compensate for the malfunctioning of the basic preparatory and employing institutions.

—Improved information is basic to improved guidance, and the federal government, in association with the states, should provide relevant data, particularly about educational and training opportunities in every major labor-market area.

—More research about labor-market institutions and operations should be financed by government and foundations and the findings adapted to enable guidance specialists to develop a better understanding of career development.

—The quality of guidance services can be enhanced by improving linkages between parents, employers, the Employment Service, and the local schools and between the Employment Service and the Armed Forces, the Veterans Administration, community agencies, and employer groups.

—The federal government should no longer be directly involved in the financing of school guidance except as part of special bloc grant funds for educational services to targeted populations; it should shift its present support for counselor education in the direction of more fellowships for advanced professional training; it should not implement the 1967 Interagency Task Force recommendation of a new federally financed training program; it should make more funds available to the Employment Service to facilitate the recruitment and retention of competent staff and otherwise strengthen its operations; it should increase its support for information gathering and dissemination and for educational and labor market research.

—State governments should mandate and help finance guidance services in all public junior and senior high schools and junior and senior colleges; eliminate the requirement of a teaching

license for certification for school counseling; discourage the
introduction of guidance into elementary schools; strengthen
supervisory structures for guidance and insist on greater
accountability; improve counselor training institutions;
strengthen Employment Services; and use their newly emerging manpower planning structures to facilitate liaison among
guidance-related institutions.

—The improvement of guidance services also hinges on the
concern and capabilities of various voluntary organizations, including foundation and community agencies, of business and
trade unions, to play an active and continuing part in charting
new directions for guidance and in working closely with government agencies to follow them.

18

TRANSFORMATIONS

AHEAD

GUIDANCE IS a mediating service. It seeks to help people find their way through established institutions so that they can better realize their aims and goals. But the people whom guidance seeks to assist live within a dynamic social and economic structure and as it changes their opportunities and their values undergo change. The effectiveness of guidance depends in the first instance on an understanding of the parameters of this changing structure and the way it can affect the formation and realization of goals.

In this concluding chapter we will seek to sketch the environment within which guidance is likely to operate in the decade immediately ahead. Rather than make long-range forecasts which cannot take into account developments that are still in gestation, we will focus on the next decade and concentrate on imminent trends and transformations whose roots already exist.

In the past guidance has failed to realize its goals because of the gap between its postulates and the world of reality. For instance, the founders of vocational guidance had little awareness that the problems created by child laborers would be solved when the school-leaving age was raised. The enthusiasts of the early 1920s whose energies were directed to improving techniques to match men and jobs were unprepared to meet the critical problem of the 1930s, which was the almost total absence of jobs for new entrants into the labor force. And as soon as the field explored how to narrow the gap between the expectations of young people and the realities of the job market, the economy took off on a vast expansion of opportunities which altered the level of aspirations.

Then came the post-World War II period with high levels of employment and a growing affluence which produced a favorable background for the transformation of vocational guidance into counseling psychology, with its emphasis on the development of the whole individual. After this change was ensconced, our society belatedly became aware of the large numbers of victims of poverty and discrimination for whom the gospel of self-concept and self-development was a mockery since they had little opportunity to shape their own lives.

Once again, in the late 1960s, guidance reverted to its earlier interests and concerns to help people improve their educational and career development. A more active stance was taken by those who sought to provide some leadership to the community with respect to the institutional reforms which were a prerequisite if the disadvantaged were to be able to see the promise of options turned into a reality.

We will begin with a consideration of the major value transformations in our society which are affecting large groups of people. Next we shall discuss how well the principal institutions involved in preparation for employment are functioning. We will then consider forces that are likely to affect the selection and pursuit of careers and how accretions to knowledge and developments in technology may affect the ways in which guidance operates. Finally we will consider certain potential developments which may alter the balance between private and public action and thereby set new challenges for guidance.

We know that we cannot foresee in detail the structure and operations of guidance in the year 1980. But we hope that the sketch which follows will provide the reader, the profession, and those who make resources available with a better understanding of the environment within which guidance must function in the coming years.

We will first consider the changing contours of *values* that are affecting the orientation of youth, of people in mid-career, and of workers approaching retirement.

In the case of youth, it is difficult to sort out the elements of continuity from those of change. Conflict, alienation, revolutionary activity, idol-smashing have always been characteristic of a minority of young people. But it is difficult to know whether the numbers involved in anti-establishment activities have vastly increased and whether our society faces a significant discontinuity in values between generations.

Let us see what is known before we begin to speculate. Many of the younger generation assume that there will be jobs available whenever they need or want to work. Large numbers of youths know that they can look forward to a period of support from home which will permit them to delay making definitive decisions about the future. Moreover, young people at the lower end of the social and economic scale realize that if they do not work, they will still eat. Survival without working for pay is a new phenomenon.

This is also the first generation to be exposed without interruption, from its earliest years, to the saccharine and discordant themes that preempt television. It would be strange indeed if this ceaseless indoctrination does not establish a heightened tension between the inherited verity that rewards come only from hard work and the version of the easy life perceived on the screen by impressionable young people. In fact, many of them have a case example before their eyes in the lives of their parents, that hard work may —and often does—end in frustration. Today's youth are worldly, if not wise.

Throughout childhood, adolescence, and young adulthood, this generation has been exposed to omnipresent impersonal organizations—schools, universities, the Armed Forces, corporations. Many youth have become alienated and disaffected, and although much of their challenge to the establishment is generic, much of it has new dimensions. We do not pretend to know what the new challenge implies for guidance, but it does suggest that counselors who are sympathetic toward youth are more likely to be effective than those who are critical and estranged. Moreover, guidance must recognize that the young are more likely to trust each other than to have faith in a representative of the adult world. Finally, guidance counselors must contend with the probability that many of their clients, especially during their developmental years, are not interested in shaping their lives to accomplish conventional career goals. This does not imply that they can ignore the young people who do not seek them out. Instead they have the difficult task of building new bridges to a suspicious and confused generation. For no matter what young people say or do, they are not disinterested in themselves nor in their future.

We have called attention earlier to the fact that more and more mature men and women are looking anew and critically at their careers and are opting for change. The decision to start again, often at considerable sacrifice of time and money, suggests that many people still look to their work as a major source of self-realization and satisfaction. Moreover, the tendency of an ever larger proportion of married women to leave their homes and return to work indicates that they too desire to function in settings that can provide more personal fulfillment.

In the 1930s, guidance was concerned about the gap between career aspirations and career possibilities. In the 1970s, growing tension may result from a new gap between increasingly higher levels of educational preparation and a fairly restricted number of positions that provide scope, challenge, and the full engagement of a individual's interests, capacities, and values. Once the extrinsic rewards from work, such as income and security, begin to lose importance as a consequence of growing affluence, the index of discontent may rise substantially.

A moderating force for many employees in jobs that do not fully engage their interests might be a shortened work-week and work-year which would enable them to undertake more satisfying activities in their off-the-job hours. The insistence of a growing number of young white and black professional and managerial personnel that their work schedules be arranged so that they can engage in community activities is one indication of what may lie ahead. The pressure for more three-day weekends is another. The demand for time off the job for additional education and training or for government service is still another. None of these alone may presage much change; together they suggest that many workers do not want to slide into old age without having had an opportunity to stretch themselves.

During the seventies, the first post-depression labor force will approach retirement. Most of their working lives have been spent in an expanding economy in which a man with skill was employable. Moreover, this is the first group reaching retirement age to have been part of the Social Security System throughout its working life. Many more people than in any previous decade will have substantial private pension benefits and will have accumulated considerable private assets and savings. While inflation may erode some of these protections, this will be a unique group of retirees in terms of both outlook and assets, harbingers of future cohorts who will make plans with retirement in view. Unlike their forebears, this group looks not to work followed by death, but to work followed by freely chosen activities.

We have already suggested that guidance, which has neglected adults in general and almost totally ignored older people in the transition between work and retirement, has a new objective for meaningful service. But this is a complex arena, since older people usually face a gamut of interrelated problems primarily concerning health, work, income, family conditions. While a few counselors have begun to acquire some expertise in this connection, the problem of the aging has barely entered the ken of the profession. Most of the response to this problem has yet to be made. But it can no longer be put off. In the decade of the seventies millions of men and women will reach the age of retirement. The years that remain for those who reach sixty-five represent between one-quarter and one-third of the years that a man spends at work, and are even longer for a woman. We cannot ignore this group; we must seek to assist them to find meaning and satisfaction in their later years.

In addition to the value transformations associated with different age groups, there are other important transformations related to sex and minority status. We have noted the changing relationship of women to the world of work. The substantial increase in the number and proportion of middle-class female workers who are mothers of young children reflects the emergence of new social values growing out of developments in the labor market, in education, and in the home. While women continue to be subject to discrimination both in school and the marketplace, the passage of federal anti-discrimination legislation in the sixties may have marked a significant turning point, especially as women increasingly organize to take advantage of it.

There is no evidence that the trend of increased female participation in the labor force will be reversed. On the contrary, it is likely to continue as government, business, and voluntary organizations contribute to a substantial increase in day care facilities for children of working mothers. Furthermore, the recent aggressiveness of young women in seeking prerogatives heretofore denied them may force the development of new vocational opportunities for females which will expand in the decades to come.

The increasing acceptance of women as workers represents a clear challenge to guidance. The field has paid inadequate attention to women at every stage of the career process: in curriculum and course selections, in career planning, and in assisting those who seek to return to the labor force after a period of homemaking and childbearing. We need not assume that women will have the identical career options as men to recognize that they have a great many and that they need help in realizing them.

The womanpower revolution dates from the onset of World War II. So does the Negro revolution. As we argued in *The Troublesome Presence,* more has happened to change the objective conditions of American Negroes since 1940 than in the 321 preceding years.[1] However, at the beginning of the 1970s many Negroes and other minority group members such as Mexican-Americans, Puerto Ricans, and American Indians still have major handicaps as they seek full citizenship and a larger share of the good things of American life.

Blacks disagree among themselves about the goals that they should pursue. Some continue to stress the classic aim of full integration; others are at the opposite extreme and advocate self-segregation; the largest number probably favor a more flexible strategy aimed at building and consolidating a power base to increase their leverage in gaining access to more opportunities. Regardless of differences over strategies and tactics, there is broad agreement as to interim objectives. All young blacks are determined to obtain their rights. They will no longer accept second-class citizenship.

There is near-certainty that the momentum of the black revolution will continue unabated in the seventies. This undoubtedly means a continuing reduction in discriminatory barriers to higher education and employment. The late sixties saw the beginning of a breakthrough and the seventies will unquestionably see many more Negroes attending professional and graduate schools and earning advanced degrees. Moreover, recent experience suggests that additional funds will be available to make it easier for black students to enter and complete higher education.

Counselors must be aware of the scale and magnitude of the changes in values in both the black and white communities and consequently must encourage every minority youngster with interest and ability to realize that he can obtain higher education or specialized training and that he will be in a favorable position to find a worthwhile job with a good future. Guidance counselors must avoid old stereotypes. For instance, five leaders among Negro medical students reported in 1969 that their guidance counselors had advised them against attempting to study medicine because the course was too long, too difficult and, particularly, to expensive for a student without strong financial backing.

If the bars of discrimination against blacks are lowered, it is reasonable to postulate that they will likewise give for other minority groups. However, for American Indians, particularly the 300,000 or so who are still living on reservations, the matter is more complicated, for it is not yet clear whether the Indian tribes, particularly the younger generation, want to protect their separation or speed their assimilation.[2] It is likely that the leadership of the American Indian tribes will make a stand for more self-determination and greater community control over their educational and related developmental institutions.

If this occurs, guidance for American Indians who live on reservations will inevitably pass into the hands of the Indian leadership. And that is how it should be. The white man should provide guidance only to those Indians who decide to tie their future to the life and ways of the majority. Alone among minority groups, the American Indian has an option between continued separation and accelerated integration and he alone should make the decision. The obligation of the white majority is to make resources available to Indians who opt for continued separation so that they can establish a reasonable level of employment and income on the reservations.

One generalization about the future can safely be ventured. There are enough matters in flux at present that the principal subgroups in the population, in terms of age, sex, and race, will hold values with respect to work and careers that differ from those held by earlier generations. It behooves guidance to be alert to this and to learn as much as possible about these changed values.

In addition, guidance must assume as its responsibility the task of alerting those in a position to alter and change institutions to the fact that some institutions operate to the serious disadvantage of various groups. To accomplish this it must strive constantly to increase its own autonomy. Professionals can criticize; employees cannot.

The second task of this concluding chapter is to look briefly at the principal institutions through which people pass as they prepare for and enter work and to consider how they are likely to change in the years ahead and the implications of these changes for guidance.

While the Great Society programs of the 1960s called attention to many long-neglected problems, particularly poverty, their limited success demonstrated that much more is required than good intentions and a few billion dollars of annual expenditures. The present administration has indicated that it will seek to improve the relief system and will act to supplement the incomes of families who are low on the income scale. Some Congressional spokesmen look to major innovations such as the introduction of a system of children's allowances or a negative income tax.

We cannot foresee how far or how fast Congress will move to increase the insufficient income of families at the lower end of the distribution, but we can reasonably postulate that it will move slowly, if only because of the large number of families always just above any minimum cutoff point. As a consequence poverty, however measured, will decline slowly rather than rapidly. We can expect that hunger will be eliminated and malnutrition substantially reduced, but there is little or no prospect that the poor will have access to adequate housing or that they will have margins above what they require for subsistence. This means that there will continue to be millions of children born into and reared in families who live in adverse circumstances.

We will probably continue such institutions as Head Start and may even expand them, unless there is clear evidence of their non-effectiveness, in the hope that early action will counter the adverse effects of poverty on the development of children. Nevertheless, the problem which John Fischer has contended American public education has never solved—the effective instruction of children from families on the lowest third of the income scale—will still confront us.[3] The present rigid structure is clearly inadequate. Reinforcing this structure by making more teachers and teachers' assistants available and reducing class size does not appear to be the answer.

The hope of the black leadership that greater community participation in local schools means better education for black children is not yet proved. We do not know the answer to the learning problems of socially handicapped groups, but we must keep trying to find one. In a world in which career opportunity is linked so closely to the mastery of basic intellectual skills, it would be conscienceless if rich America continues to permit a significant number of the children of the poor and of racial minorities to be doomed by the failure of the schools to perform their basic task of educating children in the early years.

This is no place to sketch more programs which might succeed where none has yet. But we can note the following favorable trends. The recent organization of urban parents on a community basis may force accountability on the ghetto school for its performance. Such organizations may bring the home and the school into a reinforcing relationship. If hunger is eliminated, it will be easier to attract and hold the attention of the young in the classroom. If teachers are prepared with more sensitivity to the background and thought-ways of their pupils, they should become more effective. If more principals are permitted by their school boards to organize ungraded classes, that may help. If the states and federal government assume more responsibility for educational financing and more resources become available, this will help. But while we must strive to reduce the educational failure rate, we must anticipate a continuing need for second-chance institutions for many years to come.

It has taken a long while for the negative concomitants of elongating the educational cycle to be thrown into relief. Informed people no longer believe that the schools, as presently structured and operated, can make a contribution to all teenagers until they graduate or reach eighteen. But desirable alternatives are lacking. Of all the industrial nations of the world, we have the least need for young workers. As a consequence, work-study programs at the high school level have grown slowly. Despite the disinterest and disinclination of employers to hire young workers, the U.S. Department of Labor recently announced an experimental school-work program in six states for fourteen- and fifteen-year-olds "who are unable to profit from a regular academic curriculum."[4] The federal regulations increased the hours of work that young people can engage in while school is in session from three to four hours a day, from eighteen to twenty-eight hours a week. The experimental program is to be supervised by one school coordinator for twelve to twenty pupils. The principal goal is to enable these non-academically oriented students to complete high school.

Another recent effort to find an alternative to classroom instruction for such students is an experiment in Philadelphia financed by the Ford Foundation to develop an educational program which makes use of the resources in the entire community and permits students to play a much larger role in determining what they learn. While it will require a considerably longer period before this experiment can be evaluated and its potential for replication assessed, one can note the large number of young people in the Philadelphia system who sought to enroll. This is evidence of what many have long believed, that latent discontent with the present educational structure runs deep among a significant group of the total student body.[5]

If the basic structure of secondary education is dysfunctional for a large proportion of all youngsters, there is little that guidance counselors can do to help except to feed back to the educational and community leadership what they learn about the unmet needs of their clients and to suggest, if they can, the type of institutional changes that might prove constructive. If there are additional experiments in the seventies, such as the two we have just described, guidance counselors will want to keep abreast of them in order to recommend one or another that appears suitable for their clients.

While the basic challenge rests with the community, not with the guidance profession, counselors have the obligation to stimulate action and help point it in the right direction. We do not have suitable developmental structures for many fourteen- to eighteen-year-olds. To hold them prisoner in the conventional high school until they are sixteen or seventeen and then to force them to fend for themselves is a mockery of everything that education connotes and a denial of our commitment to provide developmental opportunities for all young people, not just those on the academic track.

We do not believe that the expansion and improvement of vocational education at the high school level is the answer. Even in large cities it is difficult to organize, staff, and maintain quality programs. Moreover, the costs are high. In addition, the better programs require that the student have a capacity to deal with words, numbers, abstractions—just what the hard-to-educate lack.

If the American people realize that the conventional high school is unsuited to meet the needs of between a third and half of all adolescents, then they may mount the energy and the effort to design more suitable alternatives, including a closer liaison between school and the world of work. But the public would prefer to postpone the issue, since creating alternatives to the present school system is a formidable task. Since we are likely to have to struggle along with our existing inadequate structures throughout the seventies, improved liaison between the two largest concentrations of counselors—school counselors and counselors in the Employment Service—is a *sine qua non*. Individually they can do a little for the poorly prepared youth; together they should be able to do more.

Insofar as higher education is concerned, broadened access to college has expanded career opportunities for a large number of young people from middle- and low-income homes. However, high dropout rates indicate that these institutions are not meeting the expectations or the needs of a great many. Yet one aspect of opportunity is to offer the individual access to an educational, training, or employment situation and to permit him to take advantage of it or to fail.

We do not believe that it is wasteful for many more students to start college than to finish. But we believe that the dropout rates are so high that they point to shortcomings in preparation, expectations, and linkages between the precollege years and college. We further believe that more effective guidance services in high school and particularly early in a student's college experience might help him to develop a strategy that would enable him to relate his educational decisions to possible career alternatives and in the process to see more purpose to his putting out effort.

Partly as a response to the weakness in the conventional educational system, partly as a reflection of the preference of large employers to control the training of their work force, partly in response to the difficulties of the unskilled in the job market, the 1960s saw a rapid expansion in the large and amorphous training establishment that has been characteristic of our society and economy. Illustrative of this proliferating training effort is the almost $3 billion annual appropriation for federal manpower programs, up from a few hundred million dollars in the early 1960s. It is likely that we have not seen the end of this effort and that during the seventies further resources will be made available for establishing and strengthening training institutions and for expanding training opportunities for a still larger segment of the total population. The administration expects the states and localities to play a larger role in planning and operating the federally financed programs and in establishing and maintaining effective liaison with the many different groups of providers and users of training services.

We have noted that the guidance field has not been able to keep up to date with the fast-changing training network and we have recommended that the federal government, together with the states, seek to provide more comprehensive and relevant information about training opportunities on a local labor-market basis. But additional information is only a precondition for improved guidance services. Guidance specialists must have a better understanding about the ways in which different training opportunities are related to better jobs and better careers. They have been preoccupied with the college-bound and have neglected the mobility potentials that exist within the economy itself.

Among the interesting developments of the second half of the

1960s was the establishment under various auspices, but usually with governmental financing, of a considerable number of "second-chance" institutions. Many young people who fell off the educational track have been given another opportunity to earn high school diplomas, to acquire skill training, to enter college. The seventies will probably see more efforts along these lines, since many youth will continue to reach late adolescence poorly prepared for work and life. Guidance specialists must keep informed of these new paths to opportunity and help their clients use them. In addition, guidance counselors must offer help to trainees both during training and as they seek to make the transition into employment.

We have noted that the traditional sequence of school and work has given way to a great variety of patterns which involve the intermingling of education, training, and work, not only in the late teens and early twenties, but throughout a large part of a person's active life. We believe that the seventies will see even more of this because of the rapid expansion of general and technical knowledge. Guidance counselors therefore must be informed about the problems that young and mature adults face as they seek to move in and out of the educational and training establishment while they continue to work full-time, part-time, or withdraw from work for a time. This underscores a need for guidance centers outside the school milieu.

Finally, the President is committed to move at the earliest practical date to a voluntary military force. The expectation is that if he succeeds in accomplishing a basic withdrawal from Vietnam in 1971 the draft can be eliminated shortly thereafter. We know too little about the many diverse influences of the draft on the career planning of young men. But of this we can be sure: the plans of many will be restructured if the draft is suspended or abolished. Here is one more development that guidance counselors must be alert to in the years immediately ahead. And until this occurs, guidance counselors must be in a position to proffer assistance about draft alternatives.

This brings us to the third set of factors that is likely to affect guidance in the decade ahead—changes in the role of the professions, in knowledge, and in technology. A few words about each in turn. While the forecasts of enrollment for higher education may turn out to be too high, particularly if the draft is canceled early in the decade, the numbers and proportions of the appropriate age group who will graduate from junior college, college, and graduate school will continue to increase. Current estimates are that 9.6 million students will be enrolled in colleges and universities in 1975 and that 1.3 million will complete four or five years of college during that year.[6] This would represent more than a doubling in degree recipients within one decade.

The period since the end of World War II has been unusual in that the demand for college-trained personnel increased even more rapidly than did the rapidly expanding supply, with the result that wages and salaries of college-trained people were substantially improved. But is unlikely that these salaries will continue to increase in the seventies, at least for associate and baccalaureate holders; and salaries may not improve even for those with graduate degrees. The radical change in the demand for trained manpower in 1969–1970 should be read as a warning.

A reasonable assumption is that most professional fields with relatively limited requirements for specialized training will be in a preferred position to recruit. This surely ought to be so for the field of guidance, especially if the requirement of teaching experience for school counselor certification is eliminated and more opportunity is created for the employment of support personnel trained in junior college or even in high school. Moreover, it has been estimated that in 1971 there will be only two-thirds of a teaching job for each new graduate in education.[7] Consequently, many prospective education students may decide to enter other fields. Such a development would argue against the retention of the teaching prerequisite for school guidance; moreover, its elimination would encourage many students to enter counselor training instead of teacher training after college.

With regard to the financing of higher education, it is unlikely that during the seventies the federal government will agree to underwrite all college and graduate instruction or even all of the latter only. It is more likely to continue to make financing available for advanced professional education, to be supplemented perhaps by institutional grants to private colleges if their financial problems turn out to be as serious as the jeremiads insist.

If this turns out to be a correct forecast of the financing of higher education, the cherished hope of the guidance leadership that the basic course be lengthened to two years, preferably with an additional six-month internship, will make slow progress at best. A preferred objective, at least for the interim, would be full-time study for one year with supervised field work.

The prospects for the rapid expansion of a two-year full-time program depend on more than educational financing. They are interrelated with career opportunities for those who are trained. If there are more and better opportunities for guidance personnel to develop a career within guidance, there will be more trainees who are willing to make a greater sacrifice to obtain more and better training. The two are closely linked.

Another determinant is the extent to which the guidance specialist can succeed in widening his scope for self-determination and professional status. If his training is longer and more specialized and if the public appreciates his work, it is more likely that his employer will agree to his having a greater degree of freedom; if his training is longer, his commitment to his discipline should be greater and he can exert more pressure for autonomy. But the autonomy guidance seeks can best be exercised in educational and career spheres, not in a status-emulating therapy orientation.

The seventies will probably see a broad counter-trend. The American people are likely to insist on more accountability from every group that claims professional status and privileges. Guidance must expect to operate in a more critical environment. It can enlarge its scope for self-direction and self-determination only if it can demonstrate to the public that it is successfully meeting their priority needs.

On the knowledge front we can briefly note the following. Guidance can no longer continue to rely on dynamic psychology, not even on psychology itself. It must develop more sophisticated understanding of the sociology of institutions and the economics of the labor market. Manpower is a new discipline and, if the advances of the 1960s are projected, other advances will take place in the seventies which will underpin and give new direction to the work of guidance counselors. The sociology of institutions is both a matter of research and a matter of orientation. Systematic new knowledge will accumulate slowly, but a more active orientation will enable guidance to use what it learns from its clients in a constructive fashion in feedback aimed at institutional reform.

The links between guidance and psychology are certain to remain close. In this arena we can look forward to important new knowledge about early learning which should help reduce the malperformance of the elementary school. Guidance needs help from the more esoteric branches of psychology such as group psychology to reduce its reliance on the costly one-to-one counseling relationship and to take advantage of the learning and reinforcement that comes from effective group dynamics.

Similarly, it needs new knowledge about adolescents and young adults who account for so large a proportion of its total clientele. Many present assumptions about the improvement of career decision-making among adolescents are probably incorrect, and practices predicated on them are doomed because the tensions and turmoil of personality maturation during the teens have not been adequately charted and probed.

Guidance also needs more sociological insight into these strategic years. It may well be that youth will have little faith in advice proffered by adults, and guidance may have to adjust its priorities so that it can work with and through peer groups to help young people help themselves.

Guidance needs more knowledge about and insight into the complex determinants of the behavior of mature men and women, including those approaching retirement who must contemplate a radical restructuring of their lives. Here too psychology and the social sciences are making progress, but not rapidly. Nevertheless, guidance must attempt to broaden its services to the adult population.

The relations of guidance to technology are centered on the potentialities of the computer. We have indicated earlier our conviction that while the contribution of the computer to the improvement of decision-making may eventually be substantial—it *is* currently being effectively utilized for some placement purposes —there are many antecedent developments, particularly in the realm of conceptual clarification and information gathering, that must be made before the computer can become a major tool in guidance.

However, technology has a much broader sweep—from inexpensive paperbacks to expensive motion pictures. A paperback on *Career Guidance* modeled on Dr. Spock's *Baby and Child Care* would probably command wide parent as well as youth readership. Private and non-profit efforts have led to the production of effective motion pictures, some of which have had a recruiting objective for a particular industry, such as food services, while others have sought to broaden the horizon of young people about new career options in many different fields. Educational and commercial television have had little interest in utilizing career materials for informational purposes, although "What's My Line?" was one of the most successful shows in the history of the industry. While its purpose was recreational it may well have provided a clue to some viewers about unusual occupations. A more relevant example of the use of television for career purposes was the 1970 CBS program on job opportunities in New York in the electric-power industry.

It seems to us that there is no shortage of available data which can be more effectively exploited for career guidance. As the field begins to pay more attention to adults, recourse should be had to the wide range of technological aids from books to TV. We also expect that if private enterprise continues to lose money by using computers for guidance, it may experiment with less complex technologies.

A summary of our forecast for the seventies is that slow progress will be made toward further professionalization of guidance; new linkages will be made between guidance and manpower economics, organizational sociology, and diverse branches of psychology; existing media from inexpensive paperbacks to TV will be exploited with little contribution from computer systems.

This brings us to the last dimension that we will explore, the changing relations among the several sectors of society and particularly the extent to which government is likely to continue to dominate the field of guidance. Since well over 90 per cent of all guidance personnel are currently employed by government, there is little if any prospect that government will not be the dominant force in the field at the end of the seventies.

However, as the average income of the American family increases, it will be able and willing to spend more money on services. Moreover, government has been tried and found wanting in several areas where it has long had the responsibility to provide broad-scale services such as in education, health, transportation, recreation. A simple if disconcerting formulation would be that government is not able to provide new services of quality to the population as a whole if it must solely rely on tax revenues. But it may be able to provide services if it charges most of the consumers who want them and provides free service for the minority who cannot pay.

If this is a reasonable conclusion, then we may be approaching a turning point in the organization and delivery of guidance services. If career guidance is as useful as its enthusiasts believe it to be, more and more Americans may be willing to pay all, or at least part, of the cost for quality service. States and localities might begin to experiment with mixed patterns of financing whereby some governmental monies are made available to non-profit or profit-making enterprises which are geared to provide guidance services to a clientele that would include people who pay all, part, or none of the cost. This would not be an entirely new pattern. Most voluntary organizations have a sliding scale for fees and do some work for government under contract.

There is no denying that difficulties and complications would arise in this type of operation. But service almost exclusively financed and staffed by government has serious drawbacks. If guidance could be attached more loosely to the schools and the other governmental agencies than is the case at present, it might sprout new wings. At least it could do its work in a less constricted environment and this would have advantages for both counselors and clients.

The peace dividend which will follow termination of hostilities in Vietnam has been preempted many times—by environmental control, housing, public transportation, crime prevention, and programs to accelerate the reduction of poverty. Education will undoubtedly get a part. But the competing claimants within education include all the interest groups from proponents of preschool programs to the research establishment.

We have argued that more federal money must go into improving the guidance services of the Employment Service and into improved information-gathering and research. We have also argued in favor of more state and local expenditures for the strengthening of guidance in schools and other settings. We see no real chance for guidance to improve its services unless increased governmental funds are made available.

But if we read the history of this country correctly, quality services have always required and will continue to require money from sources beyond government. Consequently, we recommend that the American people consider new methods of financing guidance so that its future will be less dependent on the largesse of government—which has never had and cannot hope to have sufficient tax revenues at its command to meet all of its priority obligations. The future of career guidance will be determined by the willingness of the American people to seek assistance in clarifying its work goals from trained specialists and to incur the costs of high-quality services.

NOTES

Chapter 1

1. Eli Ginzberg, *et al.*, Columbia University Press, 1951. See also Eli Ginzberg, "The Development of a Developmental Theory of Occupational Choice," Chapter 4 in *Counseling and Guidance in the Twentieth Century*, ed. W. H. Van Hoose and J. J. Pietrofesa. Boston: Houghton Mifflin Company, 1970.
2. Eli Ginzberg, *et al.*, Columbia University Press, New York.
3. Eli Ginzberg, "Guidance—Limited and Unlimited," *Personnel and Guidance Journal*, 38, 1960, p. 707.
4. Buford Stefflre, "Counseling in the Total Society: A Primer," Chapter 17 in Van Hoose and Pietrofesa, *op. cit.*
5. See Preface for list of members.

Chapter 2

1. Hearings before the Committee on Education and Labor, House of Representatives. Eighty-fifth Congress, 1957–58.
2. J. B. Conant, *Slums and Suburbs*. New York: McGraw-Hill Book Company, 1961.
3. *Conference Proceedings*, Golden Anniversary White House Conference on Children and Youth. Washington, D.C., March 27–April 2, 1960, *passim*.
4. J. B. Conant, *The American School Today*. New York: McGraw-Hill Book Company, 1959.
5. *Ibid.*
6. J. W. Gardner, *From High School to Job*. Reprinted from 1960 Annual Report, Carnegie Corporation of New York.

Chapter 3

1. Henry Borow, "Milestones: A Chronology of Notable Events in the History of Vocational Guidance," Chapter 3 in *Man in a World at Work*, ed. H. Borow. Boston: Houghton Mifflin Company, 1964.
2. Frank Parsons, *Choosing a Vocation*. Boston: Houghton Mifflin Company, 1909.

3. Christopher Lasch, *The New Radicalism in America 1889–1963*. New York: Vintage Books, 1965, p. 157.
4. Lawrence A. Cremin, *The Transformation of the School*. New York: Vintage Books, 1961, pp. 110ff.
5. Lasch, *op. cit.*, p. 158.
6. Borow, *op. cit.*, p. 49.
7. Quoted in Carroll H. Miller, "Vocational Guidance in the Perspective of Cultural Change," in Borow, *op. cit.*, p. 7.
8. U.S. Bureau of the Census, *Statistical Abstract of the United States: 1969*. (90th edition.) Washington, D.C.
9. U.S. Bureau of the Census, *Historical Statistics of the United States, Colonial Times to 1957*. Washington, D.C., 1960, Chapter H.
10. Washington, D.C., American Council on Education, 1940, p. 3.
11. *Ibid.* p. 106.
12. Miller, *op. cit.*, p. 20.
13. Cremin, *op. cit.*, p. 187.
14. Quoted in *ibid.*, p. 185.
15. Yonkers-on-Hudson, N.Y.: World Book Company, 1928.
16. L. S. Feldt, "The Role of Testing in Guidance," Reprinted in *Counseling and Guidance*, ed. J. F. Adams. New York: The Macmillan Company, 1965, p. 252.
17. "The Measurement of Occupational Aptitude," in *University of California Publications in Psychology*, vol. 8, no. 2, 1955.
18. "Counseling: Self-Clarification and the Helping Relationship," Chapter 19 in Borow, *op. cit.*, p. 455.
19. "The Necessary and Sufficient Conditions of Therapeutic Personality Change," reprinted in Adams, *op. cit.*, p. 131.
20. E. Ginzberg and Associates, *The Ineffective Soldier: Lessons for Management and the Nation* (3 vols.). New York: Columbia University Press, 1959, *passim*.
21. "Transition: From Vocational Guidance to Counseling Psychology," reprinted in *Counseling: Readings in Theory and Practice*, J. F. McGowan and L. D. Schmidt eds. New York: Holt, Rinehart and Winston, 1962, p. 9.
22. E. S. Bordin, *Psychological Counseling*. New York: Appleton-Century-Crofts, 1955, pp. 11ff.
23. C. G. Wrenn, "What Has Happened to Vocational Counseling in Our Schools?" reprinted in *Vocational Guidance and Career Development*, H. J. Peters and J. C. Hansen eds. New York: The Macmillan Company, 1966, p. 309.
24. *Ibid.*, p. 305.
25. "Decision and Vocational Development: A Paradigm and Its Implications," reprinted in *ibid.*, p. 119.
26. See comprehensive analysis in J. O. Crites, *Vocational Psychology*. New York: McGraw-Hill Book Company, 1969.
27. Cremin, *op. cit.*, pp. 332ff.
28. R. H. Mathewson, *Strategy for American Education*. New York: Harper & Brothers, 1957, pp. 179–80.
29. *Ibid.*, p. 209.
30. *Harvard Educational Review*, XXVIII, No. 2 (Summer 1958), p. 279.

31. Mathewson, *op. cit.*, p. 180.
32. "The Psychological Background for Curriculum Experimentation," in P. C. Rosenbloom (ed.) *Modern Viewpoints in the Curriculum.* New York: McGraw-Hill Book Company, 1964.
33. New York, Schocken Books, 1966, p. 7.

Chapter 4

1. C. H. Patterson, "Counseling: Self-Clarification and the Helping Relationship," Chapter 19 in Borow, *op. cit.*
2. J. W. Gustad, "Test Information and Learning in the Counseling Process," reprinted in Peters and Hansen, *op. cit.*, pp. 269ff. See also Feldt, *op. cit.*, pp. 251ff.
3. A. V. Cicourel, and J. I. Kitsuse, *The Educational Decision-Makers.* Indianapolis: Bobbs-Merrill, 1963.
4. R. E. Campbell, *Vocational Guidance in Secondary Education.* Columbus, Ohio: The Center for Vocational and Technical Education, Ohio State University, 1968, p. 31. See also D. J. Armor, *The American School Counselor.* New York: Russell Sage Foundation, 1969, p. 124. See also J. S. Flanagan, *et al., Studies of the American High School.* Monograph No. 2, Project Talent Monograph Series. Pittsburgh: University of Pittsburgh, 1962, p. 7-4.
5. Armor, *op. cit.*, p. 122.
6. *Report of the Interagency Task Force on Counseling.* Washington, D.C., 1967, p. 13.
7. R. O. Stripling, "Training Institutions: Standards and Resources," in *Counselor Development in American Society,* J. F. McGowan, ed. A report to the U.S. Department of Labor and the U.S. Department of Health, Education and Welfare. Washington, D.C., 1965, p. 113.
8. *Interagency Task Force, op. cit., passim.*
9. Armor, *op. cit.*, p. 52.
10. *Interagency Task Force, op. cit.*, p. 13.
11. Campbell, *op. cit.*, pp. 65ff.
12. See Chapter 10, "Suburbantown."
13. J. L. Lister, "School Counseling: For Better or for Worse?" Unpublished manuscript. See also Halmos, *op. cit.*, pp. 84ff.

Chapter 5

1. U.S. Bureau of the Census, *Current Population Reports,* Series P-20, No. 190, "School Enrollment: October 1968 and 1967," U.S. Government Printing Office, Washington, D.C., 1969, p. 1.
2. New York: John Wiley, 1964.
3. B. S. Bloom, "A Comment on the Jensen Essay," reprinted in *IRCD Bulletin,* Vol. V, No. 4, Teachers College, Columbia University, Fall 1969, p. 5.
4. *Executive Summary.* Preliminary Draft, 1969, p. 0-5.
5. Washington, D.C.: The Potomac Institute, 1970, p. 102.
6. U.S. Bureau of the Census, *op. cit.*, p. 10.
7. Reported in J. Lederer, "The Scope of the Practice," in *The Urban Review,* Vol 3, No. 1, Sept. 1968, p. 5.

8. Quoted in C. Tree, "Grouping Pupils in New York City," in *The Urban Review, op. cit.,* p. 14.
9. *Transaction,* Vol. 5, No. 11, October 1968, pp. 45–59.
10. *Learning to Read: The Great Debate.* New York: McGraw-Hill Book Company, 1967.
11. *Pygmalion in the Classroom.* New York: Holt, Rinehart and Winston, 1968.
12. Coles, *op. cit.,* p. 87.
13. *Ibid.,* p. 106.
14. Cicourel and Kitsuse, *op. cit.,* (Chap. 4).
15. "Delinquency and the Schools," in *Juvenile Delinquency and Youth Crime.* Task Force Report, The President's Commission on Law Enforcement and the Administration of Justice, 1967, p. 231.
16. Quoted in *ibid.*
17. Staff interviews with Negro out-of-school youth living in Harlem, summer 1968.
18. J. J. Kaufman and M. V. Lewis, *The School Environment and Programs for Dropouts.* Institute for Research on Human Resources, The Pennsylvania State University, August 1968, Chapter 2.
19. "Institutional Effects on the Academic Behavior of High School Students," *Sociology of Education,* Vol. 40, Summer 1967, pp. 181–99.
20. *Manpower Report of the President,* prepared by the U.S. Department of Labor. Transmitted to the Congress March 1970. Washington, D.C.: U.S. Government Printing Office, p. 72.
21. Reported in M. S. Bedell, "Youth Corps Pay—Where it Goes," in *Manpower,* Vol. 2, No. 2, February 1970, p. 31.
22. U.S. Bureau of the Census, *Current Population Reports,* Series P-20, No. 185, "Factors Related to High School Graduation and College Attendance: 1967," U.S. Government Printing Office, Washington, D.C., 1969.
23. *Manpower Report of the President, op. cit.,* p. 320.
24. June 13, 1969.
25. *Manpower Report, op. cit.,* p. 60.
26. M. Freedman, *The Process of Work Establishment.* New York: Columbia University Press, 1969, *passim.*
27. *Education and Jobs: The Great Training Robbery.* New York: Praeger, 1970, *passim.*
28. U.S. Manpower Administration, *Occupational Licensing and the Supply of Nonprofessional Manpower.* Manpower Research Monograph No. 11, 1969, p. 1.
29. *Current Population Reports,* Series P-20, No. 185, *op. cit.,* p. 7.

Chapter 6

1. *Current Population Reports,* Series P-20, No. 185, *op. cit.,* p. 6.
2. Derived from table in *Toward a Social Report.* U.S. Department of Health, Education and Welfare. Washington, D.C.: U.S. Government Printing Office, 1969, p. 21.
3. *Current Population Reports,* Series P-20, No. 185, *op. cit.,* p. 6.
4. J. C. Flanagan, *et al. The American High-School Student.* Pittsburgh: Project Talent Office, University of Pittsburgh, 1964, pp. 11–22.

5. *Occupational Education for Massachusetts.* A Report Prepared for The Massachusetts Council on Education, June 1968, p. 22.
6. M. F. Shaycoft, *The High School Years: Growth in Cognitive Skills.* Project Talent, Interim Report 3. American Institutes for Research and School of Education, University of Pittsburgh, 1967, pp. 8–24.
7. "*Student Financial Aid—College and University.*" Manuscript of article for *Encyclopedia of Educational Research,* 4th ed., R. L. Ebel, ed., New York: The Macmillan Company. (Manuscript dated Nov. 1967, p. 15.)
8. "Transfer Students: Who's Moving from Where to Where and What Determines Who's Admitted?" in *College Board Review,* No. 72, Summer 1969, pp. 4–12.
9. U.S. Bureau of the Census, *Current Population Reports,* Series P-60, No. 68, "Poverty in the United States: 1959 to 1968," Washington, D.C.: U.S. Government Printing Office, 1969, p. 1.
10. E. Ginzberg and D. Hiestand, "The Guidance of Negro Youth," in *Employment, Race, and Poverty.* A. M. Ross and H. Hill, eds. New York: Harcourt, Brace & World, 1967, p. 439.
11. U.S. Bureau of the Census, *Statistical Abstract of the United States: 1969.* (90th edition.) Washington, D.C., p. 417.
12. U.S. Bureau of the Census, *Current Population Reports,* Series P-23, Special Studies, No. 27, "Trends in Social and Economic Conditions in Metropolitan Areas," Washington, D.C.: U.S. Government Printing Office, 1969, *passim.*
13. CED Supplementary Paper Number 26, October 1968. New York: Committee for Economic Development, 1968, p. 41.
14. J. J. Kaufman and M. V. Lewis, *op. cit.*
15. U.S Bureau of the Census, *Current Population Reports,* Series P-20, No. 183, "Characteristics of Students and Their Colleges: October 1966." Washington, D.C.: U.S. Government Printing Office, 1968.
16. H. Bienstock, "Realities of the Job Market for the High School Dropout," in *Profile of the School Dropout,* D. Schreiber, ed. New York: Random House, 1967, p. 120.
17. Shaycoft, *op. cit.,* pp. 8–26.
18. U.S. Bureaus of the Census and Labor Statistics, *Recent Trends in Social and Economic Conditions of Negroes in the United States.* Current Population Reports, Series P-23, No. 26, BLS Report No. 347. Washington, D.C.: U.S. Government Printing Office, July 1968, *passim.*
19. J. Kaufman, *et al., The Role of the Secondary School in the Preparation of Youth for Employment.* The Pennsylvania State University, Institute for Research on Human Resources, 1967, pp. 9–32.
20. *The American High School Student, op. cit.,* Chapter 5.
21. Women's Bureau, *1969 Handbook on Women Workers.* Bulletin 294. Washington, D.C.: U.S. Government Printing Office, 1969, *passim.*
22. *Ibid.,* Chapter 1.
23. U.S. Bureau of the Census, *Current Population Reports,* Series P-60, No. 66, "Income in 1968 of Families and Persons in the United States," Washington, D.C.: U.S. Government Printing Office, 1969, p. 90.
24. *Ibid.,* p. 95.
25. *Ibid.,* p. 102.

26. T. R. McConnell, Preface in C. C. Collins, *Junior College Student Personnel Programs What They Are and What They Should Be.* Washington, D.C.: American Association of Junior Colleges, 1967, p. ii.

27. *Ibid.,* p. 12.

28. *Facing Facts About the Two-Year College.* The Prudential Insurance Company of America, Newark, 1963, p. 8.

29. Collins, *op. cit.,* p. 22.

30. M. M. Levin, "The Impact of Social Class on Personal Needs and Career Choice," Chapter 1 in J. Katz, *et al., Class, Character, and Career Determinants of Occupational Choice in College Students.* Stanford University, Institute for the Study of Human Problems, 1968, p. 48.

31. Chapter V in *ibid.*

32. *Management and Improvement of Guidance.* New York: Appleton-Century-Crofts, 1965.

33. Referred to in Nash, *op. cit.,* p. 24.

34. R. J. Panos and A. W Astin, *They Went to College: A Descriptive Summary of the Class of 1965.* ACE Research Reports, Vol. 2, No. 5. American Council on Education, 1967, p. 18.

35. 1969, p. 81.

36. *Statistical Abstracts, op. cit.,* p. 106.

37. *Op. cit.,* p. 25

38. *Op. cit.,* pp. 18–20.

39. D. Hiestand, *Changing Careers.* New York: Columbia University Press, 1971.

40. U.S. Bureau of Labor Statistics, *Special Labor Force Report No. 47,* "Out-of-School Youth" February 1963—Part II, p. 1417.

41. M. W. Riley and A. Foner, *Aging and Society,* Vol. 1. New York: Russell Sage Foundation, 1968, p. 431.

42. *Ibid.,* p. 48.

43. S. Wolfbein, *Occupational Information.* New York: Random House, 1968, p. 111.

44. *Op. cit.*

45. U.S. Women's Bureau, *Continuing Education Programs and Services for Women.* Pamphlet 10. Washington, D.C.: U.S. Government Printing Office, January 1968

46. U.S. Bureau of Labor Statistics, *Work Experience of the Population in 1967.* Special Labor Force Report No. 107, A Monthly Labor Review Reprint from the June 1969 Issue, p. A-4.

47. *Op. cit.,* p. 446.

48. U.S. Bureau of Labor Statistics, *Adult Men Not in the Labor Force,* Special Labor Force Report No. 79. Reprinted from the Monthly Labor Review, March 1967, p. 7.

49. Special Labor Force Report No. 107, *op. cit.,* p. A-12.

50. *Statistical Abstracts, op. cit.,* p. 53.

Chapter 7

1. "Human Values and Work in American Life," Chapter 2 in Borow, *op. cit.,* p. 41.

2. In Peters and Hansen, *op. cit.,* p. 124.

3. "The Process of Vocational Assessment" in Borow, *op. cit.*, p. 407.
4. L. H. Stewart and C. F. Warnath, *The Counselor and Society.* Boston: Houghton Mifflin Company, 1965.
5. *The Faith of the Counsellors,* pp. 93, 105.
6. Quoted in Patterson, Chapter 19 in Borow, *op. cit.*, p. 442.
7. *Ibid.*, p. 446.
8. "Minimum Change Therapy," in J. F. Adams, *op. cit.*, p. 169.
9. A. V. Boy and G. J. Pine, "A Sociological View of the Counselor's Role: A Dilemma and a Solution," in *The Personnel and Guidance Journal,* Vol. 47, No. 8, April 1969, p. 737.
10. *Op. cit.*, p. 92.

Chapter 8

1. *Op. cit.*, p. 15.
2. H. W. Houghton, *Certification Requirements for School Pupil Personnel Workers.* OE-25050. Washington, D.C.: U.S. Government Printing Office, 1967,
3. *Ibid.* p. 19.
4. S. N. Feingold, "Issues Related to a Study of the Influence of Salary, Methods of Selection, Working Conditions, Supervision, and Mobility upon Selection, Training, and Retention of Counseling Personnel," in McGowan, *op. cit.*, pp. 132ff. See also G. L. Mangum and L. M. Glenn, *Vocational Rehabilitation and Federal Manpower Policy.* Policy Papers in Human Resources and Industrial Relations, No. 4. Institute of Labor and Industrial Relations and the National Manpower Policy Task Force, November 1967, pp. 14ff.
5. J. F. McGowan and T. L. Porter, *An Introduction to the Vocational Rehabilitation Process.* U.S. Vocational Rehabilitation Administration. Washington, D.C.: U.S. Government Printing Office, July 1967, p. 169.
6. U.S. Employment Service, *Program Letter No. 2056,* June 17, 1966, p. 4.
7. Feingold, *op. cit.*
8. U.S. Manpower Administration, *Breakthrough for Disadvantaged Youth.* Washington, D.C.: U.S. Government Printing Office, 1969, p. 101.
9. Houghton, *op. cit., passim.*
10. Feingold, *op. cit.*, p. 134.
11. *Ibid.*, p. 175.
12. H. W. Houghton and L. M. Trexler, *Inventory of Counselor Education Programs, 1965–1966.* U.S. Office of Education. Washington, D.C.: U.S. Government Printing Office, 1967.
13. E. L. Kelly and D. W. Fiske, *The Prediction of Performance in Clinical Psychology.* Ann Arbor: The University of Michigan Press, 1951. R. R. Holt and L. Luborsky, *Personality Patterns of Psychiatrists.* London: Imago, 1958.
14. R. O. Stripling, *Training Institutions: Standards and Resources,* in McGowan, *op. cit.*, p. 114.
15. *Op. cit.*, p. 16.
16. *Ibid.*
17. "Profile of ES Counselors," in *Employment Service Review,* Vol. 3, No. 12, December 1966, p. 18.

18. See for example, W. E. Hill, "Local Offices Hire School Counselors," in *Employment Service Review, op. cit.,* p. 26. Also M. P. Roche, "A School Counselor Looks at the Employment Service," in *Manpower,* Vol. 2, No. 2. U.S. Manpower Administration, January 1970, p. 22.
19. *Interagency Task Force Report, op. cit.,* p. 23.
20. Feingold, *op. cit.,* p. 138.
21. *Ibid.*
22. Interagency Task Force Report, *op. cit.,* p. 25.
23. D. L. Livers and D. Gross, "Dropouts—An APGA Membership Study," in *The Guidepost,* Vol. 11, No. 5. American Personnel and Guidance Association, June, 1969, p. 13.
24. Feingold, *op. cit.,* pp. 175, 177.

Chapter 9

1. See Chapter 10.
2. Staff interviews with black ghetto dropouts revealed that their decision to leave school was more a product of school indifference and lack of sympathy than of personal preference. They gave every indication of being "pushouts" rather than "dropouts."
3. Very few school systems collect information about student outcomes; still fewer publish their findings.
4. *The Personnel and Guidance Journal,* Vol. 47, No. 9, May 1969, p. 872.
5. "The Faculty Is Human, Too," in *The Personnel and Guidance Journal,* Vol. 35, 1956, p. 228.
6. See Chapter 10.
7. "What the School Has a Right to Expect of Its Counselor," reprinted in Adams, *op. cit.,* p. 29.
8. *Op. cit.,* pp. 25, 28.
9. G. P. Liddle and A. M. Kroll, *Pupil Services for Massachusetts Schools,* Boston: Massachusetts Advisory Council on Education, September 1969, p. 96.
10. Quoted in S. W. Gray and F. C. Noble, "The School Counselor and the School Psychologist," in Adams, *op. cit.,* p. 69.
11. See, for example, M. D. Lewis, "The Effective Elementary Guidance Worker: Counselor or Consultant," in *The School Counselor,* Vol. 17, No. 4, March 1970, p. 296.
12. *Op. cit.,* p. 30.
13. Office of the Assistant Secretary of Defense (Manpower and Reserve Affairs), Washington, D.C., April 1968, p. 2.
14. Over thirty years ago, at the conclusion of a research project at one of these colleges, I discussed the desirability of introducing educational and vocational guidance with the college president. A recent check shows the same need today!
15. E. M. Murray, "The School Counselor and the United States Employment Service," in Adams, *op. cit.,* p. 112.
16. *Hearing before the United States Commission on Civil Rights.* Montgomery, Alabama, April 27–May 2, 1968. Washington, D.C.: U.S. Government Printing Office, p. 49.

17. Staff interview with Robert Bentley, Supervisor of Counselors, Employment Division of HARYOU-ACT, October 25, 1967.
18. Manpower Administration. Washington, D.C.: U.S. Government Printing Office, 1967, p. 21.
19. See J. Gordon, *Testing and Counseling of Disadvantaged Youth*, Report to Office of Manpower Policy, Evaluation and Research, U.S. Department of Labor, 1967.
20. McGowan and Porter, *op. cit.*, Part 1.
21. "Vocational Rehabilitation: A Major Social Force," in Borow, *op. cit.*, p. 536.
22. J. E. Muthard and P. R. Salomone, "The Roles and Functions of the Rehabilitation Counselor," in *Rehabilitation Counseling Bulletin*, Vol. 13, No. 1-SP, October 1969.
23. *Department of Defense Directive*, No. 1332, 22, March 16, 1968, p. 1.
24. *The Transition Program*. Washington, D.C.: Office of The Assistant Secretary of Defense (Manpower and Reserve Affairs), January 1969.
25. U.S. Department of Defense, *Counseling in Project Transition*, August 1968, p. 29.
26. Personal communication to the author.
27. *1967–1968 Directory of Approved Counseling Agencies*. Washington, D.C.: American Board on Counseling Services, American Personnel and Guidance Association, 1967.
28. *Ibid.*

Chapter 10

1. J. B. Conant, *Slums and Suburbs*, New York: McGraw-Hill Book Company, 1961.

Chapter 11

1. L. L. Baird and J. M. Richards, Jr., "The Effects of Selecting College Students by Various Kinds of High School Achievement." *ACT Research Report, No. 23*. Iowa City, Iowa, American College Testing Program, February 1968. See also C. F. Elton and L. R. Shevel, "Who Is Talented? An Analysis of Achievement," *ACT Research Report, No. 31*, September 1969.
2. *The New York Times*, February 15, 1970.
3. S. H. Rhine and D. Creamer, *The Technical Manpower Shortage: How Acute?* New York: National Industrial Conference Board, 1969, p. 37.
4. *Measurement and Evaluation in Psychology and Education*, 2d ed. New York: John Wiley, 1961, Appendix.
5. J. Egerton, *Higher Education for "High Risk" Students*. Atlanta: Southern Education Foundation, April 1968.
6. D. R. Whitney, "Predicting from Expressed Vocational Choice: A Review," in *The Personnel and Guidance Journal*, Vol. 48, No. 4, December 1969, p. 279.
7. "Research on Instruments Used by Counselors in Vocational Guidance," reprinted in Adams, *op. cit.*, p. 273.
8. "Test Interpretation in Vocational Counseling," reprinted in Adams, *op. cit.*, p. 288.

9. See Chapter 10.
10. *Op. cit.*, p. 184.
11. Armor, *op. cit.*, Chapter 8.
12. Patterson, *op. cit.*, p. 447ff.
13. R. A. Peterson, quoted in McGowan and Porter, *op. cit.*, p. 151.
14. B. J. Dvorak, "General Aptitude Test Battery," reprinted in Adams, *op. cit.*, p. 281.
15. National Citizens' Committee for Community Relations and Community Relations Service, *Putting the Hard Core Unemployed into Jobs.* U.S. Department of Justice, 1967, p. 10.
16. S. S. Leshner and G. S. Snyderman, "A New Approach to the Evaluation and Rehabilitation of the Vocationally Handicapped," in Adams, *op. cit.*, p. 95.
17. *Op. cit.*, p. 273.
18. *Op. cit.*, p. 450.

Chapter 12

1. *Handbook of Women Workers, op. cit.*, p. 17.
2. L. Barnett, "Vocational Education" in *The Center Forum,* the Center for Urban Education, Vol. 3, No. 5, March 1, 1969, p. 14.
3. G. Kaback, "Occupational Information in Elementary Education" in Peters and Hansen, *op. cit.*, p. 200.
4. Hamel, L. B., "A Survey of the Teaching of Occupations," in Peters and Hansen, *op. cit.*, p. 220.
5. U.S. Department of Labor, *Dictionary of Occupational Titles 1965,* Vol. I, Vol. II and Supplement, 3rd ed. Washington, D.C.: U.S. Government Printing Office, 1965.
6. U.S. Bureau of Labor Statistics. *Occupational Outlook Handbook,* Bulletin No. 1550, 1968–1969 Edition. Washington, D.C.: U.S. Government Printing Office, 1968.
7. W. E. Hopke, Editor-in-Chief. Chicago: Doubleday & Company in co-operation with J. G. Ferguson Publishing Company.
8. P. A. Perrone, *A National School Counselor Evaluation of Occupational Information.* Madison, Wis.: The University of Wisconsin, Center for Studies in Vocational and Technical Education, 1968.
9. M. B. Queen (ed.), New York: The Career Resources Foundation, 1970.
10. Perrone, *op cit.* Also, G. S. DuBato, *A Feasibility Study to Investigate the Structure and Operation of a Model Occupational Information Dissemination Unit . . . ,* Albany, N.Y.: The State Education Department, Bureau of Occupational Education Research, June 1967.
11. P. A. Perrone, *op. cit.*
12. *Op. cit.*, p. 58.
13. *Current Occupational Literature: Some Antecedents.* Remarks before the National Conference on Occupational Information in Vocational Guidance, May 17, 1967, pp. 9–10.
14. DuBato, *op. cit.*
15. *Occupational Information,* 3d ed. New York: McGraw-Hill Book Company, 1967, p. 134.
16. *Op. cit.*

Chapter 13

1. St. Paul: U.S. Department of Health, Education and Welfare and Minnesota Department of Education, 1968, p. 9.
2. Conservation conference.
3. *Op. cit.*, p. 5.
4. Robert Dentler, Conservation conference.
5. *Op. cit.*
6. Flanagan *et al.*, *op. cit.*
7. *Op. cit.*
8. *Op. cit.*
9. *The Shortage of Skilled and Technical Workers.* Urbana, Ill.: Institute of Labor and Industrial Relations, University of Illinois, 1968. And *The Training of Tool and Die Makers.* Boston: Department of Economics, Northeastern University, 1969.
10. Kaufman *et al.*, *op. cit.*, and J. J. Kaufman and M. V. Lewis, *The Potential of Vocational Education: Observations and Conclusions.* University Park, Pa.: The Institute for Research on Human Resources, The Pennsylvania State University, May 1968.
11. Philadelphia: W. B. Saunders, 1965.
12. With B. A. Roens, *Guidance of American Youth.* Cambridge: Harvard University Press, 1950. Also *Guidance Practices and Results.* New York: Harper & Brothers, 1958. Also *Educational, Vocational and Social Performance of Counseled and Uncounseled Youth, 10 Years After High School.* Madison, Wis.: University of Wisconsin (unpublished), 1967.
13. "Evaluation of Guidance and Personnel Services" in *Review of Educational Research*, Vol. 30, 1960, pp. 168–75.
14. University of Florida.
15. *Op. cit.*
16. Chapter 15 in Van Hoose and Pietrofesa, *op. cit.*, pp. 223–24.
17. *Op. cit.*
18. F. E. Wellman, *National Study of Guidance, Phase I.* Contractor's Report to U.S. Office of Education. Columbia, Mo.: University of Missouri, June 30, 1968.
19. *Medical Education in the United States and Canada.* Carnegie Foundation for the Advancement of Teaching, 1910.
20. *Op. cit.*
21. *Op. cit.*
22. *The Projects CAUSE: An Evaluation.* Washington, D.C.: The School of Business Administration, The American University, May 1968.

Chapter 14

1. New York: Harper & Row, 1957.
2. *The Psychology of Occupations.* New York: John Wiley, 1956.

Chapter 15

1. *Op. cit.*
2. *Op. cit.*, pp. ix–x.

3. *Op. cit.*, p. x.
4. *Hearings on H.R. 13111*, 91st Congress, First Session. Washington, D.C.: U.S. Government Printing Office, 1969.
5. *Op. cit.*, p. 287.
6. *Op. cit.*, Preface.
7. Borow, *op. cit.*, p. 20.
8. *Ibid.*, p. 567.
9. *Ibid,* p. 20.
10. *Op. cit.*, p. 111.
11. *Op. cit.*, p. 28
12. Borow, *op. cit.*, Chapter 20.
13. Van Hoose and Pietrofesa, *op cit.*, p. 94.
14. *Ibid.*, p. 327.
15. Borow, *op. cit.*
16. *Op. cit.*, p. 11.
17. J. Jordan, *op. cit.*, Part 1, p. 1479.
18. D. R. Buckner, *Ibid.*, p. 1482.
19. J. G. Odgers, *Ibid.*, p. 1255.
20. Borow, *op. cit.*, p. 502.
21. Van Hoose and Pietrofesa, *op. cit.*, p. 76.
22. *Op. cit.*, p. 1.
23. *Ibid.*, p. 27.
24. "From a Technology of Guidance in Schools to the Profession of Guidance-in-Society: A Challenge to Democratic Government," in McGowan, *op. cit.*, p. 269.
25. *Op. cit.*, p. 5.
26. *Ibid.*, p. 3.
27. *Ibid,* p. 43.
28. *Ibid.*, p. 3.
29. Washington: The American Personnel and Guidance Association, 1962.
30. *Op. cit.*, pp. 42–43.
31. *Ibid.*, pp. 18–9.
32. *Ibid.*, p. 28.
33. *Ibid.*, pp. 45–47.
34. *Ibid.*, p. 82.
35. *Ibid.*, p. 6.
36. Borow, *op. cit.*, p. 581.
37. Van Hoose and Pietrofesa, *op. cit.*, p. 112.
38. Borow, *op. cit.*, p. 569.
39. Van Hoose and Pietrofesa, *op. cit.*, p. 113.

Chapter 16

1. *Slums and Suburbs,* and "From High School to Job."

Chapter 17

1. Washington, D.C.: Brookings Institution, 1968.
2. *Labor Market Information and the Federal-State Employment Service System.* Washington, D.C.: U.S. Department of Labor, February 1968.

3. *Education, Training, and Employment of the Disadvantaged.* Studies in Public Affairs, No. 4, 1969.
4. E. Ginzberg, "Manpower Research—The Cutting Edge of Policy," *Manpower,* Vol. 1, No. 11. U.S. Manpower Administration. Washington, D.C.: U.S Government Printing Office, December 1969.
5. *Hearings before Subcommittee of the Committee on Appropriations,* House of Representatives, Departments of Labor, and Health, Education and Welfare Appropriations for 1970. Washington, D.C.: U.S. Government Printing Office, 1969.
6. Murray Bergtraum in *The New York Times,* January 23, 1970.

Chapter 18

1. Eli Ginzberg and A. S. Eichner, New York: Free Press of Glencoe, 1964.
2. "Give It Back to the Indians: Education on Reservation and Off," *Carnegie Quarterly,* Vol. XVII, No. 2. New York: Carnegie Corporation, Spring 1969.
3. "Education for All an Unkept Promise" in *The New York Times,* Annual Education Review, January 12, 1970.
4. "Shultz Announces Experimental School-Work Program for 14 and 15 Year Olds," Washington, D.C.: Labor Press Service, November 17, 1969.
5. *The Wall Street Journal,* March 3, 1970.
6. U.S. Office of Education, *Projections of Educational Statistics to 1975–76.* Washington, D.C.: U.S. Government Printing Office, 1966.
7. J. K. Folger, H. S. Astin, and A. E. Boyer, *Human Resources and Higher Education.* Staff Report of the Commission on Human Resources and Advanced Education. New York: Russell Sage Foundation, 1969.

SUPPLEMENTAL BIBLIOGRAPHY

Adams, L. P., Axelbank, R. G., and Jaffe, A. J., *Employment of the Middle-Aged Worker.* New York: The National Council on the Aging, 1969.

Baer, M. F. and Roeber, E. C. *Occupational Information: The Dynamics of Its Nature and Use,* 3d. ed. Chicago: Science Research Associates, 1964.

Barry, R. and Wolf, B. *An Epitaph for Vocational Guidance.* New York: Bureau of Publications, Teachers College, Columbia University, 1962.

Bowles, S. and Levin, H. M. "The Determinants of Scholastic Achievement," Reprint 145. Washington, D.C.: The Brookings Institution, 1968.

Brim, O. G., Jr., *et al. The Use of Standardized Ability Tests in American Secondary Schools and Their Impact on Students, Teachers, and Administrators.* Technical Report No. 3 on the Social Consequences of Testing. New York: Russell Sage Foundation, 1965.

Campbell, R. E., Tiedeman, D. V., and Martin, A. M. (eds.). *Systems Under Development for Vocational Guidance: A Report of a Research Exchange Conference.* Columbus, Ohio: The Ohio State University, 1966.

Committee on Adolescence. "Normal Adolescence: Its Dynamics and Impact," *Group for the Advancement of Psychiatry,* Vol. VI, Report No. 68, February, 1968.

Counseling Techniques for Mature Women. Report of the Adult Counselor Program. Washington, D.C.: American Association of University Women, 1966.

Cremin, L. A. *The Genius of American Education.* New York: Vintage Books, 1966.

Downs, A. *Who Are the Urban Poor?* CED Supplementary Paper Number 26. New York: Committee for Economic Development, October 1968.

Feingold, N. S. and Swerdloff, S. *Occupations and Careers.* St. Louis: Webster Div., McGraw-Hill Book Co., 1969.

Gordon, W. E. "Vocational Guidance: Focus on the Future." Unpublished paper. Teachers College, Columbia University, 1970.

Goslin, D. A., Epstein, J. R., and Hallock, B. A. *The Use of Standardized Tests in Elementary Schools.* Technical Report No. 2 on the Social Consequences of Testing. New York: Russell Sage Foundation, 1965.

"Guidance and Counseling," *Review of Educational Research.* Vol. 39, No. 2, April 1969. Entire issue.

Harvard Graduate School of Education, *et al.* Information System for Vocational Decisions. Miscellaneous publications, 1967–70.

Hoppock, R. *Occupational Information,* 3rd ed. New York: McGraw-Hill Book Company, 1967.

Isaacson, L. E. *Career Information in Counseling and Teaching.* Boston: Allyn and Bacon, 1966.

Katz, M. *Decision and Values: A Rationale for Secondary School Guidance.* New York: College Entrance Examination Board, 1963.

Kimball, S. T. and McClellan, J. E., Jr. *Education and the New America.* New York: Vintage Books, 1966.

Krumboltz, J. D. (ed.). *Revolution in Counseling.* Boston: Houghton Mifflin Co., 1966.

Kuvlesky, V. P. and Jacob, N. L. *Educational Status Projections of Rural Youth: Annotations of the Research Literature.* Departmental Technical Report No. 3. College Station, Tex.: Texas A & M University, October 1968.

Landes, R. *Culture in American Education.* New York: John Wiley, 1965.

Landy, E. and Kroll, A. M. (eds.). *Guidance in American Education I: Backgrounds and Prospects.* Cambridge: Harvard University Press, 1964.

Landy, E. and Kroll, A. M. (eds.). *Guidance in American Education II: Current Issues and Suggested Action.* Cambridge: Harvard University Press, 1965.

Lewis, E. C. *Developing Woman's Potential.* Ames, Iowa: Iowa State University Press, 1968.

Lloyd-Jones, E. McD. and Roseman, N. (eds.). *Social and Cultural Foundations of Guidance.* New York: Holt, Rinehart and Winston, 1968.

Loughary, J. W., *et al.* (eds.). *Counseling: A Growing Profession.* Washington, D.C.: American Personnel and Guidance Assn., 1965.

Lytton, H. "School Counselling and Counsellor Education in the United States," A report to the Leverhulme Trust Fund. Exeter, England: University of Exeter Institute of Education, 1968.

"Negro Education in the United States," *Harvard Educational Review.* Special Issue, Vol. 30, No. 3, Summer 1960.

Norris, W., Zeran, F. R., and Hatch, R. N. *The Information Service in Guidance,* 2d ed., Chicago: Rand McNally, 1966.

90th Congress, 2d Session, Joint Economic Committee, Congress of the United States. *Federal Programs for the Development of Human Resources.* A Compendium of Papers submitted to the Subcommittee on Economic Progress. Washington, D.C.: U.S. Government Printing Office, 1968.

Oettinger, A. G. with S. Marks. *Run, Computer, Run.* Cambridge, Mass.: Harvard University Press. 1969.

Parnes, H. S., *et al. Career Thresholds.* Columbus, Ohio: Center for Human Resource Research, The Ohio State University, 1969.

Parnes, H. S. *et al. The Pre-Retirement Years.* Columbus, Ohio: Center for Human Resource Research, The Ohio State University, 1968.

President's National Advisory Commission on World Poverty. *The People Left Behind.* Washington, D.C.: U. S. Government Printing Office, 1967.

Roe, A. and M. Siegelman. *The Origin of Interests.* APGA Inquiry Studies, No. 1. Washington, D.C.: American Personnel and Guidance Assn., 1964.

Roth, R. M., Hershenson, D. B., and Hilliard, T. (eds.). *The Psychology of Vocational Development.* Boston: Allyn and Bacon, 1970.

Samler, J. "The Counselor in Our Time," *Madison Lectures on Vocational Rehabilitation.* Madison, Wis.: The University of Wisconsin, 1966.

The Schools and the Challenge of Innovation. Supplementary Paper No. 28. New York: Committee for Economic Development, 1969.

Sheldon, E. B. and R. A. Glazier. *Pupils and Schools in New York City: A Fact Book.* New York: Russell Sage Foundation, 1965.

Stiller, A. (ed.). *School Counseling 1967: A View From Within.* Washington, D.C.: American School Counselor Assn., 1967.

Stinchcombe, A. L. *Rebellion in a High School.* Chicago: Quadrangle Books, 1964.

Super, D. E. *The Dynamics of Vocational Adjustment.* New York: Harper, 1942.

Super, D. E. and Overstreet, P. L. *The Vocational Maturity of Ninth Grade Boys.* New York: Teachers College, Columbia University, 1960.

The Transition From School to Work. A Report Based on The Princeton Manpower Symposium. Princeton: Industrial Relation Section, Princeton University, 1968.

U.S. Department of Health, Education and Welfare. *Toward a Social Report.* Washington, D.C.: U.S. Government Printing Office, 1969.

U.S. Department of Labor. *Counselor's Guide to Manpower Information.* Washington, D.C.: U.S. Government Printing Office, 1968.

U.S. Welfare Administration. *Getting Hired, Getting Trained.* Prepared by National Committee on Employment of Youth. Washington, D.C.: U.S. Government Printing Office, 1965.

Van Hoose, W. H., Peters, M., and Leonard, G. E. *The Elementary School Counselor.* Detroit: Wayne State University Press, 1967.

Wrenn, C. G. *The Counselor in a Changing World.* Washington, D.C.: American Personnel and Guidance Assn., 1962.

INDEX

349